The Third Way and beyond

Published in our
centenary year
~ **2004** ~
MANCHESTER
UNIVERSITY
PRESS

The Third Way and beyond

Criticisms, futures, alternatives

edited by Sarah Hale, Will Leggett
and Luke Martell

Manchester University Press
Manchester and New York

distributed exclusively in the USA by Palgrave

Published by Manchester University Press
Oxford Road, Manchester M13 9NR, UK
and Room 400, 175 Fifth Avenue, New York, NY 10010, USA
www.manchesteruniversitypress.co.uk

Distributed exclusively in the USA by
Palgrave, 175 Fifth Avenue, New York,
NY 10010, USA

Distributed exclusively in Canada by
UBC Press, University of British Columbia, 2029 West Mall,
Vancouver, BC, Canada V6T 1Z2

British Library Cataloguing-in-Publication Data
A catalogue record for this book is available from the British Library

Library of Congress Cataloging-in-Publication Data applied for

ISBN 0 7190 6598 4 *hardback*
      0 7190 6599 2 *paperback*

First published 2004

11 10 09 08 07 06 05 04   10 9 8 7 6 5 4 3 2 1

Typeset in Sabon with Gill Sans display
by Servis Filmsetting Ltd, Manchester
Printed in Great Britain
by CPI, Bath

Contents

Notes on contributors

Armando Barrientos is Lecturer in Public Economics and Development at the Institute for Development Policy and Management at the University of Manchester, UK.

Paul Cammack is Professor of Government at the University of Manchester.

Stephen Driver is Principal Lecturer in the School of Business and Social Sciences at the University of Surrey, Roehampton.

Eunice Goes is the London correspondent of the Portuguese weekly *Expresso* and a researcher.

Sarah Hale is Lecturer in Political Theory at the University of Portsmouth.

Colin Harris is Senior Lecturer in Human Resource Management and Organisational Behaviour at the University of Brighton.

Will Leggett is Lecturer in Sociology at the University of Birmingham.

Luke Martell is Senior Lecturer in Sociology at the University of Sussex.

Peter McCullen is Senior Lecturer in Supply Chain Management at the University of Brighton Business School.

David Morrison is Lecturer in Sociology at Filton College, Bristol, and a doctoral student at the University of the West of England.

Martin Powell is Reader in Social Policy at the University of Bath.

Simon Prideaux is Tutor and Lecturer in Sociology and Social Policy at the University of Leeds.

Eric Shaw is Senior Lecturer in Politics at the University of Stirling.

Part I

The Third Way

Luke Martell

Introduction

In the late 1990s Third Way governments were in power across Europe – and beyond, in the USA and Brazil, for instance. The Third Way experiment was one that attracted attention worldwide, and gurus of the Third Way could count on invitations to conferences and gatherings of the politically interested across the world.

Yet only a few years later the day of the Third Way seemed to have disappeared even more quickly than it had found itself in the ascendant. The New Democrats were defeated for the US presidency by Republican George W. Bush. Across Europe parties of the Right knocked out of power Third Way exponents from the Centre-Left. Blair in Britain, perhaps the Third Way's foremost advocate, remained in power but some of his Centre-Left colleagues in France, Spain, Italy and elsewhere found themselves ousted. The 'Neue Mitte' administration in Germany clung on to power by the narrowest of margins and in any case Chancellor Schröder was showing decidedly 'old' social democratic tendencies. The Right felt increasingly rejuvenated, often (but not always) speaking the language of nationalism and xenophobic populism, even to the extent of achieving a shocking level of support for far Right parties, in Austria and France, for example, but elsewhere also.

So why another book on the Third Way? This volume is based on a conference held in November 2000 at the University of Sussex.[1] It was not our intention to publish the proceedings. But the contributions to the conference generated such distinctive angles on the Third Way, and brought out so many new insights, that this book is the result. As its chapters were worked on over the next eighteen months or so, it became clearer that the Third Way had a greater longevity than a cursory glance might show.

The first marker of the continuing relevance of the Third Way is, of course, the presence of Third Way governments in power. Tony Blair in the UK was swept back into office with an emphatic victory in 2001, by a margin unusual for a prime minister years into government. Despite many opportunities to damage the Third Way New Labour Government, the opposition Conservative Party failed to make anything but the most marginal inroads into Labour's huge parliamentary majority. In social democratic Sweden the Centre-Left held on to power in 2002 – in a country sometimes credited with originating welfare-to-work and the attempt, in typical Third Way style, to combine social justice *and* economic efficiency. As mentioned, the German SPD scraped back into power, and while the US Democrats lost a presidential election it was one in which they had the most votes. Even with war – that guaranteed vote winner for some countries – George W. Bush remains, at the time of writing, open to defeat by a new Democrat challenger when his term of office ends.[2]

Beyond the facts about who holds office, the Third Way has left a legacy which plays its part in defining the theory and politics of the early twenty-first century. The Right has to fight for power on the ground laid by the Third Way – responding to the Third Way agenda to make its way back, just as the Third Way itself was built on the ground left by 'old' social democracy and the New Right. In Britain, for instance, the Conservative Party's attempt to return to power after New Labour's 1997 victory was at first based on an attempt to differentiate itself from the Third Way by a move to the Right. After its defeat in 2001 it changed strategy to move to the centre-ground and attempted to beat New Labour on what were its own issues, such as social exclusion and public services. In both cases the Right was defining itself in relation to the approach of the incumbent Third Way Government. Furthermore the social changes posited by the Third Way as necessitating a new politics, the values they have argued for and the policies proposed for achieving those values have become established parts of the political landscape and agenda, whoever is in power.

As Will Leggett points out in chapter 10 of this book, an attempt to define the Third Way purely by its values or its policies misses out a vital part of the explanation: the social changes to which the Third Way is – or at least perceives itself to be – a response. Perhaps foremost among the social changes that the Third Way has imprinted on the political consciousness has been globalisation, especially economic globalisation. How are third-wayers to deal with this? For many third-wayers the chief response has been to actively promote economic liberalisation, to encourage free trade across national boundaries, to promote competition and deregulation and to incorporate more and more nations within this framework. In this way the Third Way has further established the approach of the New Right – or neo-liberalism. This has been the case at least for the historically more *laissez-faire* USA and UK; elsewhere it promoted a liberal approach which lacked such radical antecedents. The Centre-Left was able to pursue an economically liberal agenda which under the Right might have scared its electorates. As Leggett suggests, social changes such as globalisation are open to interpretation, as are possible responses to them. But the Third Way has laid down some commonly accepted interpretations of contemporary social transformations and how politicians should react to them. This is one plank of the enduring legacy and importance of the Third Way.

The means for dealing with globalisation have been heralded as a new pragmatism, neither the automatic market solutions of the New Right necessarily (sometimes a bit of government intervention in social policy is needed) nor just the statism of the Old Left (the private sector and non-direct forms of state intervention can have a role). A Third Way is pragmatic about policies – it can combine right and left or be something which is neither. Eric Shaw's contribution (chapter 4) casts doubt on whether *pragmatism* is the right word for this – if judged on results alone, the role of the private sector in public services does not seem to deliver the goods, so it may be that there is something more ideological going on in the Third Way's predilection for private sector solutions. Nevertheless, the argument is that the policies for responding to the globalised economy and to social policy needs have to be pragmatic – neither Left nor Right but a mix of the two, which sees a role for both public and private in tackling social exclusion and the provision of public services. Third way approaches to economic and social policy have become part of the political agenda of many countries, whoever is in power.

To some, all this may sound thus far a bit more Right than Left – the politics of economic liberalisation and private sector involvement in public services. But Third Way supporters say there is more to it than this. For a start, a role remains for active government, but a redefined one. Government guarantees rather then delivers – for example, in the provision of some public services or employment opportunities. It tries to get people off welfare into work rather than judging its successes on the level of welfare payments to those dependent on the State or just leaving unemployment to market solutions. Furthermore, it brings in distinctive values of the Centre-Left. The Third Way, it is said, offers an antidote to the individualist values of the New Right. It argues for community and social inclusiveness facilitated by government, where the New Right argues that the market should solve the problems of those who were excluded, with the consequence often being that, in practice, divisions between the haves and the have-nots grow rather than shrink. The Third Way does not pursue old-style egalitarianism but also differs from the inegalitarian politics of the New Right, saying that the State has to step in to ensure opportunities for all, through education or welfare-to-work policies, for instance. As Goes notes (chapter 6), this often means establishing minimum opportunities, or sufficiency, rather than equality of opportunity. Nevertheless, it signals something different from the Right's offering – an emphatic role for government in tackling poverty and exclusion. What is more, this approach does not see economic efficiency and such social justice as in conflict – a Third Way favours not one or the other but argues that they can go together. For many, this is what is at the heart of a new communitarianism on the Centre-Left – one which tries to rebuild community through social inclusiveness. Some contributors to this book have their doubts. Sarah Hale argues (chapter 5) that the communitarianism of New Labour is nothing of the sort, at least when compared to what one of Tony Blair's supposed gurus – John Macmurray – means by *community*. Simon Prideaux establishes (chapter 7) some – in his view – inappropriate antecedents for community in the early thought of another alleged guru of the Third Way: Amitai Etzioni. Eunice Goes suggests that communitarianism may be all well and good but that it has replaced one of the land-marks in left-wing thinking – a commitment to equality, a view similar to that put forward by David Morrison (chapter 9). For Paul Cammack (chapter 8), all this is just a rhetorical cover for more neo-liberalism. However, Pete McCullen and Colin Harris (chapter 3), as well as Stephen Driver (chapter 2), see elements of an egalitarian redistributional framework in the Third Way, or at least of some sort of continuing distinctively social democratic approach.

So in terms of social change, policies and values, the Third Way has left a well-established approach and set of ideas. Where Third Way governments continue in power – as, it should be remembered, they do – or where they have a solid basis for a return to power, those ideas continue to play a role. They also play a role in establishing what it it that the Right has to respond to. Just as the Centre-Left had to evolve to respond to the New Right, so the Right now has to work within a framework that includes the social changes, polices and values set out by the Centre-Left Third Way.

So the Third Way is a living issue. This book has a number of distinctive ways of making sense of this. As its sub-title suggests, it is not a book that just lays out the contours of the Third Way: it also interrogates its origins in social theo-ries and social change – and in doing so some chapters debunk popular assump-tions about the sources for Third Way ideas. It is not just about meanings of the Third Way – although Barrientos and Powell lay out some of the perspectives on this in the opening chapter – but also about alleged influences on why the Third Way has become what it is – with the emphasis on 'alleged', given the debunk-ing just mentioned. There are some suggestions, for instance, that influences like globalisation are posited to justify certain policies or that the social changes identified by the Third Way are open to alternative normative conclusions.

The book is neither an apology for the Third Way, nor a litany of criticisms of it. In fact, it is a healthy mix of criticism and defence, some chapters attempt-ing to provide a balanced discussion which combines both. Driver, and McCullen and Harris, for instance, defend some aspects of the Third Way for its social democratic elements – in Driver's case looking at New Labour and in McCullen and Harris's case at the Third Way theorist Anthony Giddens. But in neither of these chapters is there an uncritical endorsement of the Third Way – both provide a complex and balanced picture of its merits and limits. Other chapters question the Third Way's own account of its influences or cast doubt on the veracity of its discourse. Is it as communitarian as it says it is (Hale)? Is commu-nitarianism a disguise for something else – the abandoning of equality or the endorsement of neo-liberalism, for instance (Goes, Cammack, Morrison)? Is the Third Way as pragmatic about getting the best results as it claims to be (Shaw)? How decisive are the social changes identified by third-wayers in endorsing the political programme they lay out (Leggett)? There is a mix of defence, criticism and questioning in this book.

Some of the chapters draw out the implications on what futures there may be for, or after, or as an alternative to, the Third Way. Barrientos and Powell lay out the varieties of routes left open by Third Way advocacies – there are many Third Ways not one and this leaves open the possibility of different political alternatives. McCullen and Harris suggest a greater egalitarianism that would be needed to achieve the suggested ends of Giddens's Third Way. Hale's critique points to the possibility of an alternative *real* communitarianism. Cammack's demolition of Third Way discourse implies a more radical alternative, and Leggett looks at the social changes posited by the strategists of the Third Way and how those changes may be analysed so as to lead to different political conclusions. This book is as much about the future of, and alternatives for and to, the Third Way as it is about how the Third Way has been thus far. It combines description and analysis with explanation and normative perspectives.

The book is also interdisciplinary. It does not take a purely political science approach which looks at party systems, organisations, political institutions or elections; but it is also not simply an analysis of ideas or policy, although these are discussed. The book includes contributions from people who work and research in departments of business studies, government and politics, sociology, social policy, and social and political thought. The Third Way is a complex phenomenon that is of concern to all of these disciplines. This is reflected here in the analysis of the Third Way, not just *between* chapters but often *within* them.

The style of writing throughout is accessible and often lively. The book includes outlines of key issues about the Third Way – including problems of definition – which will be of interest both to newcomers to the field and to students of diverse disciplines. But it also questions some commonly held assumptions about the Third Way and takes the field forward in some new and original ways, especially on questions of criticisms, futures and alternatives. This is a book, in style and content, which is important for both students and experts.

Part I introduces the key themes and some of the main interpretations of what the Third Way is (or 'are' as some contributors see it more as a plural phenomenon) and the routes down which it may be going. Part II looks at issues concerning economic equality. Driver, and McCullen and Harris discuss the egalitarian potential in the Third Way, whether that of New Labour or of Anthony Giddens. Shaw assesses the Third Way's attempt to combine public and private provision in the public services.

Two major themes of the Third Way are those just mentioned – the question of the continuing status of equality in the Third Way, and whether it has been shelved in preference for something else such as equality of opportunity, inclusiveness or community; and the question of the Third Way's pragmatism over private or public provision. Another important theme in advocacies and discussions of the Third Way has been that of community – the Third Way as a communitarian project intended to be an antidote to the individualism or rights-claiming of the New Right and the Old Left, respectively. In Part III, Hale, Goes and Prideaux discuss the Third Way's community – casting doubt on whether it is actually communitarian, whether communitarianism is a justification for something else and whether New Labour's communitarianism really is

true to the roots it claims in the thought of people like John Macmurray and
Amita Etzioni.

Part IV analyses the discourse of the Third Way and offers some concluding
arguments about what the book's contributors have said. One of the main criticisms of the Third Way is that it makes use of a lot of rhetoric to disguise a lack
of substance or at least that its substance is other than that which it claims.
Morrison and Cammack make such arguments, in particular that Third Way discourses are a disguise for a more neo-liberal project than they appear on the rhetorical surface. Will Leggett concludes that there is more to the Third Way than
just such a smokesecreen: critics should take the Third Way seriously, but should
look for alternative, more radical, political strategies based on the social transformations it identifies.

Notes

1 We are grateful to the Centre for Critical Social Theory at the University of Sussex for
  supporting this conference.
2 Although, in Germany, *opposing* attacks on Iraq helped win votes for the SPD and the
  Greens.

1 Armando Barrientos and Martin Powell

The route map of the Third Way

Introduction

Although the 'Third Way' has had many previous incarnations, the current version is generally said to have originated with the New Democrats and the Clinton administration, from 1992 in the USA,[1] and been taken up by Blair's New Labour Government in the UK. However, there remains widespread debate over whether the term is applicable only to the Anglo-Saxon 'liberal' welfare states of the UK and the USA, or whether it is meaningful for the 'social democratic' and 'Christian democratic' countries of continental Europe. The main aim of this chapter is to place the debate about the Third Way in the wider context of European social policy. According to Merkel,[2] at the end of the twentieth century the debate about the Third Way has become the most important reform discourse in the European party landscape. Giddens[3] claims that almost all Centre-Left parties have restructured their doctrines in response to it. Callinicos[4] writes that the Third Way has set the agenda for the moderate Left on a European, and indeed a global, scale. Gould[5] claims that it is 'now arguably the dominant political approach throughout the world'. The Third Way is seen as a trail-blazer for a new global social policy, a new model for a new millenium.[6] As President Clinton's former Secretary for Labour Robert Reich puts it: 'We are all third-wayers now.'

However, if the Third Way is important, it is also difficult to define.[7] As Pierson[8] puts it, the Third Way has been hotly contested but consistently under-specified. Clift[9] argues that it needs more rigourous definition before firm conclusions can be drawn about its compatibility with contemporary European social democracy. In the words of Przeworski,[10] how many ways can be third?

Merkel[11] claims that there are four distinct 'Third Way models' in Europe. Giddens[12] argues that social democratic parties in Germany, France and perhaps the Scandinavian countries have been following their own 'Third Ways'. Etzioni[13] sees the countries of continental Europe, the UK and the USA as 'different Third Way societies'. He points out that while societies such as the French and the Italian drive more in the Left lane with others such as the USA more on the Right, 'the road they all travel is fully distinct from the one charted by totalitarian and libertarian approaches'. Moreover, 'while the various Third Ways differ in their specific synthesis of the ways of the state and the market, they are pulling closer to one another'. The term 'Third Way society' suggests a greater permanence than a transitory 'Third Way government'. However, in the period since Etzioni and Merkel wrote, the governments of such countries as the USA, France and the Netherlands have moved to the Right.

We build on Etzioni's picture to examine the route map of the Third Way. Are different European countries travelling along the same or parallel roads? Is there any sign of convergence in the sense of travelling towards the same destination? We argue, however, that the current route map is not particularly helpful. As we show, the scale of the map tends to be very small. While broad features may be recognised, more precise details tend to be overlooked. Moreover, the road signs are not easy to read as they give information at a high level of abstraction. The key to the map is also fairly obscure and the classifications of the roads are far from clear. The discourse routes do not clearly flow into those carrying the traffic associated with values, goals or policies. Finally, it may not be possible to produce one route map to serve travellers on all the roads in Europe. Although there are some similarities between the various route maps, they are written in different national languages, with important national contextual differences. Our approach differs from some previous discussions in two main ways. First, in contrast with accounts that cover a wide range of social and economic policies,[14] we focus on social policy. Second, we develop a 'policy process' approach, with different elements of discourse, values, policy goals and policy mechanisms.[15]

We use a simple heuristic model of the policy process in which discourse and values shape policy goals that, in turn, should be compatible with policy mechanisms. This illuminates a number of the problems encountered by earlier attempts at definition. Some have taken, essentially, the 'Herbert Morrison' approach: Morrison famously defined socialism as what a Labour government does. It follows that a government, like that of Clinton or Blair, is 'Third Way' if it says so. This focuses on self-proclamation rather than any 'third party' analysis. On the other hand, Giddens,[16] writing before the recent European elections, declared that 'across the world left of centre governments are attempting to institute Third Way programmes' – whether or not they favour the term itself. He admitted that in Europe some have actively rejected it; while others have substituted different notions like that of 'the new middle' in Germany or the 'purple coalition' in Holland. He maintained that the Third Way is not to be identified solely with the outlook and policies of the New Democrats in the USA, or indeed of any other specific party, but a broad ideological stream fed by several tributaries. The changes made by Left parties in Scandinavia, Holland, France or Italy since the late 1980s are as much part of Third Way politics as those developed in Anglo-Saxon countries.[17] This converse approach seems to suggest that a government is Third Way if a third party says that it is! For 'old' social democracy, Pierson[18] points out that at times social democratic strategies were pursued by governments that would never call themselves 'social democratic', and social democratic governments pursued non-social democratic programmes.

Reading the route map of the Third Way

The problem in examining the Third Way is that the term is used in very different senses. A number of commentators have suggested broad characteristics/themes of the Third Way, or new social democracy. Many elements of the Third Way were flagged up in the report of the British Commission on Social Justice.[19] It rejected the approaches to social and economic policy of the 'Levellers' – the Old Left – and the 'Deregulators' – the New Right, and advocated the 'middle way' of 'investors' Britain'. The report also featured much of the discourse which was to become central to New Labour: economic efficiency and social justice are different sides of the same coin; redistributing opportunities rather than just redistributing income; transforming the welfare state from a safety net in times of trouble to a springboard for economic opportunity; welfare should offer a hand-up not a hand-out; paid work for a fair wage is the most secure and sustainable way out of poverty; and the balancing of rights and responsibilities. Giddens[20] suggests a 'Third Way programme' including the new democratic state, active civil society, the democratic family, the new mixed economy, equality as inclusion, positive welfare and the social investment state. White's[21] themes include: the state as guarantor, not necessarily provider; receptivity to forms of mutualism; new thinking about public finance, including increased use of environmental taxes, hypothecation at the margin, new consultative procedures on tax, and community fund; and asset-based egalitarianism. Vandenbrouke offers what Cuperus and Kandel[22] term 'the nine commandments of a post-pessimistic social democracy'. These are full employment for men and women, attention to new risks for the welfare state, an 'intelligent' welfare state, a revalorising of active labour market policies, subsidising low-skilled labour as a new redistribution target, preventing poverty traps, developing a competitive private service sector, finding non-dogmatic approaches to a fair distribution of burdens and benefits, and maintaining discipline with regard to growth of average wage levels. Blair and Schröder[23] suggest a 'new programme for changed realities' that includes a new supply-side agenda for the Left, a robust and competitive market framework, a tax policy to promote sustainable growth, adaptability and flexibility, active government that invests in human and social capital, and sound public finance. Ferrera et al.[24] list 'elements of an optimal policy mix' that consists of a robust macro-economic strategy; wage moderation; employer-friendly and efficient tax and social policy; labour market flexibility and flexicurity; investment in education, training and mobility; and new forms of fighting poverty and social exclusion. Thomson[25] contrasts six 'aims' of classic and new social democracy (though these aims are not policy goals in our terms, and are best considered as broad themes): fairness; individual rights; 'aiding the market';

individual initiative to achieve enhancement; the state as enabler; and community. Finally, Bresser-Pereira[26] distinguishes the New Left from the Old Left and the New Right from the perspective of developing countries, or the view from the South. These characteristics are: party control by the new middle class; a complementary role for the state; managerial state reform; basic social services executed by public non-state organisations; financing of basic social services by the state; state assured basic state security; neo-Keynesian macro-economic policy; globalisation seen as a challenge.

The positions of the commentators are expanded in the original sources. Clearly such a brief listing cannot do justice to the variety of arguments advanced. However, it does illustrate the problem of constructing a composite 'Third Way model'. The meaning of some elements of the lists is not fully clear. The term 'basic', for instance, appears frequently, but with little discussion of its significance. In particular, different dimensions, such as aims and mechanisms, are conflated. In other words, it is necessary to disentangle the various themes from their soundbite definitions.

Defining and differentiating 'the Third Way'

This section aims to explore the different defininitions of 'the Third Way', and ways of differentiating it from first and second ways. This may be found in discourse, in values and ideologies, in policy goals and in policy mechanisms. While this classification is far from watertight, it is conceptually useful. First, it is important to compare like with like. For example, a similar discourse can mean very different things.[27] Blair, Schröder and Jospin all 'support a market economy, but reject a market society' and all endorse 'the active state'. However, all probably place very different interpretations on this. Second, it allows the degree of 'fit' or 'flow' between the dimensions to be examined. For example, are policy mechanisms congruent with discourse? Are there gaps between 'rhetoric' and 'reality'.[28] It is important to avoid comparing, say, Blair's policy to Jospin's rhetoric.

Discourse

Much recent work emphasises that discourse is more than simply rhetoric, empty words or cheap talk. In short, discourse matters.[29] At root, the Third Way claims to be new and distinct from both traditional social democracy and neo-liberalism. According to Fairclough,[30] the Third Way is a political discourse built out of elements from other political discourses – of the Left and of the Right. For example, 'enterprise' belongs to the Right, while social justice belongs to the Left. The language of the Third Way is a rhetoric of reconciliation which talks, for example, of 'economic dynamism as well as social justice', 'enterprise as well as fairness'. These terms are not deemed antagonistic: while neo-liberals pursue the former and traditional social democrats the latter, the Third Way delivers both. The more radical claim is that of 'going beyond' or transcending such contrary themes. It is one thing to say that there may be ways of reconciling, for instance, the promotion of enterprise and the attack on poverty; it is quite another to say that the two 'themes' can no longer be in conflict. It follows that it is important to identify not just the keywords of the Third Way, such as 'new', 'tough', 'deal', 'reform' and 'partnership', but also their relationship with the rest of the discourse. The discourse contains a mix of 'Old Left' words such as 'equity' linked with New Right words such as 'efficiency' (equity *and* efficiency), and words that attempt to stamp a Third Way identity such as 'partnership' or 'contract'.

Values

The values of the Third Way remain problematical, mainly for two reasons. First, an adequate understanding of values requires more than one-word treatments. This links with an extensive ideology/political philosophy literature.[31] There is general agreement that 'equality' is a key value for social democrats, while 'freedom' and 'individualism' are the fundamental social values of the anti-collectivists. However, terms such as 'equality' denote essentially contestable concepts, meaning different things to different people. Greater specificity is needed to explain more precise meanings. It follows that *values* must be more clearly defined and linked with *goals* (see below). In other words, to suggest 'equality' as a value hides more than it reveals since many ideologies would claim to be in favour of *some type of* equality.

Second (and linked to the first point), it is not clear whether the Third Way is concerned with 'old' values, new or redefined meanings of old values, new values or with no values.[32] Blair[33] and Blair and Schröder represent the first position, claiming that the Third Way is concerned with linking traditional values with modern means. According to Blair these traditional values are equal worth, opportunity for all, responsibility and community. Blair and Schröder write that fairness and social justice, liberty and equality of opportunity, solidarity and responsibility to others are timeless values. Social democracy will never sacrifice them. White[34] suggests opportunity, responsibility and community. Le Grand[35] presents the acronym CORA: community, opportunity, responsibility and accountability, while Lister[36] offers RIO: responsibility, inclusion and opportunity.[37] As Driver and Martell[38] sum up, there is broad agreement over Third Way values, but problems emerge over their interpretation and the extent to which they define a Centre-Left political project. Critics point out, however, that terms such as 'equality' are here redefined and diluted. For example, Cammack and Morrison[39] claim that the Third Way appropriates the vocabulary and values of social democracy in the cause of neo-liberalism. Moreover, a few 'new' values appear to have been smuggled in. Positive uses of terms such as 'entrepreneurship'[40] rarely featured in the discourse of traditional social democracy.

A conflicting strand of argument stresses a move from ideology or dogma towards pragmatism, and is summed up by the phrase 'what counts is what works'. It is generally claimed that this phrase is concerned with being flexible about means. It tends to focus attention on narrow technical ('value-free' or 'neutral') questions rather than on issues of principle. Moreover, it is difficult to totally separate means and ends. The seemingly innocent 'what works' may hide deep disagreements about values concerning the choice of variable (what works in terms of *efficiency* or of *equity*?) and the distributional consequences (what works for whom?).

Policy goals

Goals or objectives may be seen as a more specific operationalisation of values. For example, 'equality' is often referred to as a value, but this may result in very different policy objectives, such as equality of opportunity or equality of outcomes. Many discussions tend to focus on discourse and values rather than on goals.[41] However, there may be a gap between discourse and values/goals. At the risk of some exaggeration, it might be suggested that while Jospin talked Left and acted Right – in some areas, such as redistribution – New Labour talks Right and acts *more* Left (see below). It follows that some of New Labour's stated policy goals, such as the abolition of child poverty and reducing health inequalities – both of them more ambitious than the stated policy goals of 'Old Labour' – are invisible in some accounts. In other words, policy goals must be taken more seriously. Blair has stated many times that he wants to be judged on results. In the final analysis, voters may judge governments more by the congruence between goals and results (e.g. reducing NHS waiting lists) rather than on discourse or values.[42] Although it is arguably too early to judge the outcomes of Third Way governments, analyses of success in meeting goals are vital even if relatively neglected.[43]

Policy mechanisms

Mechanisms constitute perhaps the most important dimension.[44] After all, the essential point of the welfare state is to make a difference to the lives of citizens, and it is policies that make a difference 'on the ground'. Context is important: it is meaningless to place the Third Way on a Left–Right continuum that exists in a timeless policy vacuum. Rather than comparing Third Way policies to what traditional social democrats did in the 'golden age', such as Keynesian full employment, the more difficult counter-factual exercise is a comparison with what they might have done in today's circumstances. Similarly, varying economic, political, social and institutional contexts in different countries will place effective limits on policy choices. Just as social democracy and neo-liberalism in practice varied from their textbook characteristics, there is unlikely to be a uniform Third Way, given the different national contexts, with their distinct histories, polities and economies.[45]

Table 1 presents a necessarily rather stylised account of the Third Way[46] that

Table 1.1 Dimensions of the Third Way in social policy

Dimension	Old social democracy	Third way	Neo-liberal
Discourse	Rights	Rights *and* responsibilities	Responsibilities
	Equity	Equity *and* efficiency	Efficiency
	Market failure	Market *and* state failure	State failure
Values	Equality of outcome	Inclusion	Equality of opportunity
	Security	Positive welfare	Insecurity
Policy goals	Equality of outcome	Minimum opportunities	Equality of opportunity
	Full employment	Employability	Low inflation
Policy means	Rights	Conditionality	Responsibilities
	State	Civil society/market	Market/civil society
	State finance and delivery	State/private finance and delivery	Private/state finance and delivery
	Security	Flexicurity	Insecurity
	Hierarchy	Network	Market
	High tax and spend	Pragmatic tax to invest	Low tax and spend
	High services and benefits	High services and low benefits	Low services and benefits
	High cash redistribution	High asset redistribution	Low redistribution
	Universalism	Pragmatic mix of universalism and selectivity	Selectivity
	High wages	National minimum wage/tax credits	Low wages

has been created from a number of conceptual accounts of the Third Way.[47] It does run the risk of some rewriting of history, caricaturing the Old Left, the New Right and the Third Way that has been a feature of both advocates and critics.[48] For example, it may be objected that 'responsibilities' reflect a conservative rather than a neo-liberal discourse. It is unclear whether 'insecurity' is a value. Equality of opportunity may be more a means of creating incentives or a result of market rewards, and so better regarded as a mechanism than a value of neo-liberalism. The next section discusses the extent to which these dimensions are found in a number of potential 'Third Way' countries.

The route map of the Third Way in Europe

This section illustrates some of the above themes in the context of Merkel's[49] different ways or paths of social democracy in Europe. Writing prior to the recent European elections, he argued that at least four distinct paths can be identified in Western Europe: the market-orientated way of New Labour; the market and consensus-orientated way of the Dutch *polder* model; the reform–welfare state way of the Swedish and Danish social democrats; and the statist way of the French socialists. He claims that no comparably clear profile can be established for Germany, the fifth country included here. All the countries are governed by 'social democratic' governments that have been in power sufficiently long for some details to emerge. In addition to evidence on particular countries (see titles listed in the References), a number of comparative studies[50] have been used.

Discourse

Blair[51] claimed that the Third Way in the UK is new and distinctive, and he reconciled previously antagonistic themes such as economic efficiency and social justice. Busch and Manow[52] pointed out that *neue mitte* in Germany was merely the slogan of the SPD's 1998 campaign platform and not one of deeper programmatical dignity: the *neue mitte* is 'a slogan in search of a programme'. Nevertheless, there were clear discursive elements of 'newness' and a reconciling of different themes. The 1998 manifesto *Work, Innovation and Justice* discussed in positive terms the market, innovation and flexibility. According to Lafontaine[53] terms such as 'innovation *and* social justice' and 'modernisation *and* tradition' were no mere *shibboleths* but core principles of policy. Schröder clearly shares much rhetoric with Blair, as shown in the joint statement on the Third Way authored by the two leaders.[54] This contained sweeping criticisms of 'old style' social democracy for imposing equality of outcome and neglecting effort and responsibility; for identifying social justice with ever-higher levels of public spending; for over-valuing the state and under-valuing the market; and for elevating rights above responsibilities. However, 'modern social democrats were not *laissez-faire* liberals. Flexible markets must be combined with a newly defined role for the active state.' Hombach[55] praises pragmatism. He claims that we need an 'alliance pledged to change – men and women who want practical solutions, are undogmatic and free from ideology' (p. xli). 'What is needed is a rigorous policy of pragmatism' (p. 19). 'We need a radical, pragmatic policy for the middle ground' (p. 38). Blair and Schröder are regarded as examples of 'pragmatism with vision' (pp. 65–73) and 'the time of dogma and ideology is past' (p. 66). However, an unfavourable reception in Germany forced Schröder to retreat from the declaration with Blair, promising to be 'more Jospin and less Blair'.[56]

Giddens[57] claimed that more than any other Centre-Left party in Europe, the French Socialists seem to have rejected the Third Way, and they certainly want nothing to do with the term itself. Nevertherless, Levy[58] argued that Jospin attempted to steer between the discredited Jacobin *dirigiste* Left and neo-liberalism, forging a 'new left' or 'Third Way' strategy that reconciled efficiency and equity, social progress and fiscal rectitude. Similarly, Clift[59] termed the Jospin project 'realisme de gauche' (Left realism) or the 'nouveau equilibre' (new balance). Jospin rejected Blair's Third Way: 'if it involves finding a middle way between social democracy and neo-liberalism, then this approach is not mine'.[60] However, a closer inspection of Jospin's rhetoric showed some similarities to Blair's. For example, Jospin (p. 7) claimed: 'Our ideals remain essentially the same . . . Nevertheless, we must pursue these ideals by different means from those we were using fifteen years ago.' He went on to argue that a commitment to redistribution must remain but one that does not override other considerations. 'We require a competitive production base in the new global market' (p. 11). The state must adopt a 'Schumpeterian' role in order to promote innovation and growth. 'Social classes can be brought together through equality of opportunity' (p. 12). 'We need to act before the event to prevent the accumulation of inequalities' (p. 12). 'We need both to preserve our values and to face reality' (p. 13). Finally, Jospin recognised the need to build new alliances, to include the middle class: 'In this, inevitably, he is not so different from Blair or Schröder'.[61]

Hemerijck and Visser[62] claimed that the Dutch or '*polder* model' became a catchphrase for progressive European politicians pondering the possibilities of a new 'Third Way' that reconciles employment growth with equity. The key 'Third Wayers' have all expressed admiration for the Dutch policy mix of fiscal consolidation, wage moderation, consensual welfare and labour market reform, and job creation. According to de Beus,[63] the most prominent characteristic of the Dutch Left is its belief in the consensual politics of 'common well-being'. He continues that Kok stressed sound public finance, communal responsibility for safety on the streets and the work ethic: the PvdA's slogans 'stern justice', 'work, work and work yet again' and 'strong and social' will have a familiar ring about them for a British audience. The Dutch approach was based not on doctrine, but on pragmatic politics (p. 65). The PvdA's cautious managerial approach does not arouse a passion for politics: its real problem may not be its departure from left-wing ideals but its failure to address – indeed its contribution to – the more profound depoliticisation of Dutch society (p. 68). Indeed, Kok declared that 'the shaking-off of ideological feathers is a liberating experience' (p. 63). The agreement on Flexibility and Security of 1996 (see below) illustrates the reconciliation of opposites.

Lindgren[64] pointed out that in Sweden the 'third' or 'middle' way between capitalism and a planned economy – which is different from the British and German use of the term – is long established and uncontroversial. However, Swedish social democracy has 'modernised' itself more than it realises, being in a period of reconstruction with the probable result of the sort of pragmatic adjustment to new circumstances which has long been the defining feature of Swedish social democracy (p. 58). Gould[65] claimed that modern social democrats are concerned with efficiency as well as equality, but they do not act as committed neo-liberal ideologues, and continue to share the aims and aspirations of their traditionalist critics.

Values

Blair and Schröder insisted that their values had not changed. However, as noted above, there are reasons to be suspicious of such claims.[66] Hardly surprisingly, in Germany Lafointaine[67] charged the SPD under Schröder with a 'radical change of direction towards a policy of neoliberalism', but such ideological claims sit uneasily with Hombach's rejection of ideology and his embrace of pragmatism (see above).

Jospin claimed that current social democratic plans in Europe were still faithful to 'all the values that lie at the heart of socialism: citizenship, social justice, democracy, the desire for progress and the will to control this progress and our collective destiny'. Further on he claimed that our ideals remained essentially the same: justice, liberty, the collective mastery of our destiny, the development of the individual without damaging collective interests, and the desire to progress'.[68]

In the Netherlands, de Beus[69] argued that the main Left criticism of the *polder* model focused on its approach to equality, particularly on the differences between active and inactive citizens, public servants and private-sector employees, and property-less and wealth-owners. This suggests that the traditional social democratic agenda of vertical rich to poor redistribution may no longer be the main or the only concern.

For Sweden, Lindgren[70] argues that the principles of universalism and redistribution have been redefined. There is talk of 'redistributing opportunities' and of obligations: the individual has to take responsibility for his or her own social security, even if this leads to increases in inequality. This view may not be radically different from the Third Way template outlined above.

Goals

New Labour set itself many detailed policy goals.[71] Key policy goals may be seen in the slogans 'Work for those who can; security for those who cannot' and 'Making work pay'. There will be 'full employment for the twenty-first century'.

Although strong on rhetoric and emphatic about what it rejects, the Blair–Schröder paper[72] contained few clear goals in the sense of policy objectives. It certainly rejected equality of outcome, favouring a widening of equality of opportunity. It also suggested the reduction of taxation on 'hard work and enterprise'. Hombach[73] was clearer: there is no way back to a politics of redistribution. We need equality of opportunity, equality at the outset, not at the outcome – a policy of second chances. However, Schröder argued that his government should be judged by its ability to tackle unemployment.[74] With regard to Jospin, as with Schröder, detailed goals were difficult to detect. However, they included the thirty-five-hour working week, redistribution from rich to poor and from workers to non-workers, job creation, and combating poverty and social exclusion.

Policies

In the UK New Labour stressed welfare reform.[75] It emphasised conditional or contractarian welfare. Rights were not 'dutiless' but tend to be given to those who have fulfilled their obligations.[76] Services were largely financed by the State, but may be delivered by private or voluntary bodies in a 'purchaser–provider split'. Rather than hierarchies or markets, co-ordination and collaboration through 'partnerships' or networks was stressed. In some cases, there was encouragement to supplement basic state services with a private or voluntary extension ladder (e.g. pensions). There was a general tendency to prioritise services such as health and education that can be preventative in nature and can increase human capital over reactive–passive 'relief' cash benefits. Redistribution was 'for a purpose' and was based on endowments rather than effected in terms of transfer payments, although there has been some 'silent' or 'backdoor' fiscal redistribution, especially to families. Work was central to the Third Way.[77] Full male and female employment were to be achieved more by 'supply-side' employability than by 'old' style Keynesian demand management. Although this contained both carrots and sticks, it tended to emphasise advice from case workers and investment in human capital rather than 'starving the poor back into work' through low or time-limited benefits. The slogan 'Making work pay' included a national minimum wage, in-work benefits of tax credits (or fiscal welfare) and making affordable high-quality child care available. Debates about universalism versus selectivity are not to be dogmatic. On the one hand, inclusion through universal services or civic welfare is stressed; though, on the other, there may be increasing selectivity in cash benefits, such as a targeting of the poorest pensioners and new area-based policies.

There were clearer policy suggestions in Blair and Schröder's 'new programme for changed realities', although they claimed to be 'presenting our ideas as an outline, not a finalised programme'.[78] There were positive references to a welfare system that promotes work; education, training, life-long learning and employability, and an active labour market policy. The balance between the State and the market needed to change. Although both supply- and demand-side policies, involving 'macro-economic stability and micro-economic flexibility respectively', were viewed as important, there was a clear message that the latter had been neglected, and there was a need for 'a new supply-side agenda for the left'. Many of these points were made in a more forthright manner by Hombach. For example,

> by distributing resources rather than opportunities the welfare state is following a collision course. We must change the welfare state from being a safety net into becoming a trampoline . . . State intervention is only justified if it encourages the individual's abilities and challenges his sense of initiative and does not merely offer him some kind of material assistance . . .

'Any job is better than none' is the new motto. 'Work, even in low-paid, menial jobs, contributes more to the individual's self-esteem than any welfare hand-out, however generous'.[79] In order to reach its employment goals, the SPD relied on a mix of short and long-term initiatives, and of long-established corporatist principles (the 'Alliance for Jobs') and supply-side measures.[80]

In France the Socialist Party had a crowded policy agenda. According to Levy,[81] this can be distilled into four main lines of action: imposing the costs of austerity on the well to do; giving a progressive twist to neo-liberal ideas; targeting tax relief at average- and low-income groups; and channelling scant resources to highly visible, progressive projects. First, partly as a result of the Maastricht EMU criteria, the Socialist Party continued the austerity budgets of Balladur and Juppé. However, Jospin attempted to place the burdens on the broadest shoulders by placing an income ceiling on family allowances. Second, some commentators noted that a government of the Left, despite campaign promises, privatised more than the previous governments of the Right.[82] However, Clift[83] explains this paradox as a result of laws passed by the previous government, a history of toleration of 'partial privatisation' and, most importantly, using privatisation as a new means of strategic control. Similarly, Levy[84] views this, and the introduction of company-sponsored private pensions as redirecting seemingly neo-liberal policies along progressive lines. Third, within a broadly revenue neutral budget the tax burden has been shifted from low to high income groups. Finally, reform of health services aimed at making healthcare freely available to low-income groups, a youth employment scheme aimed at creating some 350,000 positions in public and private organisations, and the thirty-five-hour working week were introduced. The latter has been termed 'by some way the most interventionist employment policy now being attempted in Europe'.[85]

For the Netherlands, de Beus[86] outlined the main characteristics of the *polder* model. First, it adopted a consensual mode of decision-making. Second, it used a pragmatic approach to the use of market mechanisms in the public sphere, from internal pricing to full-scale privatisation. Third, fiscal policy aimed at reducing overall public expenditure and the burden of public debt using innovative ways of financing public goods, Fourth, there were regular refinements of the agreement between employers and trade unions, leading to wage restraint and a moderation of wage inequality. A main theme was tax reform. The reform of 1990 lowered tax rates, while 1999 saw a further reduction in rates, and shifted the tax burden from workers and employers towards energy consumption. Social security reforms focused on disability pensions, sickness benefits and unemployment benefits. In general there were trends towards the tightening of eligibility criteria, and the privatisation of benefits, placing the risks on employers. There were also increasing moves towards an active labour market policy. Jobs were created in the public sector and, for target groups, subsidised in the private sector. Obligations increased, backed by penalties since 1996. Young people's entitlement to benefit was replaced by entitlement to a job. The limit for activation for single parents was reduced from the child's age of 12 to 5 years of age. Labour market flexibility was an integral part of the Dutch policies,[87] but this is linked with greater security for part-time and temporary jobs, as encapsulated in the 'flexibility and security' or 'flexicurity' law of 1996. Much of the 'Dutch miracle' of employment growth has been in part-time and temporary jobs for women. As Levy[88] pointed out, this shows a gendered division of labour: by and large, men work full-time and women work part-time; men pursue careers, while women have jobs. In conclusion, Green-Pedersen *et al*.[89] stated that the policy elements in the Netherlands closely match those outlined in the Blair–Schröder document. To some extent, the Netherlands has been practising the 'Third Way' for some years.

Finally, Sweden has long been at the forefront of left-of-centre thinking in labour market policy: 'workfare instead of welfare' has for many years been part of the Swedish Democratic Party's creed.[90] This appears to use 'workfare' in the context of active labour market policy, with clear rights and obligations for both workers and government, rather than its usual restriction to neo-liberal strategies. Flexibility has always been an element of Sweden's active labour market policy, but this is coupled with protection for 'flexible workers' such as agreements on working conditions and a minimum salary.[91] Contrary to widespread misconceptions, during the 'golden era' of the 1950s and 1960s the SAP was already pursuing supply-orientated policies more strongly than neo-Keynesian fiscal policy. In 1994 the Government reacted 'in an almost perfectly anti-Keynesian way with a combination of tax increases and expenditure cuts . . . Like almost all social democratic parties in the nineties the Swedish social democratic government declared both its programmatic and actual support for fiscal orthodoxy.'[92]

Conclusion

Our 'policy process' approach suggests that it is conceptually important to disentangle the different elements of discourse, values, policy goals and policy mechanisms. A country that 'talks' a Third Way may not have Third Way policies in place. Conversely, a country that does not use or even rejects the label may have been practising the Third Way for many years.[93] Similarly, there may be some policy drift between values and goals, or between goals and policies.

Supporters of the Third Way claim that it consists of both old and new roads that successfully bypass the different gridlocks associated with the Old Left and the New Right. However, this glosses over four main problems in reading the route map. First, the junctions of the roads do not clearly allow the traffic from the Left (e.g. social justice) to merge with the traffic from the Right (e.g. economic efficiency). Second, the classifications of the roads are far from clear: the discourse routes do not clearly flow into those carrying the traffic associated with values, goals or policies. Third, the road signs are not easy to read as they give information at a high level of abstraction: for example, active labour market policy can be seen as an important component of the Third Way, but it appears in many guises, and one variant was a distinctive characteristic of 'old' social democracy in countries such as Sweden. Finally, it may not be possible to produce one route map to serve travellers on all the roads in Europe. Although there are some similarities between national route maps, they are written in different languages, with important national contextual differences. Etzioni[94] may be correct that the road travelled by Third Way countries is fully distinct from the one charted by totalitarian and libertarian approaches, but the scale of his route map must be revised before it becomes of real value to travellers or road protestors trying to stop the highway from being built.

Notes

1 See chapter 2, this volume, by Stephen Driver.
2 Merkel 2001: 51.
3 Giddens 2002: 3.
4 Callinicos 2001: 1.
5 Gould 1998: 256.
6 McGuire 1998–99.
7 *The Economist* 1998; Powell 2000a; Callinicos 2001, but see Etzioni 2000.
8 Pierson 2001: 130.
9 Clift 2001a: 72.
10 Przeworski 2001.
11 Merkel 2001.
12 Giddens 2002: 18–19.
13 Etzioni 2000: 13–14.
14 Green-Pedersen *et al.* 2001; Krieger 1999; Thomson 2000; Pierson 2001.
15 Bonoli and Powell 2002.
16 Giddens 2001: 1.
17 *Ibid.*, pp. 1–2.
18 Pierson 2001: 19.
19 Commission on Social Justice 1994.

20 Giddens 1998: 70.
21 White 1998.
22 Vandenbrouke 1998; Cuperus and Kandel 1998: 25.
23 Blair and Schröder 1999.
24 Ferrera *et al*. 2001.
25 Thomson 2000: 159.
26 Bresser-Pereira 2001: 368.
27 See Fairclough 2000.
28 *Ibid*.; Clift 2001a.
29 See chapters 8 and 9, this volume; also Schmidt 2000, 2001.
30 Fairclough 2000: 45.
31 See George and Wilding 1985 for an application to social policy.
32 See chapters 8 and 9, this volume.
33 Blair 2001; Blair and Schröder 1999.
34 White 1998.
35 Le Grand 1998.
36 Lister 2000.
37 See chapters 5–7, this volume, for discussions of community which occur in three of these five listings.
38 Driver and Martell 2000: 151.
39 Chapters 8 and 9, this volume.
40 E.g. Blair 1998; Blair and Schröder 1999.
41 E.g. chapters 8 and 9, this volume.
42 E.g. Gould 1998.
43 Powell 2002.
44 Green-Pedersen *et al*. 2001.
45 E.g. Cuperus and Kandel 1998; Clift 2001a; Bonoli and Powell 2002.
46 Cf. Bresser-Pereira 2001.
47 Notably Giddens 1998, 2001 and 2002; Blair 1998; Blair and Schröder 1999; Driver and Martell 1998, 2000; White 1998; Vandenbrouke 1998.
48 See Pierson 2001.
49 Merkel 2001.
50 Levy 1999; Thomson 2000; Clift 2001a; Green-Pedersen *et al*. 2001; Merkel 2001.
51 Blair 2001.
52 Busch and Manow 2001.
53 Lafontaine 2000: 42, 70.
54 Blair and Schröder 1999.
55 Hombach 2000.
56 Lees 2000: 135–6.
57 Giddens 2002: 5.
58 Levy 2001: 271.
59 Clift 2001b.
60 Jospin 1999: 4.
61 Bouvet and Michel 2001: 212.
62 Hemerijck and Visser 2001: 190.
63 de Beus 1999: 60.
64 Lindgren 1999: 48–9.
65 Gould 2001: 185.

66 Blair 1998; Blair and Schröder 1999. See chapters 8 and 9, this volume.
67 Lafontaine 2000: xiv; Hombach 2000.
68 Jospin 1999: 3, 7.
69 de Beus 1999: 63–5.
70 Lindgren 1999: 51–2.
71 Powell 2002.
72 Blair and Schröder 1999.
73 Hombach 2000: xxxiii.
74 Lees 2000 112.
75 Driver and Martell 1998; Powell 1999, 2000a.
76 See chapters 2, 6 and 9, this volume.
77 See chapter 2, this volume.
78 Blair and Schröder 1999; see Green-Pedersen *et al.* 2001.
79 Hombach 2000: xxxix.
80 Lees 2000: 112–15.
81 Levy 2001.
82 Bouvet and Michel 2001.
83 Clift 2001b.
84 Levy 1999.
85 Bouvet and Michel 2001: 208.
86 de Beus 1999.
87 Hemerijck *et al.* 2000: 226.
88 Levy 1999: 264.
89 Green-Pedersen *et al.* 2001: 320; Blair and Schröder 1999.
90 Lindgren 1999: 53.
91 Thomson 2000: 105; Lindgren 1999: 55.
92 Merkel 2001: 65–6.
93 Cf. Green-Pedersen *et al.* 2001.
94 Etzioni 2000.

References

Blair, T. (1998) *The Third Way*, London, Fabian Society.
Blair, T. (2001) 'Third way, phase two', *Prospect*, March.
Blair, T. and Schröder, G. (1999) *Europe: The Third Way/Die Neue mitte*, London, Labour Party.
Bonoli, G. and Powell, M. (2002) 'Third ways in Europe?', *Social Policy and Society*, 1(1).
Bouvet, L. and Michel, F. (2001) '"La gauche plurielle": an alternative to the third way?', in S. White (ed.) *New Labour: The Progressive Future?* Basingstoke, Macmillan.
Bresser-Pereira, L. (2001) 'The New Left viewed from the south', in A. Giddens (ed.) *The Global Third Way Debate*, Cambridge, Polity Press.
Busch, A. and Manow, P. (2001), 'The SPD and the Neue mitte in Germany', in S. White (ed.) *New Labour: The Progressive Future?* Basingstoke, Macmillan.
Callinicos, A. (2001) *Against the Third Way*, Cambridge, Polity Press.
Clift, B. (2001a) 'New Labour's third way and European social democracy', in S. Ludlam and M. Smith (eds) *New Labour in Government*, Basingstoke, Macmillan.
Clift, B. (2001b) 'The Jospin way', *Political Quarterly*, 72(2).

Commission on Social Justice (1994) *Social Justice: Strategies for National Renewal*, London, Vintage Books.

Cuperus, R. and Kandel, J. (eds) (1998) *European Social Democracy*, Freudenberg, Friedrich Ebert Siftung, and Amsterdam, Wiardi Beckman Stiching.

de Beus, J. (1999) 'The politics of consensual well-being', in G. Kelly (ed.) *The New European Left,* London, Fabian Society.

Driver, S. and Martell, L. (1998) *New Labour: Politics After Thatcherism*, Cambridge, Polity Press.

Driver, S. and Martell, L. (2000) 'Left, Right and the third way', *Policy and Politics*, 28(2).

The Economist (1998) 'Goldilock politics', *The Economist*, 19 December.

Etzioni, A. (2000) *The Third Way to a Good Society*, London, Demos.

Fairclough, N. (2000) *New Labour, New Language?* London, Routledge.

Ferrera, M., Hemerijck, A. and Rhodes, M. (2001) 'Recasting European welfare states for the 21st century', in S. Leibfried (ed.) *Welfare State Futures*, Cambridge, Cambridge University Press.

George, V. and Wilding, P. (1985) *Ideology and Social Welfare*, London, Routledge & Kegan Paul.

Giddens, A. (1998) *The Third Way*, Cambridge, Polity Press.

Giddens, A. (ed.) (2001) *The Global Third Way Debate*, Cambridge, Polity Press.

Giddens, A. (2002) *Where Now for New Labour?* Cambridge, Polity Press.

Gould, A. (2001) *Developments in Swedish Social Policy*, Basingstoke, Palgrave.

Gould, P. (1998) *The Unfinished Revolution*, London, Little, Brown & Co.

Green-Pedersen, C., van Kersbergen, K. and Hemerijck, A. (2001) 'Neo-liberalism, the third way or what?', *Journal of European Public Policy*, 8(2).

Hemerijck, A., Unger, B. and Visser, J. (2000) 'How small countries negotiate change', in F. Scharpf and V. Schmidt (eds) *Welfare and Work in the Open Economy*, vol. 2: *Diverse Responses to Common Challenges*, Oxford, Oxford University Press.

Hemerijck, A. and Visser, J. (2001) 'Dutch lessons in social pragmatism', in S. White (ed.) *New Labour. The Progressive Future?*, Basingstoke, Palgrave.

Hombach, B. (2000) *The Politics of the New Centre*, Cambridge, Polity Press.

Jospin, L. (1999) *Modern Socialism*, London, Fabian Society.

Kreiger, J. (1999) *British Politics in the Global Age*, Cambridge, Polity Press.

Lafontaine, O. (2000) *The Heart Beats on the Left*, Cambridge, Polity Press.

Le Grand, J. (1998) 'The third way begins with CORA', *New Statesman*, 6 March.

Lees, C. (2000) *The Red–Green Coalition in Germany*, Manchester, Manchester University Press.

Levy, J. (1999) 'Vice into virtue? Progressive politics and welfare reform in continental Europe', *Politics and Society*, 27(2).

Levy, J. (2001) 'Partisan politics and welfare adjustment: the case of France', *Journal of European Public Policy*, 8(2).

Lindgren, A.-M. (1999) 'Swedish social democracy in transition', in G. Kelly (ed.) *The New European Left*, London, Fabian Society.

Lister, R. (2000) 'To RIO via the third way', *Renewal*, 8(4).

McGuire, S. (1998–99) 'Brave New Left world', *Newsweek*, 28 December–4 January.

Merkel, W. (2001) 'The third ways of social democracy', in A. Giddens (ed.) *The Global Third Way Debate*, Cambridge, Polity Press.

Pierson, C. (2001) *Hard Choices. Social Democracy in the Twenty First Century*, Cambridge, Polity Press.

Powell, M. (ed.) (1999) *New Labour, New Welfare State?*, Bristol, Policy Press.

Powell, M. (2000a) 'Something old, something new, something borrowed, something blue: the jackdaw politics of New Labour', *Renewal*, 8(4).

Powell, M. (2000b) 'New Labour's third way in British social policy: a new and distinctive approach?', *Critical Social Policy*, 20(1).

Powell, M. (ed.) (2002), *Evaluating New Labour's Welfare Reforms*, Bristol, Policy Press.

Prowse, M. (2000) 'Mind the gap', *Prospect*, January.

Przeworski, A. (2001) 'How many ways can be third?', in A. Glyn (ed.) *Social Democracy in Neoliberal Times*, Oxford, Oxford University Press.

Schmidt, V. (2000) 'Values and discourse in the politics of adjustment', in F. Scharpf and V. Schmidt (eds) *Welfare and Work in the Open Economy*, vol. 1: *From Vulnerability to Competitiveness*, Oxford, Oxford University Press.

Schmidt, V. (2001) 'The politics of economic adjustment in France and Britain: when does discourse matter?' *Journal of European Public Policy*, 8(2).

Thomson, S. (2000) *The Social Democratic Dilemma*, Basingstoke, Macmillan.

Vandenbrouke, F. (1998) 'Globalization, inequality and social democracy', in Cuperus and Kandel (eds) *European Social Democracy*.

White, S. (1998) 'Interpreting the third way', *Renewal*, 6.

Part II

The Third Way, economics, equality and the State

Introduction

One major theme in discussions of New Labour and the Third Way more generally has concerned the Third Way's credibility as a social democratic force. As Part III shows, that credibility is based in part on its appeal to community, although there are some doubts about whether the appeal is a convincing one or whether community is genuinely social democratic, especially if it displaces values like equality. But the Third Way has also hung its social democratic credentials on its claim to promote a more equal society and save public services.

There is some controversy over its promotion of social equality, however, because the Third Way also says that it is no longer concerned with the Old Left's concern for equal outcomes and because saving public services requires private sector involvement. These two propositions go against traditional Left support of redistribution in creating more equal outcomes in society. They also challenge the Left's perception of public services as something that should be run by public actors according to social need, without the involvement of the private sector and profit. The controversy goes further when some critics see the replacement of equal outcomes by equality of opportunity as not even that. Equality of opportunity seems to envisage *minimum* opportunities and *sufficiency* for all as a baseline beyond which opportunities will not be equally shared, especially in the absence of some sort of redistribution of income and wealth. Stephen Driver, and Pete McCullen and Colin Harris investigate such issues, with an emphasis on defending the Third Way's egalitarianism, although not without their own reservations about the Third Way. Public–private partnership, furthermore, has been defended in the name of pragmatism – the Left should not be so dogmatic in its antipathy to private sector involvement in public services. If the public sector can be improved through private sector investment, then the Left should be open-minded about such investment. Eric Shaw, however, questions whether New Labour's pragmatic arguments actually work. For him, the pragmatic case for the Private Finance Initiative does not stand up. It seems that there may be more than a merely pragmatic belief in the private sector among the politicians of the Third Way.

Welfare reform has been central to the Third Way in both the USA and UK.

Stephen Driver asks whether New Labour's US-influenced welfare reforms involve a continuation of the New Right, rather than a Third Way break from them. Can an approach based on social exclusion and 'work first' promote egalitarian social democratic goals? Driver argues that there are continuities between Labour and Conservative approaches to welfare reform. However, he suggests that there are important social democratic elements in New Labour policy which cast doubt on a straightforward 'neo-liberal convergence' thesis. There *is* some egalitarianism and social democracy in New Labour's Third Way.

For McCullen and Harris equality is what differentiates the Left from the Right, and they suggest that the redefinition of equality by Giddens and by New Labour marks a significant departure from post-war social democratic goals. Giddens's Third Way rests on a social theory of modernisation and globalisation and uses the notion of 'generative equality' to propose a new model for social policy. McCullen and Harris critically assess this idea of 'generative equality' from a managerial perspective. On the positive side, they argue that Giddens's prescriptions for generative welfare policies and equality have much in common with those of the management literature of the last two decades which emphasises the importance of individual responsibility and 'empowerment' over Taylorist command and control approaches. It is argued, however, that Giddens's use of Maslow's hierarchy of needs as a model for the creation of 'happiness' and 'self-actualisation' is open to misinterpretation and that a stronger egalitarianism is needed for the realisation of generative equality and happiness, and for self-actualisation.

Eric Shaw discusses New Labour's Private Finance Initiative (PFI), which separates the commissioning of public services through public authorities from the provision of those services which the private sector is encouraged to undertake. PFI has been seen as an important part of the government's strategy to modernise public services and an economically feasible way of rebuilding the decaying public infrastructure, especially in the health service. It is presented as a pragmatic approach, which goes beyond both the right-wing dogmas that the private sector should own and provide public services and the leftist belief that the State should be the sole provider. Partnerships between public and private, it is argued, can secure higher public sector investment. The New Labour Government argues that PPP–PFI 'works best'. Shaw, however, argues that there is little substance to the British Government's claim that the PFI is, on pragmatic grounds, the most effective way of renewing the capital infrastructure of the NHS. There must be other reasons for the Government's preference for private sector involvement. The alleged pragmatism of the Third Way is cast into doubt.

2 Stephen Driver

North Atlantic drift: welfare reform and the 'Third Way' politics of New Labour and the New Democrats

Since the early 1990s welfare reform has been at the heart of the Centre-Left's search for a new political middle way between post-war social democracy and Thatcherite Conservatism. For Tony Blair, welfare reform was key to establishing his *New* Labour credentials – just as it was for Bill Clinton and the *New* Democrats in the USA.[1] In government, Labour's welfare-to-work programme has been the centrepiece of this welfare reform drive – and of Labour's attempt to mark out a new 'Third Way' for the Centre-Left. But some (for example, Cammack, in chapter 8 of this book) see New Labour's US-influenced welfare reforms as marking a consensus, not a break with the New Right. This chapter examines whether a policy strategy based on social exclusion and pushing 'work first' can sustain a commitment to egalitarian social democratic values, something on which Goes (see chapter 6) casts doubt. While I acknowledge the continuities between Labour and Conservative approaches to welfare reform, I argue that there are important social democratic elements in New Labour policy which cast doubt on a straightforward 'neo-liberal convergence' thesis.

Social exclusion, social justice and the Third Way

The core objective of the Labour Government's social exclusion strategy is to shift individuals from welfare to work using a mix of carrots and sticks. The aim is to get back into employment those capable but currently not working. Policies like the Working Families' Tax Credit and the minimum wage to 'make work pay' are designed, first and foremost, to remove the disincentives to take jobs for those on benefits. Making low-paid work more attractive is key. The Labour Government has also changed the rules of entitlement and introduced new time-limits.

For the Labour Government, tackling social exclusion is part of a broader strategy to promote social justice.[2] For Chancellor Gordon Brown, this means government creating greater equality of opportunity over people's lifetimes.[3] Getting the unemployed back to work – social inclusion – is one thing. But the bigger picture is about equipping individuals ('education, education, education', as Tony Blair put it) with the tools to make the most of their lives – social justice. A more equal society is about widening opportunities to work. Helping people become more employable – 'employability' – has both the short-term goal of getting the unemployed into the labour market and the long-term one of building the stocks of human capital that shape an individual's life chances, including earning capacities.[4]

By and large, this supply-side strategy rejects fiscal means – at least in terms of higher income tax rates and benefit levels for those out of work – to promote equality. Globalisation, it is argued, has undermined the fiscal powers of the state to equalise income.[5] Instead, this strategy addresses egalitarian concerns by promising a range of policies to alter the supply of labour. These, it is hoped, will redistribute work opportunities to the benefit of those less well-off in society. Policies such as the New Deal, the National Childcare Strategy, 'individual learning accounts' and 'baby bonds' are about enhancing life chances, especially for the least well-off, to find work and to increase earning capacities. This human capital strategy is an attempt to influence the market-determined distribution of resources, giving poorer individuals more leverage in the labour market by enhancing their tradable skills. In this way, opportunities are connected, in New Labour thinking, to outcomes.

So, for New Labour, welfare strategies to promote social justice and social inclusion overlap and complement one another. Social exclusion is not having a job. But it also encompasses the many ways in which individuals and families are cut off from the sources of social capital, especially education, which are seen as the main determinants of individual opportunity. The new egalitarians look to the stock of individual endowments that help shape individual lives – and the distribution of rewards in society.[6] For some Labour modernisers, the question of social exclusion is bound up with a wider debate about equality and distributive justice. Including the socially excluded by way of the labour market can be part and parcel of a wider redistribution of opportunities – and even incomes – across society.

The notion of social exclusion does not, then, in itself preclude a more egalitarian understanding of social justice. It could well be part of a re-thinking of social democracy rather than its abandonment. But some see New Labour's social exclusion agenda crowding out the Left's traditional concern with equality and social justice.[7] Moreover, whatever the intentions, doubts remain whether the Government's human capital strategy can really deliver on social justice.

The price of the Third Way: giving up on equality?

The debate about Labour's welfare reforms – and the 'Third Way' more generally – has the question of equality at its core. While Gordon Brown has robustly defended New Labour's position on equality,[8] critics have accused Labour modernisers of abandoning the Left's traditional concern with the distribution of wealth and income – and with equality of outcome.[9] New Labour stands accused of embracing a meritocratic, as well as individualistic,[10] model of equality that is both spurious and not in itself of the Left. And in giving up on fiscal redistribution – in particular, higher rates of income tax and benefit levels – the Labour Government has thrown away the central policy tools with which to redistribute resources across an unequal society. The concept of social justice has been stripped of its radical egalitarianism, in place of which there is a concern with minimum levels of opportunity that will never challenge entrenched inequalities of wealth and income. For many – even those in sympathy with New Labour – the danger of Third Way ideas is that they can all too easily lead Labour away from social democracy and the values of the Left.[11] As Carey Oppenheim – herself a moderniser – insists, equality must be central to Labour's welfare reforms: 'At the very least, the traditional social democratic goal of improving the relative position of the worst off in relation to the average has to remain a crucial objective.'[12]

For many on the Left, the debate about paid work and social inclusion in New Labour thinking ignores wider inequalities in the labour market. As Ruth Lister argues: 'it is questionable how far genuine social inclusion can be achieved without addressing the inequalities which are the motor of social exclusion'.[13] Both Lister and Ruth Levitas argue that the Labour Government's social exclusion strategy is too narrowly defined in terms of paid work. The socially excluded get to be included by becoming employed. This is crowding out the Left's traditional concern with equality and a notion of citizenship defined in egalitarian terms. Redistributive justice gets lost in worries about welfare dependence and social integration. Where the Left stands for greater equality of outcomes, New Labour believes in little more than minimum opportunities. In the hands of New Labour, then, social justice has lost its distinctively egalitarian – and socialist – value.

Some of the blame for this loss of critical edge has been put down to the American influence on British social policy – an influence felt first under the Conservatives and continued under Labour. The rest of this chapter examines whether the Government's welfare-to-work programme is undermining Labour's commitment to social justice. Like most welfare reformers in the USA, the Labour Government in Britain appears to be putting work, rather than education and training, first in its welfare-to-work programme. But putting 'work first' has no inherent interest in outcomes other than to increase work levels among those on welfare. Any job is better than no job because work is always better than welfare. But can the Labour Government combine a commitment to putting work first with a human capital strategy that genuinely creates a more level playingfield of opportunity – and which convinces critics that New Labour remains committed to making society more equal?

From welfare to work

'Work not welfare' has wide support among Western leaders of all political per-
suasions. But important differences in approach remain: the spectrum of welfare-
to-work programmes is wide.[14] On the one hand, there are active labour market
strategies – especially those rooted in European welfare regimes – that focus on
education and training as prerequisites for finding employment. On the other
hand, there are strategies now prevalent in the US that give priority to labour force
attachment: that is, to work as a necessary first step to developing the right kinds
of skills and habits – those required for success in the labour market.

Between 1987 (the start of Labour's policy review) and the mid-1990s, the
European – and European social democratic – influence on Labour thinking was
obvious. Modernisers inside and outside the party were working with a model
of political economy distinct from the neo-liberal–Anglo-American one. But
sometime in the mid-1990s the tide of influence turned. A North Atlantic policy
drift set in.[15] Welfare reform under Bill Clinton had already left its mark on
Labour modernisers – for example, the policy of tax credits to 'make work pay'.
But by the 1997 general election, New Labour had ditched a continental
European model of political economy for a North American one. Once in power,
Tony Blair and Gordon Brown began to lecture fellow European Union leaders
on the need to follow the Americans on issues such as welfare and labour market
reform. Martin Powell and Armando Barrientos are right to argue (chapter 1 in
this volume) that in practice many of those policy elements now seen as typical
of Third Way politics, such as active labour market strategies, are also characteristic of 'old' European social democracy. But despite Labour's attempts to
build bridges with European social democrats, the Third Way – and the policy
reforms that underpinned it – looked increasingly like an Anglo-American affair.

The American influence on British welfare reform and, in particular, New
Labour's social policies has been widely commented on.[16] While Alan Deacon
reminds us that '[p]olicy makers in Britain and the US operate in very different
cultural, political and institutional contexts', he adds that those same policy-
makers are 'seeking to achieve similar objectives and draw upon a similar range
of policy instruments in order to do so'. In both countries, Deacon argues,
welfare reformers have focused on welfare dependence and welfare obligations;
and, on both sides of the Atlantic, work requirements have been introduced and
attempts made to 'make work pay'. These approaches are, Deacon argues, 'inte-
grative in that they draw upon and incorporate elements from quite different perspectives on the purpose of welfare'.[17]

Just how far down the American route – in the words of King and Wickham-
Jones – is the Labour Government prepared to go? What are the implications for
Labour's fundamental objectives that are the focus of this chapter? There are two
basic positions on what New Labour has learnt from the USA. The first is that
New Labour has gone all New Democrat, that Blair and Brown are following in
the footsteps of Clinton – especially the early Clinton – and marking out a new

progressive agenda on welfare based on 'tough love'. This agenda is distinct from the conservative Right in its support for welfare entitlements; but also distinct from the liberal Left in insisting that those entitlements must be conditional: welfare rights must be matched by welfare responsibilities. This view of welfare reform sees the real possibility of tackling both social exclusion and social justice within the framework of a competitive free market economy.[18]

The second position is that New Labour has simply gone all New Right, that Blair and Brown have caved in to the Right's welfare agenda – just as Clinton did in the USA[19] – and that all talk of a welfare 'Third Way' is so much hot air: the Anglo-American consensus is really a neo-liberal consensus. Labour has abandoned a human capital model of welfare reform rooted in European social democracy and fundamental to the Commission on Social Justice. In its dash to learn lessons from the USA, the Labour Government is importing a neo-liberal model of welfare reform – 'work first' – that is at odds with its commitments to social justice, because labour force attachment strategies reinforce labour market divisions, especially for the low-paid.[20] In the UK, the USA and elsewhere, the 'welfare state' is giving way to the 'workfare state'. Any possibility of the Labour Government delivering on the traditional objectives of the Left has been lost.

Is 'work first' making it worse?

Has New Labour changed its mind on welfare reform? Has there, in particular, been a shift in emphasis from a human capital model to a 'work first' model? And what are the implications of any change for Labour's fundamental objectives – and for those of the Left more broadly?

Welfare politics in the twentieth century on both sides of the Atlantic operated within a political and institutional culture that gave priority to managing social security and which neglected human capital.[21] In the 1980s, the Labour Party nailed its employment policy colours to the education and training mast, commitments that have since been watered down.[22] Certainly, work not welfare became the central theme of New Labour's social policies in the mid-1990s, but that was tempered by the party's continuing commitment to education and training in supporting those looking for work.[23] Gordon Brown's announcement, made in opposition, that a Labour government would require young people after six months on its welfare-to-work programme to participate in one of the New Deal's four options, is rightly considered a milestone in New Labour thinking on welfare reform. The compulsion and increased conditionality of the New Deal mark off the reforms from the post-war social democratic welfare paradigm, if not from an older ethical socialist tradition.[24]

Jamie Peck suggests that Labour leaders squared the party and the trade unions on the introduction of compulsion by promising that government would offer New Dealers 'a range of high quality options' backed by hard cash. Labour's New Deal would be just that – and not another Tory Youth Training

Scheme. For Peck, however, Labour in government has shifted ground. He accuses the Labour Government of failing to deliver on its up-market version of welfare-to-work. Peck was open to the 'progressive possibilities' of Labour's New Deal.[25] And while Peck and Nikolas Theodore concede that there is more to the New Deal than most US versions of welfare-to-work, they argue that the Government has fallen for 'work first': 'While significantly more broadly based and service-rich than US-style "work first" programmes, the New Deal for 18–24-year-old unemployed people nevertheless places overriding emphasis on assisting transitions into paid employment.'[26] This reinforces what they see as the neo-liberal policy orthodoxy on flexible labour markets, and it erodes, not builds, the stock of human capital. Such programmes run against the grain of traditional approaches to welfare provision:

> [I]n contrast to the welfarist logic of providing temporary shelters outside the labour market for designated social groups, this workfarist logic dictates that targeted social groups are driven into the labour market, where they are expected to remain, notwithstanding systemic problems of under-employment, low pay and exploitative work relations.[27]

The implication, then, is that as the Labour Government's New Deal becomes orientated more around 'work first', its 'progressiveness' declines because it reinforces existing labour market inequalities. As a result, New Labour has moved away from the Left–liberal social agenda that addresses low-paid work, labour market inequalities and the issues addressed by philosophical egalitarianism.

A number of questions need to be addressed here. First, is the message really as bleak from the USA: does 'work first' necessarily exclude 'progressive possibilities' in the way that Peck and Theodore suggest? Second, is the New Deal really so orientated around 'work first'? Are there, in fact, more 'progressive possibilities' to Labour's welfare reforms – and to its Third Way – than many on the Left give it credit for?

Evaluating welfare-to-work in the USA

'Work first' has become the dominant welfare-to-work paradigm in the USA among Democrats and Republicans, especially where it matters at state government level. Support for human capital-based welfare-to-work programmes has declined.[28] Getting welfare recipients quickly back into the labour market – rather than encouraging them to take education and training courses prior to work – has become the overwhelming priority. However, the question remains whether 'work first' models of welfare-to-work are too exclusive and whether they are incapable of operating alongside other models.

In America, welfare-to-work programmes, which have been going since the early 1980s, are judged against work levels among those on welfare; and the evidence they afford is mixed. Studies of the post-1996 reforms suggest that welfare reform has had a positive impact in reducing welfare rolls – though a lot of the credit goes to the long boom in the US economy during the 1990s. In terms of the main themes of this chapter, however, the evidence also shows that the majority of those leaving welfare do so to work in low-skill, low-wage jobs.[29] Indeed, welfare-to-work is really a process of welfare-to-work plus welfare. Welfare benefits, in terms of both working tax credits and benefits in kind like food stamps and medical insurance, remain.

Within the American political debate, this evidence tends to reinforce the liberal Left's view that welfare-to-work is about 'flipping hamburgers'; and that these 'McJobs', rather than leading on to something better, are more likely to be either 'McJobs for life' or a revolving door back to welfare. In either case, welfare-to-work does little or nothing to address fundamental issues of inequality and poverty, especially among families. American egalitarians want more from welfare reform.[30]

None of this is a problem to supporters of 'work first' – or is it? Peck rightly argues that the essence of labour force attachment strategies is that any job is better than no job. What really matters is the 'work participation rate'. In this sense, 'work first' is 'outcome-indifferent'. But does this mean that advocates of 'work first' ignore broader issues such as in-work poverty and child-care provision – issues that generally fall within the progressive framework?

In the 1980s, American conservatives like Lawrence Mead argued that welfare must be made more conditional.[31] Progressives too were shifting ground. David Ellwood supported time-limited welfare alongside more training and efforts to 'make work pay'.[32] A measure of bi-partisanship on welfare-to-work emerged. Democrat and Republican state governors alike – and Bill Clinton as chair of the state governors in the late 1980s was a leading figure – championed the new approach as welfare reform was increasingly devolved to states under the policy of federal waivers.[33] By the mid-1990s, however, doubts were being raised on the means by which to deliver welfare-to-work. Support for labour force attachment strategies grew. In states like Wisconsin, this support crossed party lines. Labour force attachment was seen as a better way of getting people back to work, especially those (the majority) who had recently become unemployed and who had the necessary skills to find another job quickly. Progressives continued to believe in active government. They agreed with the 'big government conservative' Mead that those on welfare needed to be hassled – and this meant making welfare conditional by introducing time-limits. But they remained committed, unlike the libertarian Charles Murray,[34] to government help for those on welfare in the form of training, family and child-care support and in-work benefits.

So, while many American progressives – and conservatives – became critical of human capital strategies, what they were critical of was those strategies' ability, of themselves, to deliver welfare-to-work. For them, the problem was one of means. For many progressive supporters of 'work first', getting welfare recipients back into work quickly could be combined with human capital strategies that had broader objectives and progressive assumptions about the role of government in providing welfare. Rather than one big 'race to the bottom', welfare reform in the USA, albeit in incredibly favourable economic times, has seen considerable investments in welfare-to-work programmes by state governments – including job search, short-term training and family and child-care support. Those hoping that welfare reform – even on 'work first' principles – would simply save money have missed the point: welfare-to-work programmes are expensive.[35]

The essence, then, of the New Democrat position was to combine what had been thought of as distinctively progressive or conservative political positions by insisting that welfare reform could combine additional services for those on welfare with strict expectations about their behaviour.[36] Bill Clinton's promise, in 1992, 'to end welfare as we know it' reflected a bi-partisan consensus on welfare reform that had emerged in the USA in the late 1980s, especially at state level.[37] The package of reforms drawn up in Washington by Ellwood and Mary Jo Bane for President Clinton between 1992 and 1994 sought not, as the slogan suggested, to 'end welfare', but rather to insist that after a certain period those on welfare would be expected to work for their welfare cheques in a subsidised job at a private firm, public agency or non-profit organisation. This, essentially, is the welfare reform strategy pursued by the Labour Government in the UK.[38] It marks the *reform* of the welfare state, not its demise.

New Labour's New Deal

What is happening to Labour's New-Dealers?

In Britain, as in the USA, early studies of the Government's New Deal have been broadly positive.[39] After six months on Job Seeker's Allowance, young people aged between 18 and 24 are allocated a personal advisor whose job it is to provide assistance with an intensive job search. This 'gateway' period has been 'intensified' to boost 'soft skills' like punctuality, appearance and communication. At the end of four months, those individuals who have not found jobs are offered one of four options: full-time education and training for twelve months without loss of benefit for those without basic education; a six-month voluntary sector job; a job on an environmental task force; or a subsidised job (plus one day a week training). If an individual refuses one of these options, sanctions apply, including loss of benefits. It is important to note, however, that while the New Deal now covers most of the workless – including lone parents – the rules covering time-limits, compulsion and sanctions differ from programme to programme.[40]

Peck and Theodore argue that the structure and ethos of the New Deal for Young People is biased toward the employment options – either in the initial gateway period or in the choice of options after four months. In fact, of those who joined the New Deal prior to the end of April 1999, 47.1 per cent were on the education and training option and 20.5 per cent on the employment option.[41] According to the House of Commons Select Committee on Education and

Employment, by the end of April 2000, 470,000 young people had started the New Deal for Young People and approximately 330,000 had left the programme. Of these 800,000, just over 215,000 individuals had found work – and 139,000 were in 'sustained and unsubsidised jobs' lasting more than thirteen weeks. Around 30 per cent of destinations are unknown – though some survey evidence suggests that more than half of that figure found work.[42] There is also a very high (over 80 per cent) drop-out rate from the full-time education and training option.

The New Deal, which aims to get individuals back to work as quickly as possible, is supported by the Working Families' Tax Credit (including child-care support) and the minimum wage. The primary aim of these 'carrot and stick' policies is to reduce the disincentives to take up a job, especially low-paid work. In many cases, the unemployed have found work with or without the New Deal: the economy has been growing for more than five years – there are vacancies nationwide; and, while a significant minority of young people in the New Deal have problems with basic numeracy and literacy, the majority clearly have the skills and ability to find work. The relative success of the New Deal has been such that it has faced a recruitment problem. While the number of New Deal programmes has risen, the size (and the cost) of the main New Deal for Young People has decreased, largely due to lack of demand and the higher proportion of individuals leaving the programme.[43]

In many respects, 'work first' is a product of good economic times: many of those on welfare are 'work-ready', and since 1997 there have been jobs to be had in a buoyant labour market. As in the USA, the question remains whether such programmes will work as the UK's economy turns down and unemployment rates creep up. The challenge for social policy-makers is how welfare-to-work programmes deal with those who have very real problems in finding and holding down work, especially those in localities with deep-seated economic and social problems. The global economic downturn after 2001 will test the limits of welfare-to-work programmes in the UK and across the rest of the world.

Welfare reform beyond Thatcherism

New Labour modernisers insist that welfare reform can deliver on Old Left goals like social justice while sustaining an efficient market economy. New policies to enhance levels of human capital, especially of the poor, can bring a measure of social justice to society by promoting opportunities in the labour market. The Left, however, while acknowledging the Blair Government's belief in some measure of social justice – on combating poverty and social inclusion – insists that Labour's commitment to egalitarian values has evaporated. In particular, the Left insists that Labour has given up on any attempt to make economic outcomes more equal.

The data on welfare-to-work transitions gives some credence to the Government's critics. The fact that the New Deal results in a relatively high level of unsustained jobs – about 25 per cent of those who enter employment through the New Deal for Young People do not last thirteen weeks – would appear to support Peck and Theodore's view that there is a 'revolving door' between welfare and part-time, temporary and low-paid work. The USA's evidence on welfare-to-work destinations supports the view that those leaving welfare usually end up at the bottom of the labour market. The New Deal is meant in part to offer the unemployed across all age groups – including the long-term unemployed – the opportunity to enhance their human capital as a means not just of getting work but increasing their chances of finding better paid and more secure work – and in this way, enhancing the life chances of those who start with least in society. The fact that a quarter of young New Dealers enter employment that does not last thirteen weeks, or that the vast majority of young people on the education and training option fail to finish their courses, suggests that something is wrong. It is too early to determine whether the New Deal is enhancing the human capital of those at the bottom of the labour market. The challenge for any future government is to provide, for those who do find work, the support necessary to keep their jobs and to start building ladders to better positions in the future.

But does the New Deal help New Labour pass the Oppenheim test: that is, does it improve the relative position of the worst-off relative to the average? Simply in terms of relative rates of wealth and income, the answer must be no. After a period of stabilisation in levels of income inequality in the UK in the 1990s, the end of the decade saw the gap between rich and poor widen as the economy boomed and wage differentials opened.[44] It is certainly true that the Labour Government, especially after the 2000 Comprehensive Spending Review, has pursued a fiscal policy that redistributes the fruits of a booming economy to poorer groups in society, especially those in low-paid work and families. The effect of Labour's fiscal reforms has been to make the tax and benefit systems more equalising.[45]

But, even if in the longer term the Government's welfare-to-work programmes and its wider reforms to education and training do boost the human capital of the poor, it is very unlikely that this would lead to a reduction in inequality, as average incomes are also likely to rise. Those already well-stocked in human capital are always going to have the edge where education and training attracts a premium in the labour market. As David Miller concedes, 'supply-side egalitarianism' may be 'an excellent approach, but it will probably work much more effectively as an anti-poverty device, preventing people from dropping out of the bottom of the labour market, than as a device for reducing inequality between top and bottom'.[46] For that reason, many egalitarians like Miller remain committed to the kind of government interventions in the capitalist economy, in terms of both the ownership of property and the fiscal powers of the State, specifically ruled out by New Labour. Moreover, those who support a more modest 'asset egalitarianism' make very limited claims, insisting that the objective is to guarantee minimum starting-points, not equal starting-points, let alone equal shares.[47] As Andrew Glyn and Stewart Wood argue, policies concerned with the absolute position of the least advantaged can co-exist with policies that tolerate and even encourage the pursuit of wealth. As a result, society may become less egalitarian, even if more meritocratic. According to Glyn and Wood:

> In this respect New Labour has disentangled the traditional social democratic aims of promoting equality and eliminating poverty in ways that many on the left find both unacceptable (in respect of greater inequality in the top half of the distribution) and unconvincing (in respect of the near-exclusive emphasis on the labour market).[48]

In the end, the Government's critics on the Left have a point: the New Deal and its associated policies are primarily about a policy agenda narrowly focused on social exclusion and paid employment – a view readily conceded on the 'big government' Right.[49] As Raymond Plant argues, there is nothing inherently social democratic about the New Deal: enhancing the marketable skills of the poor still leaves the market as the final arbiter of the value of those skills. But neither is the New Deal very neo-liberal (say, of a Charles Murray vintage). There is something third-wayish about the New Deal in terms of how it conceives of citizenship, the labour market and the role of the State (see also chapter 9 of this volume, by David Morrison).

For that reason, lumping the Labour Government's welfare reforms into one big political pile with those of previous Tory governments – and the New Right generally – has limited value. In the end, New Labour is more than just Thatcherism Mark 2.[50] There is, to be sure, a degree of continuity between Labour and Conservative approaches to welfare (to work) over the past two decades.[51] But there are important social democratic elements in New Labour's policy-making that betray a continued commitment to social justice – and which cast doubt on a straightforward 'neo-liberal convergence' thesis.[52]

Central to the 'Third Way' politics of New Labour and the New Democrats is the notion that different policy approaches, whether from the Left or the Right, can in some way be combined, if not actually reconciled.[53] The welfare reforms of the Labour Government reflect this political strategy. They combine policies on incentives, prevention and rehabilitation, as well as a new paternalism.[54] On incentives, New Labour, like Clinton's New Democrats, has moved to 'make work pay' by introducing in-work tax credits and a minimum wage, to provide support (such as child care) to enable individuals to take up jobs, as well as subsidies to support low-paid employment (in the New Deal, for example). On prevention and rehabilitation, the Labour Government has introduced policies to enhance the human capital of those on welfare and those in work. All of these policies fit, though not exclusively, a progressive social democratic agenda on welfare reform – and, in sum, they mark out a substantial role for the State in providing welfare.

At the same time, New Labour, again like the New Democrats, has drawn on the 'new paternalism' of some (e.g. Mead), but by no means all, of the New Right. The Labour Government has made the rights of citizens to welfare even more contingent on responsibilities – in particular, the responsibility to find work. New Labour's welfare reforms demand, as the new paternalism requires, certain types of behavioural response and sanction those forms of behaviour deemed 'irresponsible'. Third way politics is not neutral on the 'good citizen'. This element of new paternalism in New Labour and the New Democrats led to the policy of work requirements and marks an obvious break with the old progressive agenda, on both sides of the Atlantic, which believed that rights to welfare should not be contingent on work requirements. But while New Labour and the New Democrats have broken with the post-war progressive Left, they have retained a distance from sections of the Right – in particular, that element (e.g. Murray) of the New Right advocating a deterrence strategy. This strategy considers that welfare entitlements should be withdrawn to prevent undesirable behavioural outcomes (like teen pregnancy). It is a strategy that seeks the *end*, not the reform, of the welfare state.

Pursuing such a welfare middle way, especially for progressive politicians, brings threats as well as opportunities. As Kent Weaver argues, Bill Clinton's repositioning of the Democratic Party widened the policy options on poverty and welfare for a Centre-Left party.[55] The 'modernisation' of the Labour Party has done much the same. But these new opportunities bring with them dangers when the policy-making door is opened to reforms far more radical than those initially envisaged. In 1996, after having largely ceded the legislative initiative to Congress, President Clinton signed the Republican welfare reform bill. Welfare politics in the US took a giant leap to the Right. Crucially, the 1996 legislation ended federal entitlements and introduced a five-year time-limit to the newly devolved state welfare support.

But must the ideological concessions made by New Labour and the New Democrats inevitably lead to further shifts to the Right, as Weaver warns is possible? As Steven Teles argues, the New Democrat position on welfare – after a certain period, benefit claimants should work or study for their welfare – reflects contemporary public opinion. Most Americans, Teles shows, want those on welfare to work, but they don't want the government to cast them adrift.[56] Such a view underpins Mead's 'new politics of poverty'.[57] This shift in public policy from welfare to employment, as Mead concedes, re-legitimises the welfare state – and this is just as likely to promote a shift to the Left as one to the Right. Once the voters know that those on welfare are going to be hassled to find jobs, they are more than happy to help them – even generously.

After its first term in government since the 1970s, New Labour's attack on the so-called 'something for nothing' welfare culture is starting to pay political dividends. The flip-side of getting tough on social security entitlements – always that part of the welfare budget least popular with voters – is a series of budgets that has set the Blair Government on a more traditional Labour course to increase spending on the public services, especially on health and education, as well as increasing the incomes of the 'working poor', especially those with children. These increases in spending are being paid for by higher taxes – both in terms of higher tax rates and a higher tax take. While Brown's budgets have been embraced by the Left as 'redistribution by stealth', there is nothing very underhand about the Labour Government's commitment to increasing the income of those at the bottom of the labour market and to those with children. The Government has remained true to its *New* Labour colours by not raising the income tax rates of high earners, although national insurance rates were increased by the chancellor in his 2002 budget. But the extra money flowing into Treasury coffers after four years in office of New Labour has been targeted on those households at the bottom of the income scale. After two years of sticking to Tory spending limits, a measure of egalitarian public policy is back on the political agenda.

The fact that the Clinton presidency did not mark a liberal counter-revolution after the Reagan–Bush years rather misses the point about what being a New Democrat is all about.[58] By the same token, that Blair has not turned the welfare clock back to a pre-Thatcher era – he never said he would – is to miss what is really new about New Labour. Like the New Democrats, New Labour's welfare reforms cross ideological lines. But there remains, despite those overlaps, a distinctively progressive and social democratic side to the reforms. This is not a Government in thrall to the New Right. Yes, there are continuities between Labour's welfare-to-work programmes – and with its broader political economy – and those of previous Conservative administrations. But putting 'work first' on its welfare reform agenda is not to exclude more progressive policy reforms on family poverty, opportunities in the labour market and social inclusion. Indeed, the 'new paternalism' in New Labour's Third Way, rather than being the thin end of a conservative wedge, may in fact help to sustain social democratic values and egalitarian public policy-making – not undermine them. There is, after all, room for social democratic politics after Thatcherism.

Notes

1 See Teles 1996; Weaver 1998.
2 See Oppenheim 1999.
3 Brown 1997.
4 HM Treasury 1999; Brown 2000; see also Mulgan in Hills *et al.* 1998.
5 CSJ 1994.
6 Kelly and Gamble 2000; Nissan and Le Grand 2000.
7 See the chapters by Goes, Cammack and Morrison in this volume.
8 Brown 1997.
9 See Cohen 1994.
10 See Phillips 2000.
11 White 1998.
12 Oppenheim 1999: 5; see also Oppenheim 2001.
13 Lister 2000a; see also Lister 2000b.
14 See Finn 1999.
15 See Driver and Martell 1998: chapter 2.
16 See King and Wickham-Jones 1998.

17 Deacon 2000a:16; see also Deacon 2000b.
18 On the 'Blair–Clinton orthodoxy', see also Jordan 1998.
19 See Lo and Schwartz 1998.
20 Peck and Theodore 2000.
21 King 1995.
22 King and Wickham-Jones 1998.
23 See Labour Party (undated).
24 See Deacon and Mann 1997, 1999; Field 1995.
25 Peck 1999; see also Peck 1998.
26 Peck and Theodore 2000: 126.
27 Peck and Theodore 2000: 131–5.
28 See Wiseman 1996.
29 Brauner and Loprest 1998; US General Accounting Office 1999.
30 See Jencks 1997; Lo and Schwartz 1998; Teles 1996.
31 Mead 1986.
32 Ellwood 1998.
33 See Weaver 1998; also Weaver 2000.
34 Murray 1984.
35 Wiseman 1996.
36 Teles 1996.
37 Wiseman 1996.
38 See Glennerster 2000.
39 Anderton, Riley and Young 1999; see also Institute for Fiscal Studies 2000.
40 See Finn 2001.
41 Institute for Fiscal Studies 2000: 99.
42 Select Committee on Education and Employment 2000: 1–2, 5.
43 Select Committee on Education and Employment 2000.
44 Office for National Statistics 2001.
45 Clark, Myck and Smith 2001.
46 Miller 1997: 89.
47 Kelly and Gamble 2000.
48 Glyn and Wood 2001: 64; see also White 1997.
49 Mead 1997.
50 Driver and Martell 1998; Driver and Martell 2002.
51 See Grover and Stewart 1999.
52 Rhodes 2000; see also Crouch 2001.
53 See Driver and Martell 2000; Deacon 2000b; see also Barrientos and Powell (chapter 1 this volume) who stress the 'traffic flow' problems as Left and Right merge on the Third Way.
54 See Weaver 1998.
55 *Ibid*.
56 Teles 1996
57 Mead 1992.
58 O'Connor 1998.

References

Anderton, B., Riley, R. and Young, G. (1999) *The New Deal for Young People: Early Findings from the Pathfinder Areas*, London, Employment Service and National Institute of Economic and Social Research (ESR 34).

Brauner, S. and Loprest, P. (1998) *Where Are They Now? What States' Studies of People Who Left Welfare Tell Us*, Washington, DC, Urban Institute.

Brown, G. (1997) The Anthony Crosland Memorial Lecture, 13 February, London, Labour Party.

Brown, G. (2000) The James Mead Memorial Lecture, 8 May, London, HM Treasury.

Clark, T., Myck, M. and Smith, Z. (2001) *Fiscal Reforms Affecting Households, 1997–2001*, London, Institute for Fiscal Studies (IFS Election Briefing Note 5).

Cohen, G. A. (1994) 'Back to socialist basics', *New Left Review*, 207.

Commission on Social Justice (1994) *Social Justice: Strategies for National Renewal*, London, Vintage Books.

Crouch, C. (2001) 'A third way in industrial relations', in S. White (ed.) *New Labour: The Progressive Future?*, Basingstoke, Palgrave.

Deacon, A. (2000a) 'Same ingredients, different recipes? Comparing the British and American approaches to welfare reform', Paper presented at the APPAM Fall Research Conference, Seattle, WA, 4 November.

Deacon, A. (2000b) 'Learning from the US? The influence of American ideas on New Labour thinking on welfare reform', *Policy and Politics*, 28(1).

Deacon, A. and Mann, K. (1997) 'Moralism and modernity: the paradox of New Labour thinking on welfare', *Benefits*, September–October.

Deacon, A. and Mann, K. (1999) 'Agency, modernity and social policy', *Journal of Social Policy*, 28(3).

Driver, S. and Martell, L. (1998) *New Labour: Politics After Thatcherism*, Cambridge, Polity Press.

Driver, S. and Martell, L. (2000) 'Left, Right and the third way', *Policy and Politics*, 28(2).

Driver, S. and Martell, L. (2002) *Blair's Britain*, Cambridge, Polity Press.

Ellwood, D (1998) *Poor Support: Poverty in the American Family*, New York, Basic Books.

Field, F. (1995) *Making Welfare Work*, London, Institute of Community Studies.

Finn, D. (1999) 'Job guarantees for the unemployed: lessons from Australian welfare reform', *Journal of Social Policy*, 28(1).

Finn, D. (2001)'Welfare to work? New Labour and the unemployed', in S. Savage and R. Atkinson (eds) *Public Policy Under Blair*, Basingstoke, Palgrave.

Glennerster, H. (2000) *US Poverty Studies and Poverty Measurement: The Past Twenty-Five Years*, London, London School of Economics (CASE Paper 42).

Glyn, A. and Wood, S. (2001) 'Economic policy under New Labour: how social democratic is the Blair Government?', *Political Quarterly*, 72(1).

Grover, C. and Stewart, J. (1999) 'Market workfare: social security, social regulation and competitiveness in the 1990s', *Journal of Social Policy*, 28(1).

Hills, J., Mulgan, G., Piachaud, J. and Wilson, W. J. (1998) *Welfare Reform: Learning from American Mistakes*, London, London School of Economics (CASE Report 3).

HM Treasury (1999) *The Modernisation of Britain's Tax and Benefits System 4: Tackling Poverty and Extending Opportunity*, London, HM Treasury.

Institute for Fiscal Studies (2000) *Green Budget*, London, Institute for Fiscal Studies.

Jencks, C. (1997) 'The hidden paradox of welfare reform', *The American Prospect*, May–June.

Jordan, B. (1998) *The New Politics of Welfare: Social Justice in a Global Context*, London, Sage.

Kelly, G. and Gamble, A. (2000) 'Stakeholding and individual ownership accounts', Paper presented to the Political Studies Association Conference, London, 10–12 April.

King, D. (1995) *Actively Seeking Work: The Politics of Unemployment and Welfare Policy in the United States and Great Britain*, Chicago, IL, University of Chicago Press.

King, D. and Wickham-Jones, M. (1998) 'Training without the State: New Labour and labour markets', *Policy and Politics*, 26(4).

King, D. and Wickham-Jones, M. (1999) 'From Clinton to Blair: the Democratic (Party's) origins of welfare to work', *Political Quarterly*, 70(1).

Labour Party (undated) *Getting Welfare to Work*, London, Labour Party.

Levitas, R. (1998) *The Inclusive Society? Social Exclusion and New Labour*, Basingstoke, Macmillan.

Lister, R. (2000a) 'Towards a citizens' welfare state: the 3 + 2 Rs of welfare reform', Paper presented to the Social Policy Association's Annual Conference.

Lister, R. (2000b) 'To Rio via the third way: New Labour's welfare reform agenda', *Renewal*, 8(4).

Lo, C. Y. H. and Schwartz, C. (1998) *Social Policy and the Conservative Agenda*, Oxford, Blackwell.

Mead, L. (1986) *Beyond Entitlement: The Social Obligation of Citizenship*, New York, Free Press.

Mead, L. (1992) *The New Politics of Poverty: The Nonworking Poor in America*, New York, Basic Books.

Mead, L. (1997) 'From welfare to work: lessons from America', in A. Deacon (ed.) *From Welfare to Work: Lessons from America*, London, Institute of Economic Affairs.

Miller, D. (1997) 'What kind of equality should the Left pursue?', in J. Franklin (ed.) *Equality*, London, Institute for Public Policy Research.

Murray, C. (1984) *Losing Ground: American Social Policy, 1950–1980*, New York, Basic Books.

Nissan, D. and Le Grand, J. (2000) *A Capital Idea: Start-Up Grants for Young People*, London, Fabian Society.

O'Connor, J. (1998) 'US social welfare policy: the Reagan record and legacy', *Journal of Social Policy*, 27(1).

Office for National Statistics (2001) *Social Trends*, London, HMSO.

Oppenheim, C. (1999) 'Welfare reform and the labour market: a third way?, *Benefits*, April–May.

Oppenheim, C. (2001) 'Enabling participation? New Labour's welfare-to-work policies', in S. White (ed.) *New Labour: The Progressive Future?*, Basingstoke, Palgrave.

Peck, J. (1998) 'Workfare in the sun: politics, representation and method in US welfare-to-work strategies', *Political Geography*, 17(5).

Peck, J. (1999) 'New Labourers? Making a New Deal for the "workless class"', *Environment and Planning C: Government and Policy*, 17.

Peck, J. and Theodore, N. (2000) '"Work first": workfare and the regulation of contingent labour markets', *Cambridge Journal of Economics*, 24.

Phillips, A. (2000) 'Equality, pluralism, universality: current concerns in normative theory', *British Journal of Politics & International Relations*, 2(2).

Rhodes, M. (2000) 'Desperately seeking a solution: social democracy, Thatcherism and the "third way" in British welfare', in M. Ferrera and M. Rhodes (eds) *Recasting European Welfare States*, London, Frank Cass.

Select Committee on Education and Employment (2000) *New Deal for Young People: Two Years On*, London, House of Commons.

Teles, S. (1996) *Whose Welfare? AFDC and Elite Politics*, Kansas, University Press of Kansas (softback pub.1998).

US General Accounting Office (1999) *Welfare Reform: Information on Former Recipients' Status*, Washington, DC, USGAO.

Weaver, R. K. (1998) 'Ending welfare as we know it', in M. Weir (ed.) *The Social Divide*, Washington, DC, Brookings Institution and Russell Sage Foundation.

Weaver, R. K. (2000) *Ending Welfare as We Know It*, Washington, DC, Brookings Institution.

White, S. (1997) 'What do egalitarians want?', in J. Franklin (ed.) *Equality*, London, Institute for Public Policy Research.

White, S. (1998) 'Interpreting the third way: not one road, but many', *Renewal*, 6(2).

White, S. (2001) *New Labour: The Progressive Future?*, Basingstoke, Palgrave.

Wiseman, M. (1996) 'Welfare reform in the United States: a background paper', *Housing Policy Debate*, 7(4).

Generative equality, work and the Third Way: a managerial perspective

Introduction

Equality has been 'the polestar of the Left',[1] and the redefinition of this concept by Giddens and New Labour marks a significant departure from post-war social democratic goals. Giddens's Third Way rests on his social theory of modernisation and globalisation, and employs the notion of 'generative equality' to propose a new model for social policy. This chapter explores Giddens's idea of 'generative equality' in the form of a critique from a managerial perspective. It is shown that Giddens's prescriptions for the creation of generative welfare policies and generative equality have much in common with the management literature of the last two decades, which emphasises the importance of individual responsibility and 'empowerment' over Taylorist command and control approaches. However, it is argued that Giddens's use of Maslow's needs' hierarchy as a model for the creation of 'happiness' and 'self-actualisation'[2] is open to the accusation of misrepresentation.

From 'productivism' to 'productivity'

Political traditions can be analysed in terms of their explanatory framework,[3] their values and their institutional plans. Giddens's explanatory framework is both social and political. In *Beyond Left and Right* he draws on the social theory which he developed in a series of books published in the early 1990s; including: *The Consequences of Modernity* (1990); *Modernity and Self-Identity* (1991); *The Transformation of Intimacy* (1992); and *Reflexive Modernisation* (1994).[4] Giddens's social theory employs a historical periodisation which distinguishes the current era of 'reflexive modernisation' from the 'simple modernisation' which preceded it. Modernisation involves the application of scientific knowledge to production and warfare, and the diffusion of new forms of transportation and communications technology. The period of simple modernisation extended from the Enlightenment to sometime after the Second World War, the year of the first satellite TV broadcast being sometimes identified as a watershed. Aspects of simple modernisation include the control of nature, administrative power, industry, the mechanisation of war, the growth of the nation state, liberal democracy, state monopolisation of the means of violence, and capitalist economic relations.[5]

Despite the far-reaching consequences of simple modernisation, many aspects of traditional society remained unscathed. Traditional societies are mediated by ritual and reproduce themselves in a relatively unquestioning way because they are, in some senses, isolated by the 'situatedness of place'.[6] The locale is minimally affected by external media, and individual members of traditional societies rarely interact with people from other settings because transportation is, compared to the current epoch, both expensive and slow. The traditional locale therefore acts as a sort of 'cultural container'. Members of traditional societies are rarely exposed to other, different, societies, and have little cause to question either their role or identity. Consequently religious beliefs, eating habits, gender roles, kinship relations and class identities pass from one generation to the next without much modification.

The period of simple modernisation profoundly changed peoples' lives through industrialisation, mechanised warfare, bureaucratisation, democracy and capitalism but, according to Giddens, left relatively unchanged fundamental aspects of peoples' lives. He argues that the religious practices, patriarchy, gender roles and kinship ties of traditional society were remarkably persistent in the face of these modernising forces. It is the persistence of tradition in the period of simple modernisation that distinguishes it from the subsequent period of reflexive modernisation. A negative characteristic, which he identifies with simple modernisation, is 'productivism', by which he means a psychological tendency towards compulsive and uncritical behaviour in areas of work and consumption.[7] In the economic sphere 'productivism' is connected with Taylorist mass production[8] and therefore, by association, with Keynsian demand management.

Giddens's account of the process of modernisation includes an analysis of the effect of transport and communications technology on social relations, and this is the essence of his theory of globalisation. The twentieth-century development of rapid transportation, instantaneous broadband communications and global media has facilitated numerous interconnections between geographically distant individuals and societies. These extensive linkages have profoundly affected the relatively impervious locale of the traditional society. Globalisation means that social relations are 'lifted out' of their local setting and re-articulated across 'indefinite tracts of time-space'.[9] The linear relationship between space and time, say the distance travelled by the Pony Express in one day, is completely transformed in the twentieth century.[10] Accessible jet travel, telephone, internet, email and satellite communications have the effect of 'annihilat[ing] space through time'.[11] The process of globalisation means that the locale is now thoroughly permeated by interconnections to other, distant, places. The extensiveness of these linkages also has the effect of 'emptying out' the locale. These profound changes alter the 'weft and weave' of social relations and are most corrosive to the social patterns which sustained traditional society. Giddens argues that the accelerated process of globalisation and associated 'distanciation' of social relations in the twentieth century is leading to the development of a post-traditional society:[12] a society in which tradition no longer has a hold. The 'detraditionalisation' wrought by the communications revolution is augmented by the generalised application of scientific method (or the Enlightenment principle of radical doubt) to almost all areas of life. Individuals are now invited to question most of what passes as received wisdom, even to the extent of rewriting their own lives' narratives through counselling, psychotherapy or self-therapy.[13] Taken together, the exposure to other cultures and value systems, and the extension of scientific method to almost all areas of life, lead to a thoroughgoing reflexivity. And it is reflexivity that Giddens identifies as the defining characteristic of the current epoch.

> Given the extreme reflexivity of late modernity, the future does not just consist of events yet to come. 'Futures' are organised reflexively in the present in terms of the chronic flow of knowledge into the environments about which such knowledge was developed.[14]

It may be helpful here to illustrate Giddens's use of 'reflexivity' with an example. In a traditional society peoples' understanding of marital difficulties might be informed by a recollection of marriage vows and by the married lives of forebears, relations and friends. In the current epoch a couple experiencing such difficulties would have access to research-based information about the marriage relationship (perhaps via a large survey), and this information would be likely to influence the conduct of the relationship, the possible future scenarios and the steps taken to improve or dissolve the relationship.

According to Giddens *detraditionalisation* means that everything is now open to question in the discursive space of the global media. Individuals are faced with an unprecedented degree of choice in areas like food, clothing, sexuality, religion,[15] physical appearance and gender,[16] lifestyle and, for the more privileged, work. Intimate relationships are open to question in a way that would have been unthinkable for our grandparents' generation. Indeed, programmes like *Ricky Lake* and *Tricia* involve trials by television of peoples' intimate relationships in a manner which is indeed consonant with Giddens's 'democracy of the emotions'.[17] In the society wrought by globalisation the cultural containers of the old order are placed under the spotlight and, unless defensively cordoned off, are thoroughly permeated by external influences and critically appraised by global media. It is no longer sufficient to refer to the ritual practices and traditions of our forebears, for every choice must now be defended and justified. A defining characteristic of this detraditionalised society is a thoroughgoing reflexivity through which individuals are constantly faced with choices in an era of *self-construction, not situation*.[18]

Giddens regards increased social reflexivity as a thoroughly positive development which he associates with the self-actualisation of Maslow[19] and Murray.[20] He believes that most people live their lives in a much more active way than, say, in the 1950s. Detraditionalisation means that people can make active choices in the 'reflexive project of the self', forming, and sometimes reforming, their own identities in the light of aspirations and changed circumstances.[21] Social relations must also be actively forged in an era where the social interactions of the locale are less reliable and, where individuals routinely communicate and travel over long distances. In the globalised setting of the current epoch trust must be actively fostered in a way which was previously unnecessary. Thus, in most areas of life people are actively involved in managing their own destinies. In contrast to the compulsive work and consumption orientation of the previous epoch, which Giddens calls 'productivism', many peoples' lives are now characterised by 'productivity' in a new 'post-scarcity' order:

> Productivity stands opposed to compulsiveness and to dependency, not only in work but in other areas, including personal life. There is a close tie between autonomy and productivity. A productive life is one well lived, but it is also one where an individual is able to relate to others as an independent being, having developed a sense of self-esteem.[22]

By extension, 'productivity' may be taken to mean the displacement of compulsion by active choices made in the areas of work, diet, body, clothing, identity, sexuality, relationships, lifestyle and politics.[23]

A further distinction which might be drawn between the periods of simple and reflexive modernisation is the move, in almost all areas of life, from a merely reactive to a positively proactive *modus operandi*.

Social reflexivity and the generative welfare state

In *Beyond Left and Right* Giddens identifies an inversion of Left–Right politics and an exhaustion of post-war political traditions in which the Conservatives have appropriated the radical agenda through their adoption of neo-liberalism. Social democrats in the Labour Party, on the other hand, have retreated into a backward defence of the welfare state. Giddens's response to neo-liberalism, particularly in later books like *The Third Way and its Critics* (2000), is to accept economic arguments concerning supply-side economics over Keynsian demand management, and the tacit knowledge and democracy of the market[24] over central planning. He also appears persuaded by neo-liberal criticism of the welfare state and the dependence it fosters. However, he is opposed to the aggressive individualism of neo-liberalism and wishes to repair damaged solidarities, to find new bases for solidarity, and to reconcile autonomy and independence. He argues that the 'external' problems of the current epoch are essentially man-made. Environmental crises and war constitute 'manufactured uncertainty' and are reflexively managed,[25] in the sense that every action is undertaken in the light of some knowledge concerning its consequences.

While Giddens embraces socialist values of solidarity, community and social responsibility, he believes that the changes wrought by globalisation render the centralised socialist state redundant. He characterises post-war social democracy as 'cybernetic' and inappropriate to the new conditions described by his social theory.[26] Welfare institutions are in crisis precisely because they are designed to address the conditions of simple modernisation. For example, they assume their recipients will be drawn from relatively homogeneous working-class families where patriarchy is the norm.

Giddens employs his analysis of post-industrial society to propose the notion of positive/generative welfare to create 'generative equality'. Generative equality emphasises self-development. This is where the welfare state moves away from *control* of individuals towards the *development* of individuals. According to Giddens, the original purpose of the welfare state was to bring about desired outcomes as determined 'from the top';[27] as Kaspersen notes, the state acts as the provider of a 'repair mechanism' which is utilised when things go wrong.[28] In line with the 'New Right' movement of the 1980s,[29] Giddens implies that traditional welfare has created coercion, dependence and diminished levels of individual liberty, and has thus placed constraints upon individual action. However, his solution is not 'less state' but a challenge to the existing role of the state. Generative policies seek to create conditions that free individuals from constraints and enhance individual happiness and, crucially, allow the autotelic self to develop and to flourish, where

> the autotelic self is one with an inner confidence which comes from self respect, and one where a sense of ontological security, originating in basic trust, allows for the appreciation of social difference. It refers to a person able to translate potential threats into rewarding challenges . . . does not seek to neutralise risk or suppose that someone else will take care of the problem; risk is confronted as the active challenge which generates self-actualisation.[30]

Generative policies aim, therefore, to facilitate change that transforms an alienating welfare system, which dictates outcomes from above, into an enabling welfare system that allows individual growth to occur. According to Giddens there are four basic prerequisites for achieving this. First, government must set into motion programmes designed to shift power towards those most in need of the help the welfare system offers. This requires a wholesale recognition that the welfare system exists not to decide on and attempt to create *ends*; rather, it is there to provide *means*. Second, in order that effective individual development can take place, conditions must be brought into existence where recipients of welfare can freely exchange information with the providers of welfare about their needs, desires, ideas, and so on. According to Giddens this requires the decentralisation of political power as a 'condition of political effectiveness because of the requirement for "bottom up" information flow (as well as the recognition of autonomy)'.[31] Third, the prerequisite for this effective information flow must be the creation of an active and sustainable trust between the recipients of welfare and the providing agencies.[32] And, last, recipients of welfare must, in order for them to effectively function and successfully interact with expert systems, be given extended individual autonomy – a prerequisite of effective personal development.

It can be seen that Giddens is proposing wholesale reform here. The implication is that for generative policies to be successful a 'mental revolution' must take place. A mental revolution is required of those 'at the top' as well as those 'at the bottom'. The point is that if existing mindsets prevail – according to which providers of welfare seek control of outcomes and the beneficiaries of welfare are required to satisfy the outcomes set them – then generative policies are 'dead in the water'. It is therefore pertinent to examine how Giddens sees this mental revolution being achieved. On this specific issue, the parallels between the managerial literature on human resources management (HRM) and Giddens's prescriptions for generative equality become apparent. The remainder of this chapter explores these parallels.

A managerial interpretation of Giddens's 'generative welfare policies'

From a managerial perspective, Giddens's prescriptions for generative welfare in a post-scarcity society engender a strange sense of *déjà vu*. That is not to deny its utility in its context; but, from the perspective of the managerialist literature of the last two decades on issues such as the management of change,[33] it strikes some familiar tones. What Giddens argues for, in the context of generative welfare policy, bears a striking resemblance to the fairly prescriptive management literature from the early 1980s onwards.[34] This is usually viewed as a response to the globalisation of capitalism typified by competition from Japan and, more currently, from China and in the Pacific Rim. One of the recurring issues within the HRM literature concerns organisational culture change. The literature addresses management–employee relationships and adopts the premiss that, hitherto, relations were dysfunctional and/or antagonistic.

Legge has noted that 'in the last ten years, in both the UK and USA, the vocabulary for managing the employment relationship has undergone a change. 'Personnel management' has increasingly given way to "human resources management".'[35] In common with the 'cycle of control' thesis, embryonic HRM strategies were exclusively management-led – what Salamon refers to as *descending participation* 'in so far as management invariably initiates the development for its own purposes'.[36] However, as HRM strategies have developed, more emphasis has been placed upon employee participation. In line with this, management objectives have shifted from attaining control and compliance of the workforce – as suggested by the cycle of control arguments and, more generally, by Taylorist approaches – towards securing the further commitment and co-operation of employees.[37] This has been described as a shift from 'control' models to 'commitment' models of HRM. The commitment model seeks to attain a 'mental shift' in employees' attitude to work. It aims to foster an intellectual understanding of the needs of the organisation, the needs of management, and how these link with employees' performance at work itself. Colloquially, management tends to refer to this as 'employee buy-in'; in the literature it is generally referred to as the 'mutuality model'[38] which creates 'an organisational climate in which employees feel a sense of positive identification with and commitment to goals of the organisation'.[39]

However, HRM strategies have attempted to push the firm–management–employee relationship one step further. This can be illustrated by looking at one of the more significant HRM developments in organisations in recent years – the adoption of 'total quality management' (TQM) programmes. These programmes, as well as being contingent upon 'mutuality' in the employment relationship, by their nature imply a management *dependence* on labour.[40] TQM practices based on the work of Juran, Crosby and Deming[41] dictate that companies have a strategic commitment to constantly improve the quality of their products or services.[42] For instance, in a manufacturing context TQM concentrates on driving down the number of defects; or, in the context of a service industry, it focuses on driving down the number of complaints. From the prescriptive management perspective it can be seen that TQM practices require a shift in an employee's approach in one key area – his or her orientation to the work task itself. For TQM practices to succeed, employees' autonomy in the work process must be increased, and responsibility be given for channelling information through team structures and broader interrelating expert systems. This is illustrated by Brown:

> When I went to Japan I saw they actually owned every problem belonging to their job. If a machine broke down, the operators, the members of that team owned that problem . . . if a major problem did arise during production, the entire team would stop, tackle the problem and solve it.[43]

Commonly called 'empowerment', this practice purportedly gives employees *ownership* of the work process (direct participation) and is clearly linked[44] to the development of the Hawthorne experiments in the 1930s and the development into the neo-human relations school.[45] O'Reilly argues that participatory systems, like empowerment in TQM, through offering choices in the work process, develop a sense of responsibility in individual workers. This is because 'when we choose of our own volition to do something we often feel responsible'.[46] Hence, he makes an important point about *control* of a process leading to *ownership* of that process, and he therefore proposes as the likely outcome that the responsibility thus engendered acts to encourage responsible behaviour. So, in the case of TQM, empowerment of the employee at the level of the work process directly translates into ownership of the process of work.

TQM represents the development of a literature which offers largely prescriptive 'management solutions' on how to create 'win–win' situations, or 'mutuality' or 'unitarism' or 'role convergence', within organisations. Put simply, the literature purports to represent the key to the wholesale creation of employee relations where management and those managed have, in the domain of work, shared goals and objectives. This has also been described as *Japanisation* – the most developed version of which would be the creation of the 'empowered' employee in a TQM setting.

In broad terms, this genre of the management literature has exhorted a shift away from Taylorist management principles to the more humanistic employee-centred approaches typical of the human relations school. It is this broad shift in emphasis in the management literature that is uncannily mirrored in Giddens's discourse on generative welfare policy: this is where he proposes a shift away from simple modernisation to reflexive modernisation. From the perspective of the managerialist literature, it would not be unfair to argue that Giddens is selling old wine in new bottles, albeit to a new market keen to find solutions. In managerial terms, Giddens has espoused a *Japanisation* of state welfare provision, as *productivism* (Taylorism) moves to *productivity* (self-actualisation and empowerment).

Taylorism, welfare and dependence

Taylorism, the application of 'scientific management' to the workplace has, as Giddens rightly points out,[47] proved to be historically limited. However, there is a clear parallel to be drawn in his analysis of the outcomes of state welfare and what would now be described in the management literature as 'conventional wisdom' regarding the outcomes of the application of 'scientific management'. For example, in his work on 'strategic management' Brown[48] echoes Peters[49] in his criticisms of scientific management methods. He argues that the application of these methods in an effort to enhance productivity results in the opposite effect. Taylorist methods, he stresses, preclude any chance of management utilising employees' potential. This is because in the use of such methods employees' actions are determined by management decisions about how employees should perform various functions – Taylorist techniques are inextricably linked to management control of processes. This creates employees who depend upon management for direction. Management appropriation of control in the productive process thus stifles employee initiative and takes away employees' responsibility for their actions. In the productive process employees act as they are told to act rather than how they might see fit to act if allowed autonomy. Employees are therefore disempowered by work itself because they disassociate themselves from the outcome of their actions. The upshot is that the products of the productive process are likely to be defective and need a course of corrective action which costs the organisation both time and money. This would be far less likely to happen, Brown argues, if employee initiative and autonomy were fostered rather than stifled by management. Thus, the core of this argument is that attempts to control action occasion undesirable outcomes which need correction at some later stage.

Giddens offers a parallel analysis in his assessment of the outcomes of state welfare provision. He argues that state welfare systems tend towards control, the setting out of values and the creation of dependence. Furthermore, he stresses that state welfare systems, like the application of Taylorist management techniques, may also yield undesirable outcomes requiring subsequent remedy. Giddens calls this 'precautionary aftercare', and it 'not only means dealing with situations and events after they have happened, but it is closely involved with an actuarial outlook which supposes that the future is in principle predictable'.[50] From a managerial perspective Giddens can be seen to draw from a critique of Taylorism and scientific management in his analysis of the welfare state. Both create dependence, while both are left to pick up the tab for undesirable outcomes. Both create mindsets that may not be conducive to attaining the desired outcomes.

Empowerment, self-actualisation and generative welfare

Thus far, we have attempted to draw a parallel between the managerialist critique of Taylorism and Giddens's appraisal of welfare provision. We would also argue that there is a parallel between Giddens's prescriptions for the creation of welfare provision in a post-scarcity society and the managerial prescriptions for a post-Taylorist order. To alleviate the problem of undesirable outcomes, the post-Taylorist management literature emphasises a move towards more humanistic approaches. As we have seen, this involves breaking the traditional relationship between management and employees based on management control and worker dependence, in favour of a relationship typified by interdependence and mutuality. Similarly, Giddens argues that the state must break from its traditional role where it creates dependence and move towards generative policies which break the traditional intrinsic relationship between welfare and state. Both of these perspectives see the *empowering* of the individual as a prerequisite for the releasing of human potential and thus a fundamental step towards the creation of a 'new order'. In the management context, the notion of 'empowerment' is manifest in participatory systems such as TQM, in which employees are said to develop a sense of responsibility in the workplace as they are given more autonomy and the opportunity to use their initiative in work tasks. The future prosperity of companies lies in the success of tapping this human potential. Similarly, in his analysis of state welfare, Giddens argues that '[r]esponsibility in fact accords closely with self-reliance',[51] and it is the informal economy, and not through state welfare provision, in which human action becomes autonomous and responsible, thereby showing the way for generative welfare.

Giddens uses 'lean production'[52] in an attempt to link principles underpinning new managerial production techniques to generative welfare.[53] He stresses that lean production techniques are performed in a 'rich social context'[54] and that they can be learned from in a post-scarcity society the aim of which might be to promote the pursuit of happiness. Clearly, Giddens believes that these forms of production technique tap into more intrinsically human qualities. To illustrate this he draws from management literature via Murray.[55] He employs Maslow's 'hierarchy of needs', with its emphasis on 'self-actualisation', to illustrate the 'rich social context' of lean production techniques. It is the attainment of 'self-actualisation', inextricably linked to the pursuit of happiness, that Giddens sees as a template for defining the goals of social 'welfare' in a post-scarcity society:

> Suppose we take seriously the proposition that the aim of good government should be to promote the pursuit of happiness, and that both individual and social 'welfare' should be defined in such a way. Let us also accept that happiness is promoted by security (of mind and body) self-respect and the opportunity for self-actualisation.[56]

We have little problem with the proposition that good government should promote the pursuit of happiness and provide the platform for self-actualisation. Our problem is with the use of Maslow's 'hierarchy of needs' as a framework, and the lack of clarity on how, within that framework, self-actualisation is to be achieved. Maslow identified five levels in a hierarchy of needs.[57] Briefly, these are:

1 *physiological needs*: the most basic level of 'natural' primary needs; for example, thirst, hunger, sleep. Once these needs are satisfied they no longer motivate, and it is the next level of needs that will then motivate the person;
2 *safety needs*: these are concerned with emotional and physical safety. When safety needs have been satisfied, they no longer motivate and the person is motivated by the next in the hierarchy;
3 *love needs*: these are the intermediate needs, and are best described as social needs, or the need to belong;
4 *esteem needs*: these represent higher order needs of humans – the need for power, status and achievement. Esteem is in this sense self-esteem and the esteem granted one by others; and
5 *self-actualisation*: this is the level at which individuals are self-fulfilled and have realised, or are realising through personal growth, their full potential. It is the culmination of the lower, intermediate and higher needs described above.

Maslow's model stresses that once a particular level of needs is satisfied, it no longer motivates – the next level of needs then motivates the individual. So, for example, when housing, clothing, nutrition and security needs have been achieved, they no longer motivate because the lower order physiological and safety needs have been met. Individuals will now be motivated to achieve intermediate love needs. In Giddens's use of this model to illustrate self-actualisation through generative welfare policies, *the hierarchical nature of the model is ignored*. It appears that needs from the lower order (security) through to the higher order are treated as non-hierarchical, as if all could be fulfilled simultaneously; so, for Giddens,

> [s]ecurity, self-respect, self-actualisation, these are scarce goods for the affluent as
> well as the poor, and they are compromised by the ethos of productivism, not just
> by distributive inequalities ... overcoming welfare dependency means overcoming
> the dependencies of productivism.[58]

This is problematical. It is clear from Maslow's model that if self-actualisation
is to be achieved, or at least serve as a motivator, then the lower order needs *must*
first be satisfied. It is also axiomatic that the lower order needs require adequate
financial means to be fulfilled. Therefore to argue that the possession of wealth
does not necessarily allow individuals to achieve 'security, self-respect and self-
actualisation' is, in the Maslovian sense, incorrect. If an individual does not have
the means to achieve security needs then, according to Maslow, they will continue to be motivated to achieve these needs. Until they do they will not turn their
attention to achieving self-actualisation. However, according to Giddens, it is
overcoming the *ethos* of productivism in favour of productivity that will allow
happiness and self-actualisation to be achieved. Thus, for him, it is the reorgan-
isation of a belief-system that causes this to occur. Our argument is not with this
sentiment, but with the model being used to illustrate this desired end-state.
Maslow's hierarchical model requires material means – however provided – to
enable higher order motivation to be attained. Giddens's use of self-actualisation
is, therefore, open to the accusation of misrepresentation.

In his calls for good government, Giddens stresses that conditions for self-
actualisation and the pursuit of happiness should be created. Therefore, government policy should be directed towards creating the conditions that allow
individual productivity and the autotelic self to flourish[59]. We have argued,
however, that the model used for this dictates that certain criteria need to be fulfilled if the desired outcomes are to be attained. Maslow's model tells us that
attention needs to be given to the means by which individuals can work up the
needs' hierarchy towards the goal of self-actualisation. Thus, if Maslow's is a
viable model it is inevitable that policy will need to be directed at successfully
addressing inequalities in wealth.

There is one more important issue that will require careful consideration when
formulating generative policies. In the preceding discussion we have argued that
generative politics requires a form of mental revolution to take place. Both the
providers and the receivers of welfare need to substantially alter their mindset to
allow generative equality to flourish. Giddens's work, like much of the management literature, focuses to a greater degree on the 'bottom end', namely, the recipients of welfare and 'employees'. Generally, there is less focus on those who were
previously responsible for the outcomes of policy. On this issue, the critical management literature[60] tells us that it is precisely those people who have the greatest
difficulty with policy change. It informs us that resistance to change comes not
from those who are likely to be developed by it, but from those who, as a result
of policy change that espouses mutuality and interdependence, stand to lose
power. If we can learn from the management literature here, then policy should
also take into account the barriers that might be erected at the 'top'.

Conclusions

Within Marx's idea of a communist society it is possible to see the hope of greater happiness through freedom and self-actualisation, 'to hunt in the morning, fish in the afternoon, rear cattle in the evening, criticise after dinner'.[61] These themes are reflected by Hattersley,[62] who identifies happiness as a goal and inequality as an impediment to its achievement. Giddens articulates a broadly consonant view of the good life as self-actualisation, but does not see inequality as necessarily presenting an obstacle to its achievement: 'We should want a society that is more egalitarian than it is today, but which is meritocratic and pluralistic. . .'.[63] Giddens wishes to promote equality of opportunity by 'developing people's capacity to pursue their well-being',[64] but he acknowledges that this is bound to lead to unequal outcomes, and that redistribution across generations is then necessary to counter the inequalities of inheritance. Poverty is seen largely as an impediment to autonomy, and for that reason Giddens supports redistribution: 'Modernising social democrats should accept the core importance of progressive taxation as a means of economic redistribution.'[65] The values of social cohesion and productivity expressed by Giddens certainly stand in the socialist tradition, but his explanatory framework marks a significant departure from those employed by democratic socialism.

In his critical reading of 'the new communitarianism', Prideaux[66] accuses Etzioni of coaxing the reader to accept a congenial view of American society in the 1950s, and then attempting to restore social cohesiveness through the application of social controls, and, in a manner consistent with his own organisational theory.[67] 'In reality the favourable bias assigned to past social configuration tends to sway the suggested solutions to perceived social ills back toward the reassertion of the mores and morals so predominant in the 1950s.'[68] The same accusation could not be levelled at Giddens, whose explanatory frameworks explicitly embrace social and political change. His social theory describes a type of society very different from that inhabited by the democratic socialists of the post-war period.[69] Globalisation and increased social reflexivity, he argues, make for a more active and potentially more autonomous citizenry. His political and economic analyses concede the neo-liberal tenets of market democracy and supply-side economics, although he is critical of the aggressive individualism and social fragmentation wrought under Thatcherism.

We also identify a Japanisation of welfare that is consonant with the themes of HRM. Just as Taylorist work organisation can inhibit human potential and create dependence through its orientation to control, so can the centralised welfare state. Giddens's notion of generative equality is congruent with the practices of TQM and empowerment, which aim to foster a responsibly proactive approach to business problems rather than a reactive one.

In the new type of society which Giddens describes it is possible to envisage liberty and fraternity in terms of autonomy, 'productivity' and 'active trust', and it is clear that he equates self-actualisation or the means to self-actualise with 'happiness'. The socialist preoccupation with equality as a means of achieving those ends is also present in the Third Way, and Giddens's notion of 'generative equality' is an appealing one. However, we believe that he underestimates the obstacle which inequality presents to self-actualisation, and that this is due to his misreading of Maslow, who articulates a *hierarchy* of needs. Self-actualisation is possible only where the lower order needs have been met, and there are many members of society devoid of land or capital who are as dependent on work as Marx's alienated and commodified labour. It will therefore be important for New Labour to address those security needs if they wish to foster the active and productive citizenry of Giddens's most hopeful account. We have also highlighted the need for policy to account for resistance to change from those who are required to 'give away' or 'share' their power in order to create a greater good. Giddens's generative politics requires, we have argued, a mental revolution to take place. Its success may well depend upon the depth of that revolution.

Notes

1 Greg Elliott speaking at a Social and Political Thought Graduate Seminar, University of Sussex, 28 January 1999.
2 Giddens 1994: 166.
3 Benton 1995.
4 Beck, Giddens and Lash 1994.
5 Giddens 1990.
6 See Giddens 1993.
7 Giddens 1994: 168–9.
8 *Ibid.*, p. 178.
9 Giddens 1991: 18.
10 Prior to the telegraph, letters were the main form of communication between absent others, but these communications could be transferred only as quickly as someone could travel the same distance. Written communication therefore involved time delays which were as long as the journey that would be necessary to facilitate a face-to-face meeting. The movement through space necessary to conduct social relations therefore involved a corresponding movement through time. The advent of electronic communications changed this relationship because it became possible to conduct a relationship across space without a corresponding movement through time.
11 See Harvey 1994: 299.
12 Giddens 1994: 83.
13 Giddens 1991: 72.
14 *Ibid.*, p. 29.
15 The 'new age' is sometimes described as a supermarket of religious experience.
16 The physical appearance of individuals is regularly altered through diet, 'working-out', cosmetic surgery and, in some cases, through sex-change operations.
17 Giddens 1994: 119.
18 Benton 1995.
19 Maslow 1987.
20 Murray 1988.

21 Giddens 1991: 75.
22 Giddens 1994: 180.
23 Here the use of 'politics' is associated with life political issues relating, say, to animal rights, food, health and the environment.
24 Giddens 2000: 35–6.
25 Giddens 1994: 152.
26 *Ibid.*, p. 66.
27 *Ibid.*, pp. 92–3.
28 Kaspersen 2000: 126.
29 See e.g. Green 1987: 167–74.
30 Giddens 1994: 192.
31 *Ibid.*, p. 93.
32 *Ibid.*
33 Particularly changing work cultures.
34 For example, seminal works here are Peters and Waterman (1982) *In Search of Excellence: Lessons from America's Best Run Companies* and Deal and Kennedy (1982) *Corporate Cultures: The Rites and Rituals of Corporate Life.*
35 Legge 1995: 62.
36 Salamon 1992: 346.
37 See for example Blyton and Turnbull 1998; Oliver and Lowe 1991; and O'Reilly 1991.
38 Goss 1994; Walton 1991.
39 Goss 1994: 101; see also McKenna and Beech 1995; and Legge 1995.
40 Blyton and Turnbull 1998: 220; see also see Hill 1991.
41 See Juran 1974; Crosby 1979; and Demming 1982.
42 Brown 1996: 232; Oakland 1995: 18.
43 J. Ferry, *The British Renaissance*, quoted Brown 1996: 189.
44 Sewell and Wilkinson 1998: 100.
45 This school is usually associated with the human relations school of Harvard and Chicago and Elton Mayo. The human relations approach to management can be viewed as a response to Taylorist approaches to elicit effective worker behaviour. Whereas Taylorist approaches appeal to rational, calculating, human instinct, the human relations theorists stress the appeal to individual desires for challenge, sociability and variety as more likely to result in positive worker behaviour. Worker behaviour is, therefore, best manipulated by subtle management techniques that seek to secure loyalty through team-working and schemes to encourage workers to participate in behaviour that is beneficial for them and for the well-being of the firm.
46 O'Reilly 1991: 250.
47 Giddens 1994: 178.
48 Brown 1996.
49 Peters and Waterman 1982; Peters 1987 and 1992.
50 Giddens 1994: 180.
51 *Ibid.*, p. 162.
52 'Lean production' is a phrase coined by Womack *et al.* (1990) to describe the Toyota Production System and its derivatives. This highly influential book and its successor, *Lean Thinking*, have led to a widespread diffusion of 'the lean approach', first through automotive and subsequently through other manufacturing and service sectors. The lean approach involves the workforce and suppliers in team-based improvement activities that are oriented towards improving customer satisfaction,

improving quality, reducing defects and reducing cost etc. According to Womack and Jones (1996: 15): 'Lean thinking is lean because it provides a way to do more with less and less – less human effort, less equipment, less time, and less space – while coming closer and closer to providing customers with exactly what they want.'

53   Giddens 1994: 180–2.
54   *Ibid.*, p. 179.
55   Murray 1988.
56   Giddens 1994: 180.
57   Maslow 1987.
58   Giddens 1994: 192–3.
59   *Ibid.*, p. 192.
60   See e.g. Legge 1995.
61   Marx and Engles 1976.
62   Hattersley 1987.
63   Giddens 2002: 38.
64   *Ibid.*, p. 39.
65   Giddens 2001: 184.
66   See his chapter in this volume.
67   Etzioni 1961.
68   See chapter 7, this volume, by Prideaux.
69   Post-war society is encompassed by Giddens's period of 'simple modernisation'; see Giddens 1994: 80–7.

References

Beck, U., Giddens, A. and Lash, S. (1994) *Reflexive Modernisation*, Cambridge, Polity Press.

Benton, E. (1995) '"Green", beyond Left and Right?', Paper delivered at a Joint Seminar between Social and Political Thought, Sociology, and Social Psychology, University of Sussex, 4 December.

Blyton, P. and Turnbull, P. (eds) (1998) *Reassessing Human Resource Management*, 2nd edn, London, Sage.

Brown, S. (1996) *Strategic Manufacturing for Competitive Advantage*, London, Prentice-Hall.

Crosby, P. (1979) *Quality Is Free*, New York, McGraw-Hill.

Deal, T. and Kennedy, A. (1982) *Corporate Cultures: The Rites and Rituals of Corporate Life*, Reading, MA, Addison-Wesley.

Deming, W. (1982) *Quality, Productivity and Competitive Position*, Cambridge, MA, MIT Centre for Advanced Engineering.

Etzioni, A. (1961) *A Comparative Analysis of Complex Organisations: On Power, Involvement, and Their Correlates*, New York, Free Press.

Giddens, A. (1990) *The Consequences of Modernity*, Cambridge, Polity Press.

Giddens, A. (1991) *Modernity and Self-Identity*, Cambridge, Polity Press.

Giddens, A. (1992) *The Transformation of Intimacy*, Cambridge, Polity Press.

Giddens, A. (1993) *A Contemporary Critique of Historical Materialism*, 2 vols; vol. 1: *Power, Property and the State*; vol. 2: *The Nation State and Violence*, reprinted in *The Giddens Reader*, ed. P. Cassell, Basingstoke, Macmillan.

Giddens, A. (1994) *Beyond Left and Right*, Cambridge, Polity Press.

Giddens, A. (2000) *The Third Way and its Critics*, Cambridge, Polity Press.

Giddens, A. (2001) 'The question of inequality', in A. Giddens (ed.) *The Global Third Way Debate*, Cambridge, Polity Press.

Giddens, A. (2002) *Where Now for New Labour?*, Cambridge, Polity Press.

Goss, D. (1994) *The Principles of Human Resource Management*, London, Routledge.

Green, D. (1987) *The New Right: The Counter Revolution in Political, Economic and Social Thought*, Brighton, Wheatsheaf.

Harvey, D. (1994) *The Condition of Postmodernity*, Oxford, Blackwell.

Hattersley, R. (1987) *Choose Freedom: The Future for Democratic Socialism*, Harmondsworth, Penguin.

Hill, S. (1991) 'Why quality circles failed but total quality management might succeed', *British Journal of Industrial Relations*, 29(4).

Juran, J. (1974) *Quality Control Handbook*, 3rd edn, New York, McGraw-Hill.

Kaspersen, L. (2000) *Anthony Giddens: An Introduction to a Social Theorist*, Oxford, Blackwell.

Legge, K. (1995) *Human Resource Management – Rhetorics and Realities*, London, Macmillan.

McKenna, E. and Beech, N. (1995) The Essence of Human Resource Management, London, Prentice-Hall.

Marx, K. and Engels, F. (1976) *The German Ideology*, 3rd rev. edn, Moscow, Progress Publishers.

Maslow, A. H. (1987) *Motivation and Personality*, 3rd edn, New York, Harper & Row.

Murray, C. (1988) *In Pursuit of Happiness and Good Government*, Simon & Schuster.

Oakland, J. (1995) *Total Quality Management*, Oxford, Butterworth–Heinemann.

Oliver, N. and Lowe, J. (1991) 'The high commitment workplace: two cases from hi-tech industry', *Work, Employment & Society*, 5(3).

O'Reilly, C. (1991) 'Corporations, control, and commitment', in R. Steers and L. Porter (eds) *Motivation and Work Behaviour*, New York, McGraw-Hill.

Peters, T. J. (1987) *Thriving on Chaos: A Handbook for a Management Revolution*, London, Pan Books.

Peters, T. J. (1992) *Liberation Management: Necessary Disorganization for the Nanosecond Nineties*, London, Macmillan.

Peters, T. J. and Waterman, R. H. (1982) *In Search of Excellence: Lessons from America's Best Run Companies*, New York, Harper & Row.

Salamon, M. (1992) *Industrial Relations Theory and Practice*, 2nd edn, London, Prentice-Hall.

Sewell, G. and Wilkinson, B. (1998) 'Empowerment or emasculation? Shopfloor surveillance in a total quality organisation', in Blyton and Turnbull (eds) *Reassessing Human Resource Management*.

Steers, R. and Porter, L. (eds) (1991) *Motivation and Work Behaviour*, New York, McGraw-Hill.

Walton, R. (1991) 'From control to commitment in the workplace', in R. Steers and L. Porter (eds) *Motivation and Work Behaviour*, New York, McGraw-Hill.

Womack, J. P., Jones, D. T. and Roos, D. (1990) *The Machine that Changed the World*, New York, Rawson Associates.

Womack, J. P. and Jones, D. T. (1996) *Lean Thinking: Banish Waste and Create Wealth in Your Corporation*, New York, Simon & Schuster.

What matters is what works: the Third Way and the case of the Private Finance Initiative

Introduction

There is a multitude of ways of defining and explicating the Third Way, and there is now an extensive literature on the matter. (See, in particular, chapters 1 and 8 in this volume.) I use the term 'Third Way' in a limited and, hopefully, precise manner. Policy-making is a complex and problematical matter, often entailing difficult choices in uncertain circumstances, selecting from a range of options whose consequences cannot be accurately predicted. To render the task more manageable all policy-makers inevitably rely on a cognitive map or frame of reference to help order their understanding of external reality, selecting, classifying and highlighting its most salient features, identifying those problems of social life deemed to require public intervention, explaining how they arose and providing recommendations as to how they may most effectively be remedied. They compose an 'operational code' – a set of goals and guidelines used by policy-makers to structure analysis, define priorities and set the policy agenda.[1] My suggestion here is that the most useful way of approaching the problem of the Blair Government's 'Third Way' is to apply the term to its 'operational code': the precepts, assumptions and ideas that actually inform policy choice. I propose to do this by selecting for more detailed analysis a policy strategy which has been presented by the Government as typifying the Third Way. My choice is the strategy of public–private partnership (PPP) or the Private Finance Initiative (PFI),[2] as applied to health policy.

The PFI involves a separation between the role of commissioner of public services, which remains the responsibility of public authorities, and the role of provider of those services, which the private sector is encouraged to undertake. It has been described as the 'key element in the Government's strategy for delivering modern, high quality public services'.[3] It is promoted as the most practicable and cost-effective way of remedying the country's much-neglected public infrastructure, especially in the health service. But it is also commended as exemplifying New Labour's 'pragmatism'. The PPP strategy is presented as a 'Third Way' alternative to the 'dogma of the Right' that 'insisted that the private sector should be the owner and provider of public services' and the 'dogma of the Left' that insisted the State must be the sole provider. 'The modern approach to public services' contends, to the contrary, that 'the best way forward is through new partnerships between the public and the private sectors'.[4] By the same token, critics of the PFI are dismissed as hidebound traditionalists who allow ideology (or vested interest) to obscure the fact that this new mechanism alone can guarantee 'value for money to the taxpayer' and 'the delivery of a higher sustainable level of public sector investment'.[5]

The Government's case is that it opted for the PPP–PFI approach because it delivers the goods – it 'works best'. There are indeed instances where the evidence points to one particular policy as unequivocally the most effective – in terms of meeting its objectives and serving the public good. As I hope to show, the PFI is *not* one such instance. Various factors other than its intrinsic merits – e.g. electoral issues – may persuade a government to select a policy, and I find some such reasons for the decision to back the PFI. Yet, the Government does appear to genuinely believe that it affords better value for money than any alternative. We need to know why – and in seeking the answer we are, by definition, uncovering the Third Way as operational code.

The chapter's first section outlines the PFI and highlights its political and ideological importance. The second reviews research findings on the operation of the PFI in the health service. I find that there is little substance to the Government's claim that the PFI is *on strictly pragmatic grounds* the most effective way of renewing the capital infrastructure of the NHS – the third section explains why. In the fourth section, by exploring the reasons for its adoption, I hope to shed some light on the character and contours of the Third Way as New Labour's operational code.

The PFI and New Labour's pragmatism

The Major Government launched the PFI in 1992. Under the PFI the public sector contracts to purchase services long-term from the private sector, which provides finance and accepts some of the venture's risks in return for an operator's license to provide the specified service. Within the NHS the PFI involves a consortia of construction companies, bankers and service providers contracting to finance, design, build, maintain and operate new hospital facilities which they then lease to the NHS, usually for periods of 25–35 years.[6]

Labour was from the start hostile to the PFI and as late as 1995 was still denouncing it as 'totally unacceptable' and 'the thin end of the wedge of privatisation' (Margaret Beckett, shadow health secretary, cited in *Health Service Journal*, 1 June 1995). Shortly afterwards Labour began to change its mind. In office Labour ministers found the PFI (in the words of Paymaster-General Geoffrey Robinson) to be 'floundering' – and they set about resuscitating it.[7] By 1999, with far more PFI agreements being signed than under the Tories, the Government declared that a 'revitalised PFI' had become 'a key tool in helping provide effective and good value public services'.[8] It was 'the only game in town'. The health research institute known as the King's Fund calculated that by the close of 2002 the bulk of NHS capital investment projects would be financed and managed by the private sector.[9]

The creation of the NHS is still regarded as Labour's crowning achievement. To the Government, the PFI is indispensable to NHS modernisation, indeed to its survival as a free and universal service providing health on the basis of clinical need. It has, however, provoked a storm of opposition among critics (especially, but by no means exclusively, the public sector unions) who claim that it amounts to 'privatisation by stealth'. At its June 2001 annual conference, UNISON, the country's largest union, announced a co-ordinated national campaign of strikes, demonstrations and lobbying against 'the privatisation juggernaut', with Dave Prentis, the union's general secretary, accusing ministers of having a 'depressing obsession and love affair with the private sector' (*Guardian*, 21 June 2001). In January 2002 the General, Municipal and Boilermakers' Union (GMB), a traditionally loyal union, announced that it would, in protest against the policy, cut affiliation fees by £500,000 in each of the next four years (*Guardian*, 3 January 2002). The issue threatens to be one of the most troubling in the Blair Government's second term. Indeed John Edmonds, general secretary of the GMB, warned that, by his insistence on the PFI strategy, 'Tony Blair threatens to crack the foundations of the Labour party. He has certainly tested the loyalty of Labour party members to destruction' (*Guardian*, 10 September 2001).

How, then, can we account for the Government's enthusiasm – overturning the reservations initially expressed while in opposition – for the PFI? The explanation put forward by the Government itself (and by a number of commentators) is that it reflects a crucial defining feature of New Labour – its pragmatism. Pragmatism has been defined by one sympathetic commentator as a 'a technical and hands-on orientation' focusing first on the detail of 'what works' and what can be achieved within 'the constraints of empirical and political realities'.[10] In the past (it is contended) Labour was, on grounds of dogma, stubbornly opposed to reliance on the private sector and market disciplines for supplying public services. This 'old argument' over the relative merits of public and private supply of goods and services is now dismissed as 'simply outdated', reflecting irrelevant battle lines which only distract from 'the real challenge of improving our public service'.[11] The Third Way's pragmatism stipulates an approach to policy which makes decisions according to the merits of the case, the feasibility of a policy, and a careful and scrupulous investigation of its likely consequences – and not on the basis of fixed ideological formulae.[12] According to Le Grand it reflects a Third Way agnosticism as to means: 'the best means are whatever achieves the best combination of ends, whether the means concerned involve the market, the state or some combination'.[13] In some areas the state should remain the direct provider of public goods; in an increasing number of areas, it should act in partnership with the private sector, purchasing and regulating services which the latter delivers. The great advantage of public–private partnerships is that they harness the strengths of the market – 'dynamism, innovation and efficiencies' – to the delivery of public services.

The PFI, in short, is New Labour pragmatism in action: 'what matters is what works'. To what extent can that proposition be substantiated?

Choosing what works? The PFI balance sheet to date

PPP schemes, and most notably the PFI, are seen by the Government as 'central to our drive to modernise our key services'. They have been pronounced 'a huge UK success story. We are blazing a trail that others will undoubtedly follow'.[14] Their success rests on their ability to deliver:

- investment in the public infrastructure that would not otherwise have been possible;
- higher quality projects; and
- greater value for money.[15]

The Government acknowledges that public authorities can raise capital more cheaply in the financial markets than can private concerns, and therefore that the PFI carries an initially higher financial cost. This will be more than wiped out by the efficiency gains inherent in public–private partnerships procured by:

- greater private sector access to relevant expertise and experience
- the incentive to minimise costs imposed by operating within a commercial environment
- significant performance improvement through private sector innovation and management skills.[16]

Therefore PFI deals promise 'more essential services and to higher standard than would otherwise have been the case'.[17]

Is this claim justified? The impact of the PFI on the quality of service, usually understood to refer to the ability of the NHS to meet need through appropriate treatment, equitably delivered, is very difficult to operationalise and measure. Furthermore, evaluation of the impact of the PFI on the standard of service – on outcomes – has to be tentative since PFI-built hospitals are only now beginning to open and none has a track record on which to base a firm assessment. Rather than confronting the problem directly (though I do, from time to time, quote judgements by recognised authorities), I utilise two indicators as proxies:

- *staffing*: the numbers of skilled personnel available to help in the delivery of health care; and
- *capacity*: the number of beds (which includes appropriate equipment and facilities) available.

Both these indicators are, of course, inputs, but my working assumption (reflecting a broad consensus among practitioners and experts) is that a growth in these inputs is a necessary, though not a sufficient, condition for effective needs fulfillment.

The Government insists that the money to fund a PFI hospital will not be found 'through shedding staff who are needed . . . A hospital that was not fully staffed would not be value for money and would not attract Health Authority support. In no way . . . are clinical services compromised or threatened'.[18] A number of investigations suggest, however, that this is precisely what is happening. Pollock *et al.* (2000) report that 'all of the first wave of PFI hospitals, for which figures are available, involve reductions in the number of beds'. The average reduction is of 31 per cent of current (1995–96) capacity.[19] It is estimated that the burden of meeting the costs of the new PFI hospital in Carlisle will involve a 13 per cent cut in the clinical staffing budget between 1994 and 2000 with 88 per cent of the posts lost in nursing. Similarly, when the new Edinburgh Royal Infirmary opens in 2003 'the projected staff budget will be 23% less than 1996, and there will be almost 25% fewer staff, a greater proportion of whom will be untrained and unskilled'. The result of the PFI deal at the Worcester Royal Infirmary is expected to produce a 17 per cent cut in the number of nurses and a 31 per cent cut in the number of ancillary staff.[20] This trend can be replicated elsewhere.[21] The House of Commons Select Committee on Health reported in 1999 that 'the evidence we have received leads us to conclude that on current trends the projected increases in the number of nurses and other clinical staff fall well short of what is required to deal with current shortages and future developments in the NHS'.[22]

But would these capital projects have fared any better under public procurement? The Government insists that the PFI is selected over public procurement only after a rigorous analysis of the relative costs. It is a comparative judgement: which promises better value for money, public procurement or PFI? All PFI schemes are compared against a notional publicly funded equivalent, the so-called 'public sector comparator' (PSC), using an appraisal method 'under which the cash payments associated with each option are "discounted" and costs are adjusted to reflect "risk transfer"'. The PSC takes account 'of risks which under public procurement the public sector carries itself, but which under private finance initiative it pays another agent, the private investor, to bear'.[23] These include such risks as construction-cost overruns, design faults, higher than expected maintenance costs, unexpected variations in demand and so forth. In almost every case, the PSC judges the PFI option better value for money. The method used to assess risk is the crucial factor since, as the Department of Health acknowledged in its evidence to the Health Select Committee, 'the majority of savings provided by PFI are due to risk transfer'.[24] Without this, in most cases, outright public funding would provide better value for money. 'If insufficient risk is transferred', the Government holds, 'a project will not represent value for money and will not be pursued under PFI.'[25]

A number of commentators have, however, cast doubt on the robustness of the appraisal methods used to determine risk responsibility under PFI. The best indicator of the extent of risk actually transferred is the rate of interest paid by consortia to their lenders, which reflect calculations by lending sources about their precise degree of risk exposure. In PFI schemes surveyed by Gaffney *et al.*, it was found that borrowing terms were 'extremely favourable', implying modest vulnerability.[26] Similarly, Hutton concludes that while the 'whole purpose of the PFI is to off-load government borrowing and risk onto the private sector the private sector regards itself as accepting very little risk'. Indeed, the relatively low levels of risk have allowed some PFI firms to capitalise on a 'risk premium' through the development of new risk markets. PFI contractors are increasingly undertaking 'refinancing' deals which enable them to borrow at lower interest rates and pocket the difference between the original and new financing costs: PFI 'risk' has been converted into a commercial product, priced and traded (*Observer*, 13 December 1998). Furthermore, doubts have been raised about the degree to which, in the real world, risk in large-sale public sector capital projects *can be* moved to the private sector. A project – such as a new hospital – cannot be simply abandoned if the private consortium is unable to deliver on its contract. As the National Audit Office noted, 'ultimate business risk cannot be transferred to the contractor because if the contractor fails to deliver the specified project, the public sector still has the responsibility for delivering the required public service'.[27]

Public or PFI? What determines which works?

The King's Fund report on the PFI, summarising existing findings, concludes that 'the evidence on which individual decisions were made was insufficient to justify a wholesale switch from public to private financing of investment in NHS hospitals'.[28] I would further suggest that the inadequacies of PFI funding arrangements reflect structural characteristics of the new health market. Economic theory allows us to have a stab at predicting or, at least, anticipating the circumstances and conditions in which goods and services are most efficiently and effectively supplied by the private sector. The indicators are:

- where the market for goods and services is sufficiently open and competitive to ensure that producers provide value for money;
- where transaction costs are low; and
- where there are no major externalities involved and profit-maximisation by private firms responding to market incentives produces outcomes broadly congruent with the needs and well being of the relevant publics.[29]

Competition

In conventional markets, the degree of competition is seen as a key determinant of efficiency, responsiveness and choice. This entails multiple providers, none of which should be able to influence the market price by changing their output.[30] 'Competitive tension' in the market for health contracts, the Public Accounts Select Committee stressed, 'is the key both to obtaining and to demonstrating value for money in procurement'.[31] Theoretically, PFI contracts involve the public sector client specifying the services which it wishes to purchase and, through competition, selecting private sector suppliers to provide them. However, because of the sheer magnitude of the costs incurred by a potential contractor, the number of bidders involved in any one set of project discussions is usually very small. In four of the first fifteen PFI schemes to reach financial closure there was only one final bid.[32] The Treasury Select Committee acknowledged that, in the real world, 'there is a trade-off between competition and the length and cost of [PFI] negotiations'. Few companies are large enough to cope with the size of the contracts and the complex negotiating processes involved in PFI, and the ongoing process of acquisitions and mergers is constantly reducing that number. Even where the procurement was competitive overall, the Treasury Select Committee added, the market 'may be too immature for competitive tension to provide value for money . . . In these circumstances, it may not be sufficient to rely only on competitive pressure to secure reasonable financing arrangements.'[33] In short, because of the highly imperfect operations of the competitive mechanism, there are grounds for the supposition that PFI procurement is unlikely to secure the kind of efficiency gains that may be anticipated in a more open and competitive market structure.

Transaction costs

Transaction costs are the costs involved in arranging contracts. They include 'the costs encountered in drafting, negotiating and safeguarding an exchange agreement' and 'the costs of monitoring the outcomes of the exchange to check compliance with the exchange's terms after the transaction has taken place'.[34]

Their magnitude has been recognised as a key issue in determining whether goods and services should be contracted out or handled in-house.[35] The more effectively contractual performance can be monitored and the more effectively compliance enforced, the higher the chances of promised gains being made – a key point where contracts take the form of long-term binding agreements. Transaction costs vary according to the transparency and complexity of the services offered. If the delivery of a service or product can be easily prescribed and monitored contractually, and the standard of the service provided measured with some precision, outside tendering may well make sense.[36]

The negotiation and monitoring of contracts for NHS PFI projects is, however, complex, intricate and time-consuming, requiring a range of technical expertise. Generally speaking, NHS trusts have responded by buying-in services. But the expertise required – finance, law and accounting – is very expensive. Details obtained through Parliamentary Questions revealed that the advisors' costs for the first fifteen NHS PFI hospitals represented between 2.4 per cent and 8.7 per cent of the capital cost of those projects.[37] The Public Accounts Committee expressed 'alarm' in its report on the Dartford and Gravesham Hospital contract that the health trust incurred costs from its advisors, KPMG and Nabarro Nathanson, which exceeded the initial estimates by almost 700 per cent. Boyle and Harrison concluded that in the early stages of the PFI there was a substantial increase in transaction costs over the level of pre-PFI schemes.[38] The NHS Confederation reported that NHS managers found the PFI to be slow and bureaucratic, requiring 'us to put up a vast amount of management time and consultancy fees at risk without the certainty of success'.[39] Heald and Geaughan also suggest that because the PFI process is so protracted delays longer than might have been expected under conventional procurement have occurred. Similarly, the National Audit Office found that 'there have been notable cases where PFI projects have failed or been delayed with significant adverse consequences for the public sector'.[40]

Externalities

'Externalities' are costs (or benefits) external to the terms of a contract. Parties to a contract reach an agreement which is intended to bring mutual benefits, but they incur costs which are borne by others who are not party to it. As I use the term, it refers to the negative effects on the operations of the healthcare system as a whole which, directly or indirectly, flow from the terms of the contract. PFI contracts focus on how a set of discrete procedures, typically the responsibility of an NHS trust, can be carried out in the most cost-effective way. By encouraging a multiplicity of contractual arrangements among a host of autonomous units, the PFI contributes to a fragmentation of overall service provision and to a neglect of wider needs, formal responsibility for which lies with bodies or agencies not party to a contract. An example would be adequate provision for the elderly, which requires close collaboration between suppliers of both primary and community care, responsibility for which is divided between the NHS and local government social services departments. However, it may make financial sense for NHS commissioning bodies to make savings by off-loading responsibilities to other agencies. The effect has been to displace costs on to the local health economy, reducing the amount left to finance other aspects of healthcare such as mental health, community services and primary care – despite the fact that current Government policy is to encourage the integration of all aspects of health.[41] As Boyle and Harrison comment, 'the PFI in its existing form is not a suitable means of delivering on the Government agenda to rebuild the NHS around the planned delivery of health care across a full range of provision facilities'.[42]

There are also broader long-term externalities. The Government insists that, under PFI arrangements, 'while responsibility for many elements of service delivery may transfer to the private sector the public sector remains responsible for deciding, as the collective purchaser of public services, on the level of services that are required, and the public sector resources which are available to pay for them'.[43] In fact, the commitment of a growing slice of the health budget to meet public contractual responsibilities has quite serious implications for the ability to imprint national priorities, as registered in election contests, upon future spending patterns. A growing share of the resources set aside for healthcare will be pre-committed, leaving less and less to the discretion of public authorities and democratic choice.[44] One of the first pieces of legislation passed by the new Government was the National Health Service (Private Finance) Act, which empowered NHS trusts to enter into PFI agreements and guarantee financial payments over the life of the contract, *irrespective of public expenditure totals*.[45] The *Financial Times* (17 July 1997) noted that

> future cash outflows under PFI/PPP contracts are analogous to future debt service requirements under the national debt, and, potentially, more onerous since they commit the public sector to procuring a specified service over a long period of time when it may well have changed its views on how or whether to provide certain core services of the welfare state.

Further PFI contracts will not only limit the ability to switch resources in the future but, in the event of a need to cut spending, will force non-PFI expenditure to carry proportionately deeper cuts. It is difficult to interpret this as anything other than a substantial constraint on the ability of a future government, 'as the collective purchaser of public services', to decide on how to respond to shifting social needs and new priorities. Changes in medical needs, technologies and treatments may, for instance, reduce demand for large acute PFI hospitals, but the public sector will be contractually bound to a pre-set schedule of payments.[46] As Anthony Harrison of the King's Fund points out:

> If the demand for hospital services is reduced for any reason, the NHS trust is still tied into an agreement for maintenance, facilities, and management services over and above the cost of building the hospital. This would not be the case if the hospital was built with public funding.[47]

In short, though there *may be* short-term benefits in relying on the PFI – a more rapid commitment of funds – within the time-span of the contract as a whole the NHS is binding itself to a sup-optimal allocation of resources.

The PFI and the Third Way as operational code

To some commentators, the Blair Government's backing of the PFI represents a 'pluralist approach to the delivery of public services', opening up 'established hierarchies without fetishizing the market'. It is a Third Way since it rejects 'Old Labour's 'centralism' while remaining rooted in the socialist tradition.[48] From that perspective, the Blair Government's pursuit of the PFI testifies to a new open-mindedness and hard-headed realism – to a refusal to be distracted by ideological *shibboleths* from measures which promote the more efficient and effective delivery of services. But this line of reasoning presumes what needs to be demonstrated: that the PFI, as compared to public funding, promises more and higher quality public services. The evidence provides no solid substantiation for the proposition.[49] Precisely for that reason, many within the medical profession and among health researchers have reacted with mounting apprehension. For the editor of the *British Medical Journal* 'much evidence is accumulating to show that private finance initiative schemes are costing much more than traditional public funding of capital development'.[50] Sir Peter Morris, president of the Royal College of Surgeons, warns that within a decade the cost of the PFI to the health service would land it 'in desperate trouble'.[51] Dr Peter Hawker, chairman of the British Medical Association's Consultant's Committee, expressed his anxiety about the PFI's 'poor use of public money' and its 'rash assumptions about work intensity' (quoted on BBC website, accessed 19 May 1999). And, most recently, the country's leading health research institute, the King's Fund, has pronounced the PFI-driven hospital construction programme as one of the Blair Government's 'few outright errors of policy' (*Guardian*, 9 May 2002).

What, then, does the Government's zeal for the PFI tell us about the Third Way? One possibility is that it tells us little – that it was embarked upon for considerations apart from its intrinsic merits. There is some support for that view. In part it originated (in 1992) as a financial stratagem, an accounting device to allow for some investment in the UK's decaying public infrastructure while maintaining a tight fiscal stance. While borrowing to fund conventional public procurement was counted as adding to the public sector borrowing requirement, borrowing by the private sector of the same amount of money to finance the same investment was not – even though the public body would be contractually bound to repay the private firm from its revenue budget. It was 'off-balance sheet'.[52] This had an obvious attraction for the incoming Labour Government, torn between its commitment to rigorous controls over public spending and borrowing, on the one hand, and its pledge to 'save' the NHS (and education), on the other (*Guardian*, 14 March 2000). It allowed the claim that the PFI provided for higher levels of public investment than would otherwise have been possible.[53] However, this argument is now less frequently heard. The Accounting Standards Board objected that PFI spending had to be paid from the public purse in precisely the same way as standard public procurement and should no longer be treated as off-balance sheet, a criticism which the Government appears to have accepted[54] (David Heald, *Observer*, 28 April 2002). Notwithstanding, this factor almost certainly weighed heavily in the Blair leadership's *initial* decision to embrace the PFI.

A second consideration is, we can safely surmise, electoral. 'Acquiring assets via the PFI is analogous to buying a house with a mortgage rather than paying cash for it up-front. You still have to pay for the house, one way or the other.'[55] There is, however, a disjuncture between the repayment schedule and the electoral cycle, for long before the former has been completed the ministerial incumbents responsible will have departed the political scene. In short, it makes electoral sense to stretch out the payment of the bills even if the final total is much larger. So the Government can claim (credibly) to be embarking on the largest hospital building programme in history without placing unduly burdensome claims on the public purse. The real cost will bite only later.

However, these factors fall far short of fully explaining the Blair Government's stance on the PFI, for it appears to genuinely believe that PFI offers a better deal. Why? It is rare for 'the facts' to point unequivocally in favour of any single policy. Decision-makers may vary in their willingness to take account of research findings, to engage in reasoned analysis and to question inherited policy stances. Similarly, they may differ in the flexibility and open-mindedness with which they tackle policy problems. But the stark contrast between a 'pragmatic' approach driven by an objective consideration of evidence systematically and comprehensively assembled and rationally evaluated, on the one hand, and an 'ideological' approach, on the other, is misleading. Persuasive evidence about the likely consequences of differing policies is difficult to obtain, even if commissioned; and wholly dispassionate analysis is rare. To this may be added the force of limited time and energy, of political exigencies demanding rapid action, the limited cognitive and information-processing abilities of decision-makers and the press of governmental business.[56]

As Lindblom, Simon and many other social scientists have shown, the claim that policy choice is based on 'rational, synoptic' analysis is rarely convincing. Decision-making is, at best, 'boundedly rational'.[57] All governments must, inevitably, rely upon selection principles – cognitive short cuts, criteria for determining what is feasible and practicable – for guidance in making policy decisions. As Hall suggests, they 'customarily work within a framework of ideas and standards that specifies not only the goals of policy and the kind of instruments that can be used to attain them, but also the very nature of the problem they are to be addressing'.[58] The key factor impelling policy-makers to opt for one line of action rather than another is less often a detached and meticulously analysed assessment of 'what works best' than their 'subjective view of the situation' and the way in which they 'characterise the choice situations that face them':[59] in short, their assumptions and beliefs about why some things work better than others – their 'operational code'. In essence, the argument here is that it is not 'objective' logic but the logic of the Blair Government's 'framework of ideas and standards' which renders the choice of PFI intelligible.

New Labour's support for greater private involvement in the provision of services is rooted in a diagnosis of the innate weakness of public sector service provision. As 'monopolist providers', one New Labour sympathiser commented, public institutions 'grew fat and unwieldy' and ' ran up uncontrollable bills'.[60] All this reflected *endemic* public sector failure – a tendency to bureaucratic inertia, a wasteful use of resources, over-centralisation, incompetent management, poor motivation and low commitment. 'Compared with the experience of the private sector', one cabinet minister has written, 'services in local hospitals, schools councils were often too slow and inadequate. Much of this was due to a bureaucratic and statist regime of control and command.'[61] A major injection of private sector techniques and market disciplines was deemed to be vital precisely because these faults were seen to be inherent in public provision.

On what grounds is it anticipated that a greater commercial role in the organisation and provision of services will raise their quality and reduce costs? The Government's reasoning is (as we have seen) based less on iron-clad evidence than on assumptions about the factors that 'can lead to better value services, delivered more flexibly and to a higher standard'. Thus, it is held that the corporate imperative to expand markets and maximise profits 'provides the private sector with an incentive to innovate and try out new ideas'. Equally, it renders businesses 'more adept at looking for innovative ways of delivering their services, and adapting to changing requirements and expectations'.[62] By its very nature, the public sector is less efficient and effective in managing large projects because it has ' no incentive to make a profit or recoup the cost of capital'. As a result there is an innate 'temptation to over specify, leading to gold-plated projects'. In contrast, under PFI private firms have 'every incentive for tight project management and the best use of capital'.[63] In short, the presumption is made that market disciplines and the drive to boost profit will more or less guarantee both higher quality and cost efficiencies, as corporate interest can normally be expected to mesh with the public good.

Organisational efficiency, higher standards and responsive service delivery all require that appropriate institutional incentives and disciplines are in place to motivate the required commitment. Here it is assumed that profit maximisation and performance-related financial reward offer the most potent incentives for management and employees 'to maximise efficiency and take full advantage of opportunities'.[64] The beliefs about human behaviour underpinning the Government's faith in market solutions are squarely rooted in classical political economy, with its conviction that people are *by nature* self-interested 'utility maximisers'. As Tony Blair explained to the British Venture Capitalist Association, the pressures of the market stimulate entrepreneurial behaviour, a zeal to innovate and to eliminate waste. Lacking the spur of these pressures 'people in the public sector' tended to be sluggish, unimaginative and reluctant to experiment. Importing the rhythms of the private sector can enhance motivation and therefore performance. 'Let's be honest about it', the prime minister declared, 'the private sector, in its reward and motivation, has moved on apace.' The same spirit must be instilled in the public sector.[65]

How dramatic a change in Labour's creed does all this represent? It would be wrong to infer that the Blair Government has abandoned traditional Labour values. Thus the Government remains committed to a welfare state in which core services are freely provided and financed by taxation, just as – unlike its predecessor – it seeks to promote greater social justice and social cohesiveness. This is reflected in the Blair Government's major expansion of health spending since 1999 and the great energy and political capital it is investing in building a streamlined and more effective NHS. In a sense the Third Way is, as it claims, pursuing traditional values in 'a modern setting'. But that setting is a cognitive one: a revised operational code. The Third Way is a particular type of synthesis in that it seeks to yoke neo-liberal concepts and modes of analysis to the furtherance of public purposes. It has absorbed much (though by no means all) of the 'new public management' – in effect the infusion of market norms into public admin-istration.[66] It often takes as axiomatic that profit-maximising firms operating within market environments are a more natural repository of creativity, cost-savings and organisational dynamism than are their public sector counterparts. What has occurred is a transformation in the frame of reference that Labour's leadership utilises to define and tackle political problems – in the manner in which it construes issues, in its preferred diagnoses, in its standards of judgement and in its notions of feasibility and efficacy.

What will be the impact of all this? For Will Hutton, the choice of the PFI is not, as its champions urge, simply a matter of means, for it amounts to 'the enthronement of market values in public provision'. Patients' interests have become secondary to those of ideological public accounting principles and a dynamic has been released in which 'considerations of public health, clinical need and patient care' will be progressively subordinated to the values of 'cost reduction, operational efficiency and the need to reproduce the managerial culture of a privately-owned PLC' (*Observer*, January 10, 1999).

The New Labour response is that the State should be a 'steerer' not a 'rower', a notion, Anna Coote tells us, that 'is characteristic of "Third Way" politics'.[67] In fact, this begs the crucial question: where the private sector (increasingly) owns and manages, who actually steers? In 1997 the health policy specialist Chris Ham, addressing the issue of PFI, pointed out that 'investors who put their finance at risk will want to have a big say in how the hospitals are run . . . The end of the route will be increasing privatisation' (*Independent*, 22 April 1997). There is an 'institutional logic' to the process in which the scale of private involvement steadily expands. Thus, initially, a distinction was made between core clinical and non-clinical services. In 1999 Alan Milburn reaffirmed the Government's view that while the role of the private sector in the supply of ancil-lary services could be expected to grow, 'clinical services are best delivered by public sector staff not least because the NHS is more efficient than the private sector alternative'.[68] If public sector provision has the advantages attributed to it by ministers, logic dictated its application to core as well as secondary services. As Kelly and Le Grand noted, ' to confine the role of the private sector in this way may be to lose what are supposed to be its benefits'. Indeed (as proponents of PPPs) they suggested that that the most 'impressive efficiency savings and innovations are made' where private firms are able 'to manage the whole service'.[69] By 2000 the rule limiting the PFI to non-clinical services – which ini-tially the Blair Government had adduced to demonstrate its commitment to the NHS ethos – was abandoned and Alan Milburn, the health secretary, announced that he wanted it extended 'beyond the hospital gates to include GP surgeries, community pharmacies, health centres, intermediate and long-term care facili-ties' (*Observer*, 19 November 2000). This process is set to continue.[70]

Government choice is reinforced by institutional dynamics. The relentless advance of PPPs through the NHS since 1997 has steadily increased the financial and organisational leverage available to private firms to advance the process still further. 'Once the private sector controls the operational management of facilities [it] will be in a powerful position to influence service delivery policies.'[71]

Conclusion

To New Labour a defining feature of the Third Way is its pragmatism, its commitment to evidence-based policy-making: in the pithy precept so often reiterated, 'What matters is what works.' The case of the PFI casts a rather different light on the Third Way, since self-evidently it does not work. A paper produced jointly by the King's Fund and the NHS Alliance (representing primary care groups – GPs and other community health providers) concluded that the evidence for public–private partnerships increasing funding and improving services within the NHS was 'paltry'.[72] Precisely for that reason, the case of the PFI is particularly instructive, since it affords insights into the Blair Government's presumptions about 'what works' or, more precisely, why particular policies can be expected to work better than others. The Third Way, according to the interpretation proffered here, constitutes New Labour's operational code: its cognitive structuring of the situation; its mental maps which help it clarify 'the nature of the problem, relate it to [its] previous experience, and make it amenable to appropriate problem-solving activities'.[73]

From this perspective, the Government's decision to rely upon the PFI as the main mechanism for renewing the UK's public infrastructure reflects the Blair Government's reappraisal of the appropriate role of the State. 'A seismic switch in the business of government itself', Milburn observed, has occurred. Governments are judged 'not so much on what they own – or even what they spend – but more on what they do'.[74] From this perspective the evolution of the State 'from being an owner of capital assets and direct provider of services, into a purchaser of services from a private sector partner responsible for owning and operating the capital asset that is delivering the service' seems a natural step.[75] This may represent the ultimate thrust of the Third Way's view on the future of public services. As operational code, it retains Labour's traditional commitment to the free delivery of healthcare, but within the context of a commodification of service provision. It still upholds a large public sector, but one increasingly permeated by market arrangements and a more commercial ethos. The Third Way prescribes for the State a major role in social life, but less as a direct provider than as purchaser and regulator. It would retain responsibility for guaranteeing access to services free at the point of delivery, but these would be increasingly supplied, under contract, by private firms.

David Marquand has argued that the fate of 'social democracy and the public domain are inextricably intertwined [for] without a vibrant public domain, ring-fenced from the market and private domains, social democratic politics cannot flourish'.[76] If so, in this may lie the ultimate significance of the PFI for Labour in Britain.

Notes

1 George 1967: 13; March 1994: 14.
2 I use the terms PFI and PPP as synonyms. 'PPP is a generic term used to describe part-nerships, which involve more flexible methods of financing and operating facilities and/or services', while PFI is 'a particular method of financing private investment, which requires the private sector to design, build, finance and operate facilities' (Centre for Public Services 2000).
3 HM Treasury 2000.
4 Milburn 1999a.
5 Robinson 1998.
6 Pollock, Price and Gaffney 1999; Gray 1997.
7 Robinson 1998.
8 Milburn 1999a; Smith, A. 1999.
9 Boyle and Harrison 2000: 24.
10 Halpern 1998.
11 HM Treasury 2000; Blair 2001.
12 Temple 2000: 320.
13 Le Grand 1998.
14 Milburn 1999b.
15 Robinson 1998.
16 Department of Health 1999.
17 HM Treasury 2000, Foreword by the chief secretary.
18 Department of Health 1999.
19 Pollock, Price and Gaffney 1999). In Hereford the number of beds available will fall from 351 to 250; in Norfolk, from 1,600 beds to 1,000; in Worcester, from 540 to 380, in Carlisle from 520 to 440, in Edinburgh from 1,300 beds to 800. The BMA estimates that 5,000 beds will be lost to the system once the 38 PFI hospitals, costing more than £3.6 billion, are built. Gaffney, Pollock, Price and Shaoul 1999a; *Observer*, 27 August 2000; Cohen 1999.
20 Pollock, Price and Gaffney 1999; Pollock, Price and Dunnigan 2000.
21 Gaffney, Pollock, Price and Shaoul 1999a.
22 Health Select Committee 1999.
23 Gaffney, Pollock, Price and Shaoul 1999b.
24 Boyle and Harrison 2000: 22.
25 HM Treasury 1999.
26 Gaffney, Pollock, Price and Shaoul 1999b; Shaoul 1999.
27 National Audit Office 2001.
28 Boyle and Harrison 2000: 34.
29 Buchanan 1985: 14–15; Bartlett and Le Grand 1993.
30 Bartlett and Le Grand 1993: 19.
31 Public Accounts Select Committee 1999.
32 Boyle and Harrison 2000: 19.
33 Treasury Select Committee 2000.
34 Bartlett and Le Grand 19993: 27.
35 Williamson 1985.
36 Coulson 1998: 30.
37 *Hansard*, written answer, 28 February 2000, quoted in Centre for Public Services 2000.

38 Public Accounts Select Committee 2000; Boyle and Harrison 2000: 19.
39 Health Select Committee 1999.
40 Heald and Geaughan 1997: 230; National Audit Office 2001.
41 Boyle and Harrison 2000: 34; Lister 2001; Will Hutton, *Observer*, 13 December 1998.
42 Boyle and Harrison 2000: 34.
43 HM Treasury 2000.
44 Pollock, Shaoul, Rowland and Player 2001.
45 Centre for Public Services 2000.
46 Dawson 2001.
47 Cited in MacDonald 2000. According to a King's Fund report, Labour had 'entered a massive building programme without an assessment of future requirements and without transferring any substantial risk from the public to the private sector' (quoted, *Guardian*, 9 May 2002).
48 Bevir and O'Brien 2001.
49 See e.g. Boyle and Harrison 2000; Sussex 2001; Health Select Committee 1999.
50 Smith, R. 1999.
51 Revill 2001.
52 Centre for Public Services 2000.
53 'PFI is enabling Government to support a significant number of additional projects beyond what can be provided through the public purse', according to Robinson 1998.
54 Smith 2000a: 'Unlike the last Government, we use PFI where it offers best value for money – not to move public sector investment off balance sheet.'
55 Sussex 2001.
56 Simon 1985; March 1994.
57 See e.g. Lindblom 1979; Simon 1985; March 1994.
58 Hall 1993: 279.
59 Simon 1985: 300.
60 Coote 1999: 117.
61 Hewitt 2001.
62 Smith, A. 1999.
63 HM Treasury 1999. One of the Government's main objections to public procurement schemes has been major cost overruns and the heart of its case for the PFI is that 'it offers best value for money' (Smith 2000b). In fact, the PFI has performed no better, as a clear pattern of serious cost escalation is now emerging. Among the more dramatic increases in prices from original plan to final PFI deals are: Greenwich: up from £35m in 1995 to £93m; UCLH, London: up from £115m to £404m; Leicester: up from £150m to £286m; South Tees: up from £65m to £122m; and Swindon: up from £45m to £96m (Lister 2001).
64 Smith, A. 1999.
65 Blair 1999.
66 Dunleavy 1994.
67 Coote 1999: 148.
68 Milburn 1999b.
69 Kelly and Le Grand 2000.
70 Notably via the 'concordat' under which the NHS contracts to buy services from commercial organisations.
71 Centre for Public Services 2000.
72 Kmietowicz 2001.

73 George 1967: 16.
74 Milburn 1999b.
75 HM Treasury 1999.
76 Marquand 2000.

References

Bartlett, W and Le Grand, J. (1993) 'The theory of quasi-markets', in W. Bartlett and J. Le Grand, *Quasi-Markets in Social Policy*, London, Macmillan.

Bevir, M. and O'Brien, D. (2001) 'New Labour and the public sector in Britain', *Public Administration Review*, 61(5).

Blair, T. (1999) Speech to the British Venture Capitalist Association, London, July.

Blair, T. (2001) Speech on public service reform, October.

Boyle, S. and Harrison, A. (2000) *Investing in Health Buildings: Public–Private Partnerships*, May, London, King's Fund.

Buchanan, A. E. (1985) *Ethics, Efficiency and the Market*, Oxford, Clarendon Press.

Centre for Public Services (2000) *Private Finance Initiative and Public Private Partnerships: What Future for Public Services?* Available online: www.centre.public.org.uk.

Cohen, N. (1999) 'The Private Finance Initiative: how Britain mortgaged the future', *New Statesman*, 15 October.

Coote, A. (1999) 'The helmsman and the cattle prod', *Political Quarterly* (special issue), 70: s1.

Coulson, A. (ed.) (1998) *Trust and Contracts*, Bristol, Policy Press.

Department of Health (1999) *PFI Questions and Answers*, December, London, Department of Health.

Dawson, D. (2001) 'The Private Finance Initiative: a public finance illusion?', *Health Economics*, 10(6).

Dunleavy, P. and Hood, C. (1994) 'From old public administration to new public management', *Public Money & Management*, July–Sept.

Gaffney, D., Pollock, A. M., Price, D. and Shaoul, J. (1999a) 'Planning the new NHS: downsizing for the 21st century' *British Medical Journal*, 319.

Gaffney, D., Pollock, A. M., Price, D. and Shaoul, J. (1999b) 'PFI in the NHS: is there an economic case?', *British Medical Journal*, 319.

Gaffney, D. and Pollock, A. M. (1999) *Downsizing for the 21st Century: A Report to UNISON Northern Region on the North Durham Acute Hospitals PFI Scheme*, 2nd edn, London, UNISON.

George, A. (1967) *The Operational Code: A Neglected Approach to the Study of Political Leaders and Decision-Making*, Santa Monica, CA, Rand.

Gray, A. (1997) 'Editorial: Private Finance Initiative', *Public Money & Management*, July–September.

Hall, P. (1993) 'Policy paradigms, social learning and the State: the case of economic policy-making in Britain', *Comparative Politics*, 25(3).

Halpern, D. (1998) *The Third Way: Summary of the NEXUS On-Line Discussion*, available at: www.netnexus.org/library/papers/3way.html.

Heald, D. and Geaughan, N. (1997) 'Accounting for the Private Finance Initiative', *Public Money & Management*, 17(3).

Health Select Committee (1999) *Future NHS Staffing Requirements. Third Report*, vol. 1, London, Stationery Office.

Hewitt, P. (2001) 'The principled society: reforming public services', *Renewal*, 9(2–3).

HM Treasury (1998) *Modernising Public Services for Britain*, London, Stationery Office.

HM Treasury (1999) *Economic Briefing. Issue 9: The Private Finance Initiative*, London, Stationery Office.

HM Treasury (2000) *Public–Private Partnerships: The Government's Approach*, London, Stationery Office, available online at www.hm-treasury.gov.uk.

Kelly, G. and Le Grand, J. (2000) 'Should Labour go private?', *New Statesman*, 11 August.

Kmietowicz, Z. (2001) 'News roundup', *British Medical Journal*, 323.

Le Grand, J. (1998) *UK Policy: The Appropriate Role of the State*, available: www.netnexus.org/library/papers/3way.html.

Lindblom, C. (1979) 'Still muddling, not yet through', *Public Administration Review*, November–December.

Lister, John (2001) *PFI in the NHS: A Dossier*, Researched for the General, Municipal and Boilermakers Union, London, GMB.

March, J. G. (1994) *A Primer on Decision-Making: How Decisions Happen*, New York, Free Press.

Marquand, D. (2000) 'The fall of civic culture', *New Statesman*, 30 November.

Milburn, A. (chief secretary to the Treasury) (1999a) Speech at the Private Finance Initiative Transport Conference, February, available online: http:www.hmtreasury.gov.uk/pub/html/speech/cft202999.

Milburn, A. (chief secretary to the Treasury) (1999b) Speech at the launch of the Institute of Public Policy Research Commission into Public–Private Partnerships, HM Treasury News Release 152/99, September.

Milburn, A. (health secretary) (2001) Speech to the NHS Confederation Conference, July.

National Audit Office (2001) *Managing the Relationship to Secure a Successful Partnership in PFI Projects*, November, London, NAO.

Pollock, A., Price, D. and Dunnigan, M. (2000) *Deficits Before Patients: A Report on the Worcester Royal Infirmary PFI and Worcestershire Hospital Reconfiguration*, London, School of Public Policy, University College.

Pollock, A., Price, D. and Gaffney, D. (1999) *The Only Game in Town? A Report on the Cumberland Infirmary Carlisle*, Carlisle, UNISON Northern Region.

Pollock, A., Shaoul, J., Rowland, D. and Player, S. (2001) *Public Services and the Private Sector: A Response to the IPPR*, Catalyst Working Paper, London, Catalyst Trust.

Public Accounts Select Committee (1998) *Forty-Second Report: The Skye Bridge*, June, London, House of Commons Committee Office.

Public Accounts Select Committee (1999) *Twenty-Third Report: Getting Better Value for Money from the Private Finance Initiative*, London, House of Commons Committee Office.

Public Accounts Select Committee (2000) *Twelfth Report: The PFI Contract for the New Dartford and Gravesham Hospital*, April, London, House of Commons Committee Office.

Revill, J. (2001) 'Hold on, where did that £21bn go?', *New Statesman*, 7 December.

Robinson, G. (paymaster-general) (1998) Speech to the Private Finance Initiative Conference, 27 April.

Shaoul, J. (1999) 'The Private Finance Initiative: looking-glass world of PFI', *Public Finance,* January 29–February 4.

Simon, H. A. (1985) 'Human nature and politics: the dialogue of psychology with political science', *American Political Science Review*, 79.

Smith, A. (chief secretary to the Treasury) (1999), Speech to 'The Partnerships UK' Conference, HM Treasury News Release 209/99, 7 December.

Smith, A. (chief secretary to the Treasury) (2000a) Speech to the IPPR Seminar on Public Private Partnerships HM Treasury News Release 50/00, 5 April.

Smith, A. (chief secretary to the Treasury) (2000b) 'Benefits of public–private partnerships', HM Treasury News Release 39/00, 15 March.

Smith, R. (1999) Editorial: 'PFI: perfidious financial idiocy', *British Medical Journal*, 319.

Sussex, J. (2001) *The Economics of the Private Finance Initiative in the NHS: A Summary*, London, Office of Health Economics, available online at www.ohe.org/private_finance_initiative.htm.

Temple, M. (2000) 'New Labour's third way: pragmatism and governance', *British Journal of Politics & International Relations*, 2(3).

Treasury Select Committee (2000) *Fourth Report: The Private Finance Initiative*, March, London, House of Commons Committee Office.

Williamson, O. (1985) *The Economic Institutions of Capitalism*, New York, Free Press.

Part III

Community and the Third Way

Introduction

The idea of community forms a significant part of the positive content of the Third Way. Anthony Giddens, in his account of the Third Way, says that 'the theme of community is fundamental to the new politics'.[1] For Amitai Etzioni, 'cultivating communities where they exist and helping them form where they have been lost ... should be a major priority for future progress along the Third Way',[2] while community is one of the four values placed by Tony Blair at the heart of his Third Way.[3]

Linked to the idea of community is the doctrine of communitarianism, which appears in a number of forms. The prominent juxtaposition of rights and duties, or rights and responsibilities, in the Third Way – for example, Giddens suggests, 'as a prime motto for the new politics, *no rights without responsibilities*',[4] while Blair's Third Way has responsibility as a key value and features the claim that 'the rights we enjoy reflect the duties we owe'[5] – a key aspect of some versions of communitarianism, particularly that of Etzioni – and thus feeds back into ideas about community. The different forms taken by communitarianism can, at the most basic level, be categorised as political and philosophical. Both have been linked with New Labour.

While the narrative of community is central to New Labour's message, there is little consensus among commentators as to either the form or the significance of the concept in this context. Closely linked, and similarly vague, is the idea of communitarianism and its role in the 'newness' of New Labour. The chapters in Part III both reflect and assess some of the approaches, attitudes and assumptions surrounding the role of community – and of communitarianism – in the Third Way as manifested in Britain by New Labour.

Sarah Hale examines the role of communitarian philosophy in New Labour's Third Way, challenging the view that contemporary academic communitarian philosophy has played a significant part in informing the party's approach, and critically assessing the claim, made by Blair himself and endorsed and promulgated by commentators, that the British moral philosopher John Macmurray has influenced New Labour's approach.

Eunice Goes and Simon Prideaux consider the role of political communitarianism, and the contribution of its most noted exponent, Amitai Etzioni. Goes argues that New Labour has not, as is often suggested, adopted communitarian values, but has used them strategically in developing a Third Way which moves away from a traditional commitment to equality, particularly in the context of the party's welfare-to-work agenda.

Simon Prideaux traces the provenance of Etzioni's 1990s communitarianism and finds that it is little different from the organisational theory which that author espoused as a functionalist sociologist in the 1960s. This, Prideaux argues, makes for a highly inappropriate basis for a Third Way supposedly of the Left.

Taken together, the chapters in Part III provide, on a number of fronts, a challenge to accepted beliefs about the role of community – and of communitarianism – in New Labour's Third Way.

Notes

1 Giddens 1998: 79.
2 Etzioni 2000: 18.
3 Blair 1998: 4.
4 Giddens 1998: 65.
5 Blair 1998: 4.

References

Blair, T. (1998) *The Third Way: New Politics for the New Century*, London, Fabian Society.
Etzioni, A. (2000) *The Third Way to a Good Society*, London, Demos.
Giddens, A. (1998) *The Third Way: The Renewal of Social Democracy*, Cambridge, Polity Press.

5 Sarah Hale

The communitarian 'philosophy' of New Labour

When, in February 2002, Tony McWalter, an obscure Labour backbencher,[1] asked Tony Blair, at Prime Minister's Questions, to 'provide the House with a brief characterisation of the political philosophy that he espouses and which underlies his policies',[2] it was in the apparent belief that he was asking his leader an easy question. However, Blair's evident confusion and his eventual reply, that 'the best example I can give is the rebuilding of the national health service under this Government – extra investment', led to a few days' ridicule in the broadsheets' parliamentary sketch columns. 'Tony Blair with a philosophy?' Simon Hoggart asked incredulously in the *Guardian*. 'You might as well . . . inquire of Vinnie Jones[3] whether dualism was an apt response to pre-Cartesian thought'. In a more serious response, Roy Hattersley suggested that '[u]ntil Tony Blair came along, Labour had an implied philosophy' based around egalitarianism and support for 'the bottom dog', but that once this implied philosophy 'was formally renounced by the prophets of "the project" it needed replacing with a set of overt beliefs'.[4]

The development and academic study of the 'Third Way' since the mid-1990s represents the most consistent and durable attempt to develop those overt beliefs on behalf of the 'Centre-Left' in general and New Labour in particular. The wording of McWalter's question made explicit the idea that a politician's guiding idea is expected to be a *political philosophy*. Yet the oft-cited 'gurus' of the Third Way – Anthony Giddens way out in front, with Amitai Etzioni leading the pack following a good distance behind – are not political philosophers, but sociologists. When Blair said, at the launch of the Social Exclusion Unit, 'My political philosophy is simple. Individuals prosper in a strong and active community of citizens. But Britain cannot be a strong community, cannot be one nation, when there are so many families experiencing a third generation of unemployment', he was making an empirical claim about 'the dangers of a society that is falling apart',[5] not a philosophical point. It is nonetheless hard to imagine any politician, friendly or otherwise, asking Tony Blair about the sociology underlying his policies, even though beliefs about the dynamics of society are more easily discernible in policy than is any political philosophy.

However, farther down the field, the names of philosophers have been mentioned in connection with New Labour, and these philosophers are the subject of this chapter. The philosophy in question is *communitarianism* – a term popularised by Etzioni and generally – often misleadingly – associated with him. Etzioni's communitarianism is not a political philosophy but, as Simon Prideaux shows in chapter 7, a sociology, and a sociology of a particularly narrow and unsatisfactory kind. Five names crop up when communitarian philosophy is cited by Third Way commentators: Alasdair MacIntyre; Michael Sandel; Charles Taylor; Michael Walzer and John Macmurray. The first four are a well-known quartet who, although very diverse, were brought together under the communitarian label in the 1980s as all of them were seen to offer a critical response to an inherent individualism in liberal political philosophy since Rawls. They have all, with varying degrees of vehemence, objected to being called communitarian. When these four names come up in relation to New Labour, it tends to be simply because of this label. If we look a little more closely at communitarian political philosophy we find not only great variety and diversity in the writers' approaches, concerns and starting-points, but a range of philosophical positions which, insofar as they can be related to it, are inherently opposed to – rather than supportive of – New Labour's approach. The fifth philosopher linked with the party, John Macmurray, was not known in his lifetime as a communitarian (the term's current use in political philosophy dates only from the early 1980s and Macmurray died in 1976); he thought of himself as a Christian socialist. Nonetheless, because of his stress on the idea of community he has been closely linked with 'New Labour's communitarianism' and that of Etzioni. He is also cited as an influence by Blair himself. More surprisingly, perhaps, in the light of this, a closer examination of his philosophy again reveals much that is the antithesis of what New Labour believes and does.

The Third Way and contemporary communitarian philosophy

The development of communitarian political philosophy was characterised at the time as a debate with liberalism, with the communitarian side identified most closely with books by four writers, published during the 1980s: Alasdair MacIntyre's *After Virtue* (1981); Michael Sandel's *Liberalism and the Limits of Justice* (1982); Michael Walzer's *Spheres of Justice* (1983); and Charles Taylor's *Sources of the Self* (1989). These are not the only works of the four writers which are significantly communitarian: in particular, Taylor's 1985 article 'Atomism' does much to set out what is recognisably communitarian in his approach; but the publication of four books within a clearly defined decade usually proves too neat a boundary to resist. Although *After Virtue* had been published a year earlier, 'it was Sandel's book that first elicited the label "communitarian" and brought about the retrospective recruitment of other writers to that flag'.[6] Even as political philosophy has moved in recent years beyond this 'debate', its terminology has crept into political discourse.

Although these academic philosophers do not have a high profile, their names do crop up in relation to 'communitarian politics' and New Labour, frequently via an assumed connection with Etzioni. Anthony Giddens, in a review of Etzioni's *New Golden Rule*, has suggested that Charles Taylor is Etzioni's 'illustrious predecessor', and that Etzioni takes the former's work to a greater level of detail.[7] Etzioni himself promotes the idea of a link, comparing his 'responsive communitarianism' with the work of 'old communitarians' – Taylor, Sandel and Walzer, and the sociologists Philip Selznick and Robert Bellah.[8] Philip Collins, writing in *Renewal*, calls communitarianism 'a loose set of ideas . . . usually associated with' Etzioni, but goes on to say that the 'more substantive body of communitarian thought was named and given its most eloquent advocacy in Michael Sandel's *Liberalism and the Limits of Justice*. It includes in the canon Alasdair MacIntyre, Charles Taylor, Michael Walzer and Joseph Raz.' Other commentators, whether academics or journalists, suggest a direct link between contemporary communitarian philosophy and New Labour. Driver and Martell include MacIntyre and Sandel (along with Macmurray, Tawney, Hobhouse and T. H. Green) as 'communitarian influences [which] are clearly apparent among Labour modernizers'.[9] Writing in the *Independent*, Demos director Geoff Mulgan suggests that the communitarian philosophy of the four writers is one of 'several diverse currents' upon which the party's 'shift, towards what can loosely be termed communitarianism, has drawn' and has given 'intellectual backbone' to a backlash against both individualism and the insecurity engendered by rapid social change. Melanie Phillips, herself sometimes considered a populariser of communitarian thought, introduces MacIntyre's name in an article which examines 'what the talk of morality and community really means'. Although she conceives of communitarianism in terms very similar to Etzioni's – it 'attempts to forge a new equilibrium between rights and responsibilities' – she does not see Etzioni as a direct influence on New Labour or Blair, although she does believe that MacIntyre's thought feeds directly into Etzioni's. Rather, she suggests that '[i]t was Gordon Brown who brought the MacIntyre position into the Labour Party', and that this 'chimed with his own Scottish ethical tradition, as it did with Blair's particular Christian perspective'.

These claims tend to give the impression, firstly, that there is a continuum between communitarian philosophy and the political communitarianism of Etzioni, through which it has filtered into the ideas of the Third Way; and, secondly, that communitarian philosophy has been a direct source of ideas for New Labour. A closer look at communitarian philosophy and New Labour policy suggests this to be far from the case.[10]

What, then, do these communitarian philosophers have to say? It is impossible here to give more than a very brief and superficial account of each writer's position where it has relevance to New Labour's policies and attitudes – and that with two caveats: firstly, this area of philosophy does not on the whole concern itself with the quotidian business of politics, making direct comparisons problematic; and, secondly, although the same terms occur (for example, *community*, *contract*, *person*), they frequently carry different meanings, which can be a trap for the unwary.

Michael Sandel

While some commentators[11] tend to define communitarianism in relation to John Rawls's *A Theory of Justice*, Sandel is one of only two (the other being Walzer) of the four philosophers under consideration who specifically take it as their starting-point. Sandel's approach has been seen as epitomising a communitarianism in which justice and community are in conflict.[12] He questions Rawls's assertion that 'justice is the first virtue of social institutions',[13] claiming instead that it is a 'remedial' virtue, necessary only when other social virtues, such as benevolence or solidarity, are lacking. Too great a reliance on Rawlsian justice is likely to cause these communal virtues to atrophy still further – or, at the very least, to 'reflect a lessening of the moral situation, rather than a moral improvement'.[14]

While Tony Blair has shown no sign of familiarity with communitarian philosophers like Sandel, he has referred to Rawls – suggesting that *A Theory of Justice* epitomises a highly individualistic model of human behaviour which began to take root in the 1960s and, by implication, led to the excesses of selfishness and greed widely perceived to characterise the 1980s. According to Blair, 'the Left was captured by the elegance and power' of Rawls's work. His comment on it is intriguing: '[Rawls's] manifesto for an egalitarian society is a brilliant exposition of the argument that an equal society is in the interests of anyone who does not know which position in that society they would occupy. *But it is derived from a highly individualistic view of the world.*'[15] That derivation is apparently sufficient to condemn the theory in Blair's eyes, but this reflects a confusion between the theory's 'philosophical anthropology' – 'its general account of the human person' and other background factors – and its 'prescriptive principles'.[16] Rawls's theory may be implicitly individualist at the anthropological level, but the political and social arrangements yielded by its explicit prescriptive principles are anything but. There is one obvious point on which Rawls and New Labour clash: Blair's avowed support for meritocracy is at odds with Rawls's view that people should not benefit[17] from 'arbitrary' attributes like talents which happen to be marketable. However, in that respect it is Rawls's egalitarianism rather than his individualism which Blair is rejecting; and the egalitarian principle is one which many communitarians, including Sandel, share with Rawls.

Alasdair MacIntyre

MacIntyre describes *After Virtue* as having arisen from his 'negative view of late twentieth century bureaucratised consumer capitalism and the liberal individualism which is its dominant ideology', and concludes that

the moral philosophy which informs that ideology had been generated by the fragmentation of an older moral tradition concerning human goods, virtues and the
social relationships in and through which goods can be pursued, of which the classical expression is the ethics of Aristotle.[18]

MacIntyre's criticism of liberalism is thus far broader than Sandel's. His objections are to the entire post-enlightenment liberal tradition, rather than to any
specific work, and he expresses concerns about liberalism's substantive moral
implications, in addition to questioning its conceptual coherence. His thesis is
that liberal societies are in a state of confusion, clinging to the vestiges of traditions destroyed by liberalism itself, which thus no longer make sense. Liberal
societies are beset by effectively irresolvable moral arguments – irresolvable
because there is no one set of basic premises, shared by the whole society, on
which to base moral judgements. Instead, there is a plurality of incommensur-
able moral assertions,[19] which must ultimately be arbitrary, but are cloaked in the
antiquated language of moral authority – vestiges of a tradition of which only
the language remains.

True human morality, destroyed by the enlightenment project of seeking its
rational justification, must, for MacIntyre, be teleological, directed towards the
end that is the good life, and this, for any individual, cannot be separated from
the social roles which that individual holds and which prescribe what is 'good'
for a person who inhabits those roles. MacIntyre uses the analogy of a watch: we
cannot judge whether a watch is a good watch or not unless we know what it is
that a watch is meant to do – what its role is, in other words. Human potential
cannot be realised, nor human ends fulfilled, in isolation from such communal,
social and moral roles.

To illustrate how we are to understand these roles and the ends they offer,
MacIntyre introduces the concepts of 'tradition' and 'practice'. Inherent to the
concept of practice is the notion of an 'internal good': a good which can be realised only through (or, rather, within) that practice.[20] These then provide an internal standard against which to make moral judgements about human action, and
which itself, unlike liberal moral assertions, is not arbitrary. It is because such
practices and traditions are realisable only in society that the concept of community is vital to MacIntyre's thought, and this is one of the reasons why his criticism of liberalism is a communitarian one, although it is also neo-Aristotelian
and, in subsequent work,[21] neo-Thomistic.

A third aspect of MacIntyre's communitarianism is his insistence on the 'narrative unity' of a human life.[22] What this means, in part, is that people make
choices not in the vacuum of the moment but in the context of a whole life, and
thus, again, in terms of their ultimate human ends.[23] For MacIntyre, therefore,
the possibility of attaining, or even identifying, any kind of good, but particularly the good life for human beings and the possibility of moral behaviour, is
dependent on the standards given by traditions and practices, which are, in turn,
social phenomena, requiring membership of a community.

The virtues whose loss MacIntyre laments are again those of Aristotle's political ideal.

> The notion of the political community as a common project is alien to the modern liberal individualist world. This is how we sometimes at least think of schools, hospitals or philanthropic organizations; but we have no conception of such a form of community concerned, as Aristotle says the *polis* is concerned, with the whole of life, not with this or that good, but with man's good as such.[24]

Although in appeals to the ideas of 'one nation' and 'national community'[25] it might appear that New Labour is pursuing this ideal, it is not, on two counts. While New Labour does have a clear view of the good citizen – one who works for a living and brings children up properly – this only reflects its narrow view of citizenship, which is defined in those very terms. It does not reflect a conception of what is good for 'man as such', or of the human *telos*. Rather, it reflects a view of what is good for the British nation or society – economic competitiveness and social order. People's *human* fulfilment, on the other hand, is to be sought on the basis of individual choice, sometimes in the public sphere but equally possibly in the private, and subject only to the liberal constraints of not impinging on others' ability likewise to seek fulfilment: 'We seek', Blair says, 'a diverse but inclusive society, promoting tolerance within agreed norms.'[26]

Government and politics simply do not concern themselves with what is good for man *as such*, i.e. as an entity with given ends. MacIntyre is right to say that we no longer think of people in this way. In the terms of MacIntyre's particular brand of communitarianism (although we must not forget that he himself has eschewed the label) New Labour, like every other major Western political party and polity, is irredeemably and inescapably liberal; they are among his 'barbarians'.[27]

In the same way that New Labour's invoking of the idea of citizenship superficially but misleadingly suggests congruence with MacIntyre's communitarianism, so too might Blair's frequent appeals to 'tradition', a key anchor for the modernisation of the party in the early years of his leadership. However, in a very significant sense New Labour understands this concept also in a different way from MacIntyre, because, for Blair, tradition (and its continuation) is something which is consciously *chosen* – impossible on MacIntyre's conception of it. Furthermore, Blair suggests that we can chose rationally between different traditions, or between 'values' and 'attitudes':

> When I think of the values and attitudes of my parents' generation, I distinguish between the genuine values that underpinned the best of Britain and the attitudes we can safely and rightly leave behind. Old-fashioned values are good values. Old-fashioned attitudes or practices may simply be barriers that hold our values back.[28]

'Values' worth keeping here include good manners, respect for others, courtesy, rejection of crime, respect and support for teachers, and doing voluntary work, while 'other things from the past' which Blair chooses 'to leave behind' include opposition to women working, to wearing jeans in church and failure to be 'fair-minded to gay people'.[29] Nowhere does Blair give any basis – other than personal preference or an intuition of the spirit of the age – for these distinctions: they are essentially arbitrary. In this, Blair is actually exhibiting what MacIntyre condemns as one of the manifestations of the modern age. In addition, in suggesting that it is possible rationally to chose to keep some traditions and reject others Blair is utilising a conception of 'tradition' wholly different from MacIntyre's.

Charles Taylor

In *Sources of the Self*, Taylor sets out to 'define the modern identity in describing its genesis'.[30] This modern identity, the ways in which we understand ourselves, is central to any understanding of 'modernity' in general. Taylor's approach is a historical one, because he believes that this question of identity can be understood only in the context of past conceptions. A central issue is where we find apparently objective standards of right and wrong – those standards which go beyond mere preference and enable us to undertake what Taylor calls 'strong evaluation'.[31] Morality, or 'the good', is strongly intertwined with the idea of 'selfhood', but, Taylor claims, modern moral theory focuses on 'what it is right to do' rather than what it is 'good to be'.[32] Ideas about the good, and strongly evaluative standards, must come from a social or communal context. This context provides 'frameworks' which enable us to judge by standards that are above and beyond our own immediate reactions and that can give us something to which to aspire. We can recognise such standards without necessarily being able to articulate why we subscribe to those particular ones. The kinds of communities which give such meaning to our lives, and which here mark Taylor out as a communitarian, are far broader and deeper – encompassing history, culture, religion and, above all, language – than what is generally understood by the term 'community', and the conception of it employed by New Labour.

A key feature of modernity, in Taylor's thesis, is the elevation of 'ordinary life'. In the past, ordinary life was not an end in itself, but a necessary prerequisite for the pursuit of 'the good life': a life which is fully human (compared to the life of a slave, in the classical model). In ancient Greece, or under the Italian republican revival, this was epitomised by a 'citizen ethic': to be a good citizen was to aspire to far more than the domestic necessities of ordinary life[33] – but in New Labour's conception, being a good citizen is identified very closely with the two most fundamental activities of ordinary life: working for a living; and taking care of one's family. This identification is made explicit in Blair's announcement to his party conference that once given the 'chance' to join the labour market, single parents, 'no longer the butt of Tory propaganda, [. . .] will be the citizens of New Britain who can earn a wage and look after the children they love.'[34]

Taylor claims that in modern societies 'the individual has been taken out of a rich community life and now enters instead into a series of mobile, changing, revocable associations, often designed merely for highly specific ends'.[35] Taylor clearly considers this a matter for regret, but when those 'revocable associations' take the form of short-term employment contracts and other manifestations of the 'flexible' employment market that is the Third Way response to its perception of globalisation, this is a model of society endorsed by – or at least acceptable to – New Labour. For Blair, community is not the framework which provides us with our bearings, but is itself a means to an end; for example, helping people in 'the struggle of balancing work and a family' and in the adjustment to a global economy: 'to become the masters of change, not its victims, we need an active community'.[36] Taylor notes that 'a society of self-fulfillers, whose affiliations are seen as more and more revocable, cannot sustain the strong identification with political community which public freedom needs'.[37] This means that two aspects of what New Labour wish to achieve are, in communitarian terms, in conflict with each other. Moreover, Taylor continues in a direct reference to policy,

> the atomist outlook which instrumentalism fosters makes people unaware of these conditions [i.e. the conditions 'for the public health of self-governing societies'], so that they happily support policies which undermine them – as in . . . neo-conservative measures in Britain and the US, which cut welfare programmes and regressively redistribute income, thus eroding the bases of community identification.[38]

Taylor wrote that in 1989, but policies of this sort have been implemented to increasing degrees since then on both sides of the Atlantic; New Labour in government has, for example, implemented cuts in lone-parent benefits and increased (regressive) indirect taxation. The Labour Government has more recently put into place a range of measures – among them the 2002 budget – which have redistributed resources to the least well-off. Nonetheless, that was not the case in the party's first years in office – when claims about its communitarianism were at a height. Furthermore, help for the worse-off has been in the form of the minimum wage, child-care provision and tax credits, all of which are available only to those in work, thus underscoring the conception of citizenship and inclusion rejected by Taylor. Neither Taylor's theory in general nor his specific allusions to policy offer any comfort to New Labour, and his communitarianism is not one with which the party could identify.

Michael Walzer

Like Sandel, and unlike MacIntyre and Taylor, Walzer writes in direct response to *A Theory of Justice*. According to Walzer, the way in which different social goods are distributed, and by whom, depends on particular cultural understandings of those goods, and the 'idea that principles of justice must be culture-specific entails a hostility to any political theory that embodies claims to universality', such as Rawls's theory of justice and many other liberal positions. The next stage of Walzer's argument is that different criteria for distribution are appropriate in different 'spheres' – injustice arises when, say, a criterion for the distribution of goods in one sphere intrudes into another:

> Every social good or set of goods constitutes, as it were, a distributive sphere within
> which only certain criteria or arrangements are appropriate. Money is inappropri-
> ate in the sphere of ecclesiastical office; it is an intrusion from another sphere. And
> piety should make for no advantage in the marketplace . . .[39]

By keeping the spheres separate, Walzer seeks 'complex equality', by which,
although simple inequalities of wealth and all sorts of social goods will remain,
they will lose their capacity to 'dominate'. (A dominant good is one which reinforces inequality by commanding goods from other spheres.[40]) What kinds of
goods belong to which sphere, and what principles of distribution are then
appropriate, can be the product only of shared cultural understandings, which
will vary across cultures. It is this 'radically particularist'[41] view, as well as the
cultural particularity of his principles of justice and his concomitant rejection of
universalism, rather than any substantive objections to liberalism, that mark
Walzer out as a communitarian.

Even a society as diverse as Britain's was in the late twentieth century has a
stock of shared understandings, in Walzer's terms. These are socially constructed meanings and ways of understanding things that depend as much on
history and tradition as on current agreement; they govern what *feels* natural and
right. These shared understandings can be, and are, called upon to decide which
criteria are appropriate for the distribution of certain goods, and the criteria
which those understandings yield are sometimes in conflict with the potential
outcomes (intended or otherwise) of government policies. In a booklet published
by Demos in 1996 John Gray explores some of the implications for policy of
Walzer's account. For example, he notes:

> In Britain most people think it unfair that access to decent medical care should be
> restricted by income rather than need, or that the provision of such care should be
> distorted by market forces. This common understanding condemns the neoliberal
> commercialisation of the NHS, if – as available evidence strongly suggests – the
> introduction of market mechanisms within it has partly decoupled patient care
> from medical need and made access to care to a significant degree and accident of
> the policies of the NHS trust currently in force in one's locality. Moreover, it
> demands the reversal of these policies, insofar as they have effects which violate it.[42]

Written in 1996, this clearly refers to the policies of the Conservative administration, but while Labour in government have amended the internal market in the
health service, market mechanisms play an increasing and more direct role,
through the Private Finance Initiative (PFI; see below) and the increasing use of
private health facilities for NHS patients.

Another policy in which New Labour itself has arguably violated the shared
understandings of the society it governs is by its extension of the PFI and
'public–private partnerships' (PPP) in the NHS and other areas of public provision (the London Underground being a recent high-profile example), under which
profit-making companies operate public services. This suggestion is borne out by
the widespread unease and opposition which the proposals have met from the

public. It is seen as simply wrong – or inappropriate – that public services should be run for private profit, *even if* this would result in the cheaper delivery of those services (which, as Eric Shaw points out in chapter 4, is often not the case).

This is illustrated by the case of prison policy. In opposition, Jack Straw opposed private prisons on the grounds that it is morally wrong for anyone to profit from people's incarceration. A 1995 policy document unequivocally stated that the 'Labour Party is opposed in principle to the privatisation of prisons . . . It is not appropriate for people to profit out of incarceration.'[43] In government, however, this was outweighed by economic considerations, and existing prisons continued to be in effect privatised while considerable amounts of new prison building were undertaken by the private sector. Inspectors' reports suggest that, in at least some cases, the private prisons, as well as being cheaper, provide better facilities and conditions for inmates. None of this, however, assuages public unease at the *idea* of making profits from public services.

In everyday terms, this might be described as a case of the Government 'moving too fast', in introducing policies for which the public are not yet ready. While there is often a case to be made for governments doing this, any government so doing is failing in that instance to legislate according to our shared understandings, and is thus not communitarian in Walzer's terms.

While abstract political philosophy may not offer much in the way of concrete policy proposals, the ideas expressed by these four writers do offer different ways of understanding the problems facing politics in the modern age; a far broader range of understandings than that of which politicians avail themselves. However, even a very superficial examination is sufficient to show that contemporary communitarian philosophy has contributed little to the development of Third Way thinking and New Labour's understanding of politics.

John Macmurray

John Macmurray was until recently unremarked upon and unremembered, being already unfashionable by the time of Tony Blair's interest in him. Yet from the 1930s to the 1950s he was widely known as a populariser of moral philosophy through radio appearances and lecture series, collections of which were being published into the 1960s,[44] and pamphlets/short volumes on a number of topics.[45] As well as this relatively popular work, he wrote more academic volumes[46] and held chairs at London and Edinburgh, and in South Africa and Canada. The publishers of the 1968 edition of *Freedom in the Modern World* (first published in 1932) claim that the work 'has probably had a deeper and more lasting effect than any other book of a philosophical character published this century'.[47] Even allowing for publishers' tendency to hyperbole, Macmurray was clearly considered a very important figure in mid-twentieth-century Britain.

Tony Blair himself has referred to Macmurray as an influence, and these few comments have been picked up on by commentators and have led to a minor revival of interest in his work. According to Blair's biographer, John Rentoul, Macmurray is Blair's 'philosophical mentor',[48] and 'Blair's idea of community, which is perhaps his most distinctive theme as a politician, derives directly from Macmurray'.[49] This claim is repeated and reinforced by Driver and Martell, who note that 'Blair read and discussed the communitarian philosophy of John Macmurray'[50] while at Oxford, and, elsewhere, they refer to Macmurray as 'the Scottish philosopher who influenced Tony Blair'.[51] In another biography, Jon Sopel notes that Blair 'became fascinated by [Macmurray's] work [which] introduced him to an idea that would later become central to his political thinking, the notion of 'community'.[52] Sopel also refers to Macmurray as 'the Scottish philosopher . . . whom Blair was so influenced by when he was an undergraduate at Oxford'.[53] Elizabeth Frazer states, similarly, that 'Tony Blair's communitarianism was influenced by the philosophy of John MacMurray'.[54] More recently, the *Observer* has described Macmurray as 'an important influence on the Prime Minister'.[55]

At Oxford, Blair's interest in Macmurray came about via Peter Thomson, an Australian theology student some years older than Blair and his contemporaries. Blair was an enthusiastic contributor to an informal Christian discussion group which coalesced around Thomson, and it is from this period and this friendship that Blair's own Christianity dates. Thomson was an enthusiast for Macmurray's particular brand of active Christian socialism. Legend has it that Blair and Thomson made a pilgrimage to Edinburgh to visit Macmurray in 1974, shortly before his death, although in the event only Thomson went into his home and met him.[56]

Blair's own references to Macmurray date from July 1994, just days after Blair's election to the party leadership, and before the modernisation project had got underway. 'If you really want to understand what I'm all about', he is quoted as saying, 'you have to take a look at a guy called John Macmurray',[57] going on to say that 'he was influential – very influential. Not in the details, but in the general concept.'[58] Blair also mentions Macmurray as one of many writers to have influenced his 'interest in religion and philosophy', alongside Kierkegaard, Jung and Kant, saying: 'One of the best things I have read on the subject of Christian duty was an essay by the Scottish philosopher John Macmurray, a socialist thinker whose writings I was introduced to as a student at Oxford.' What Blair understood Macmurray to mean in this (unidentified) essay was that 'there is a human impulse within, which can be fulfilled only through duty'.[59]

Community

The obvious connection between Blair and Macmurray is the importance for both of them of the idea of community. The problem lies in that 'the general concept' cited by Blair – which most commentators understand as referring to *community* – is notorious for the broad range of interpretations which it invites. Blair himself employs a number of different conceptions, evident in this single paragraph:

> At the heart of my beliefs is the idea of community. I don't just mean the villages, towns and cities in which we live. I mean that our fulfilment as individuals lies in a decent society of others. My argument to you today is that the renewal of community is the answer to the challenges of a changing world.[60]

Nonetheless, throughout discussions of Macmurray's perceived influence on Blair 'community' is treated as if it is an uncontested, unambiguous term.

The main thrust of Macmurray's work is his assertion that people's humanity and human potential are realised only through their relations with others – but only through certain kinds of relationships. Relations, according to Macmurray, may be either social or communal. Where people come together to co-operate for common ends, a *social* relationship is formed. In this, we

> associate with others in order to achieve some purpose that we all share. Out of this there springs a life of social co-operation through which we can provide for our common needs, and achieve common ends. We may define this social life in terms of purposes. That is its great characteristic.[61]

Social relationships are, in other words, instrumental. The definition of society is that it is founded upon, and composed of, instrumental relationships. This is highly necessary to human survival, but it is not the form of relationship which expresses and realises humanity itself.

> The satisfactory working of social life depends upon entering into relationships with other people, not with the whole of ourselves, but only with part of ourselves. It depends upon suppressing . . . the fullness and wholeness of our natures.[62]

The '*personal* life', in contrast,

> demands a relationship with one another in which we can be our whole selves and have complete freedom to express everything that makes us what we are. It demands a relationship with one another in which suppression and inhibition are unnecessary.[63]

The personal life is in contrast to both the social life and the individual life.[64] Whatever we call this kind of relationship (and Macmurray points out that all the possible terms, such as 'friendship', 'fellowship', 'communion' and 'love', have taken on partial meanings too specific to that purpose), at the heart of it

> is the idea of a relationship between us which has no purpose beyond itself; in which we associate because it is natural to human beings to share their experience, to understand one another, to find joy and satisfaction in living together; in expressing and revealing themselves to one another.[65]

This is Macmurray's highly specific conception of community. Certainly, in Macmurray's view, society and community are two very different things, defined in opposition to each other. Society arises through external pressures and needs; community from internal human impulses, and 'the difference between a community and a mere society is . . . clear cut'.[66]

Society is built on interdependence, but any kind of dependence is, for

Macmurray, corrosively destructive of *community*. If we are dependent on other people – however much it may be mutual – we cannot be in true fellowship with them, but only in an instrumental relationship which diminishes our humanity.[67] For Blair, on the other hand, community is a recognition of interdependence: 'The idea of community resolves the paradox of the modern world: it acknowledges our interdependence; it recognises our individual worth',[68] while Gordon Brown 'think[s] of Britain . . . as a community of citizens with common needs, mutual interests, shared objectives, related goals. . .'.[69]

The entire point of Macmurray's advocacy of community is as a contrast and necessary complement to social relations. His work cannot be used to confer the value that he ascribes to his conception of community on what he calls 'mere society'. However, New Labour tends to conflate the two concepts and use the terms 'community' and 'society' interchangeably – as, for example, in: 'At the heart of my beliefs is the idea of community . . . that our fulfilment as individuals lies in a decent society of others'.[70] In doing this, New Labour rejects the distinction which is at the very heart of Macmurray's work, and thus negates everything he has to say about the desirability of community.[71]

Individualism

Many of the themes and ideas *attributed* to Macmurray, most explicitly by Rentoul, and by Driver and Martell,[72] are closer to modern communitarian philosophy than to Macmurray's own work. For example, Rentoul claims that

> Macmurray saw his purpose as being to challenge the starting point of modern philosophy, the idea that people are individuals first who then choose how to relate to others. He insisted that people exist *only* in relation to others . . . he argued that the liberal self was incomplete, because people's personalities are created by their relationships to their families and communities.[73]

Driver and Martell also present Macmurray's position as 'a direct attack on liberalism',[74] although nowhere does Macmurray overtly attack liberalism. Indeed, in *The Self as Agent*, he defends liberalism against communism.[75] Macmurray's attacks are directed primarily towards capitalism and tradition, and generally towards those forces which *suppress* the individual human impulse.

Communitarian politics is often presented as an antidote to the selfish individualism perceived to have been engendered under Thatcherism. For Macmurray, however, individualism – which he perceived in his own time – was not the cause of social ills, but a symptom of them, and of insecurity in particular, in a world dominated by fear rather than love.

> Fear accomplishes [the] destruction of life by turning us in upon ourselves and so isolating us from the world around us. That sense of individual isolation which is so common in the modern world, which is often called 'individualism' is one of the inevitable expressions of fear.[76]

For Macmurray, individualism is an expression of fear, while society is an expression of mutual need, and community an expression of love.[77]

Duty, responsibility and rights

Blair is frequently labelled communitarian because of his continual emphasis on duties and responsibilities and the prioritising of these over rights. The idea of 'no rights without responsibilities' is also one of the defining 'values' of Giddens's Third Way.[78] Recent examples from New Labour include Blair's assertions: 'If we invest so as to give the unemployed person the chance of a job, they have a responsibility to take it or lose benefit';[79] and 'For every new opportunity we offer, we demand responsibility in return.'[80] These reflect Blair's view that 'a decent society is not based on rights. It is based on duty.'[81] However, this finds few echoes in Macmurray, who talks about rights far more than about duties, and whose references to responsibilities show a very different understanding from Blair's.

Peter Thomson is quoted by Rentoul as saying that Macmurray

> was onto a concept of community. He used to say that the noblest form of human existence is friendship and that instead of being on a debit and credit ledger idea of 'If you do this for me, then I'll do that for you,' we ought to develop a sense of community where people were committed to the welfare of one another.[82]

This is a long way away from New Labour policy, in which the language of rights in exchange for duties; opportunity in exchange for responsibility, and 'contracts', 'compacts' and 'covenants'[83] strongly reflects the 'debit and credit ledger idea' rejected by Macmurray in his advocacy of the spontaneous generosity of truly human relations. For Macmurray, the provisions of the welfare state *are* unconditional rights, which he compares here with charitable provision:

> [G]etting rid of unemployment, providing hospitals and recreation grounds and better schools for the poor and so on . . . is a matter of bare justice, and it has got to be done . . . What the unemployed need is not pity from a distance, but their bare rights as members of an astonishingly wealthy community. We have to see that they get their rights, and not pat ourselves on the back for our benevolence when we are merely being honest and decent.[84]

While *duty* is a term which occurs only rarely in Macmurray's work, responsibility for oneself does play a part in his thought, but one different from the Third Way's understanding of it. For Macmurray, the ability to take responsibility for oneself is a privilege; even, perhaps, in an ideal world, a right, but certainly not a burden. For example, in a discussion of democracy, Macmurray says that '[democracy] opposes privilege and social distinction, because these mean that some people or some classes of people are cornering freedom and responsibility for themselves at the expense of others'.[85] Responsibility is a precondition of freedom,[86] and people will grasp it if only given the opportunity; it is not something which has to be imposed on them by, say, New Deal-type conditions. It might be argued that this reflects an overly optimistic view of human nature. But it cannot be argued that New Labour's conception of responsibility is anything like Macmurray's.

'Active community'

One aspect of the Government's brand of communitarianism is the attempt to foster community by encouraging people to serve others. This ethos underlies the notion of 'active community', which encompasses voluntary work and charitable giving, and is a key plank in the proposals for the teaching of citizenship in schools. It is also widely promoted and practised by Christianity of a traditional kind. For Blair and his Government, '[v]olunteering and community activities are central to the concept of citizenship and are the key to restoring our communities'.[87] Such a sentiment reflects, almost word for word, pre-election Labour Party policy documents.[88] The idea that '[c]learer expectations need to be set about the importance of people participating in their communities . . . Children should grow up with these expectations', and the proposal that 'by 2010 all first degree courses should provide for a small element of credit towards the degree for approved community activity; and all universities and colleges should use community involvement as part of the criteria for entrance',[89] appear to bring us a little nearer to the compulsory community service advocated by contemporary communitarians like Etzioni.[90] Macmurray scathingly condemns such an ethos of service to others, and in doing so unambiguously rejects the accepted communitarian conception of the individual's relationship to the rest of society. To understand why, we must return to Macmurray's philosophy.

Macmurray describes three kinds of morality: mechanical; social (or organic); and human.[91] The second of these, social morality, is very close to the communitarian morality endorsed by Etzioni and promoted by New Labour. Macmurray sets out what social morality says. For example, social morality

> will talk a great deal about purpose. Each of us ought to have a purpose in life and to work for its achievement, it will say. Then whatever draws us aside from out purpose will be bad and whatever advances it will be good . . . If human life is to be good, it must not forget that the purpose which it serves is not its own purpose but the purpose of life as a whole.[92]

Macmurray outlines ideas behind this morality which bear some resemblance to aspects of modern communitarianism:

> Each of us is born into a society and our lives are bound up with the community to which we belong . . . We owe all we have and all we are to the community to which we belong. The community is our real environment and we live only in it and through it. Therefore the purpose which ought to control our lives is not our own selfish purpose, but the social purpose. We are part of a community of social life, and the goodness of our individual lives depends upon our devoting them to the

common good . . . The good man is the man who serves his country, serves his generation, identifies himself with the good of the community and devotes his life to the accomplishment of the social purpose.[93]

However, *this* morality is being set out by Macmurray only to be condemned. Such a 'morality of service . . . is a false morality. It is false because it thinks of human life in biological terms, as if we were animals, not persons.'[94] Furthermore, it is 'a denial of human reality. It treats everybody as a means to an end' and 'subordinates human beings to organization.'[95] In sum: 'The first thing we have to stop is the false idea that it is a good thing to serve society and its institutions. It isn't. *It is an evil thing.*'[96] Thus Macmurray unambiguously rejects a morality and a view of the individual's relationship with his or her society which has been at the heart of New Labour thinking.

This is not to say that Tony Blair was lying when he claimed, in 1994, to have been influenced by Macmurray's ideas; nor even to suggest that he misunderstood the writer. After all, it was Blair who said that,

at its best, socialism corresponds most closely to an existence that is both rational and moral. It stands for co-operation, not confrontation; for fellowship, not fear. It stands for equality . . . because only through equality in our economic circumstances can our individuality develop properly.[97]

But he said that in 1983, as a newly elected Labour MP. Such sentiments – strongly evocative of Macmurray – may once have been Blair's, but they are not those of New Labour or the Third Way.

This, perhaps, provides a clue to the more general lack of influence of communitarian philosophy: maybe there is simply no room in government, or even in the serious politics of opposition, for the precision which political philosophy demands and the abstraction by which it is attained. As Adam Swift points out, while politicians are happy to employ, in a strategic way, philosophical concepts like 'community' or 'freedom', 'the pursuit of truth and the pursuit of votes are very different enterprises' requiring 'not just different but incompatible virtues'.[98] The real question is why we expect politicians to espouse 'a philosophy' – why McWalter, himself formerly a philosophy lecturer,[99] thought his question to be even reasonable, let alone helpful.

Notes

1 Tony McWalter, MP for Hemel Hempstead.
2 *Hansard* for 27 February 2002: col. 698.
3 British footballer turned film actor, renowned in both contexts for violence rather than intellect.
4 Hattersley 2002.
5 Blair 1997a.
6 Mulhall and Swift 1992: 40.
7 Giddens 1997: 11.

8 Etzioni 1998: x.
9 Driver and Martell 1997: 28.
10 Some commentators do mention communitarian philosophy while acknowledging its distance from politics - an example is Bowring 1997: 96.
11 Mulhall and Swift 1992 explicitly do this.
12 By Kymlicka 1993: 367.
13 Rawls 1972: 3.
14 Kymlicka 1993: 367.
15 Blair 1996a: 299.
16 This distinction is made by David Miller (1999: 172), who suggests that any political theory 'contains two analytically separable elements': a 'philosophical anthropology', and a 'set of prescriptive principles'. The philosophical anthropology, which may be explicit or implicit, but is always present, is 'a general account of the human person, of the conditions of moral agency, of the nature of human relationships and so forth', while the prescriptive principles 'specifying how social relationships are to be ordered, how the state is to be constituted and so on'. The relationship between the two is one of support rather than entailment, so one kind of anthropology could be associated with a number of different sets of principles (and vice versa).
17 Unless allowing them to do so will benefit the worst off.
18 MacIntyre 1997: 332.
19 Mulhall and Swift 1992: 72.
20 MacIntyre 1985: chapter 15.
21 MacIntyre (1997: 332) has 'continued the project initiated in *After Virtue* . . . in *Whose Justice? Which Rationality?* (1988) and in *Three Rival Versions of Moral Enquiry* (1990)'.
22 Mulhall and Swift 1992: 86.
23 *Ibid.*, p. 88.
24 MacIntyre 1985: 156.
25 See e.g. Blair 1996a: 298: 'To recover national purpose we need to start thinking and acting as one nation, one community again.'
26 Blair 1998.
27 MacIntyre 1985: 263.
28 Blair 2000a.
29 *Ibid.*
30 Taylor 1989: x.
31 *Ibid.*, p. 4.
32 *Ibid.*, p. 3.
33 *Ibid.*, p. 213.
34 Blair 1995.
35 Taylor 1989: 502.
36 Blair 2000a. This is just one of many possible examples.
37 Taylor 1989: 508.
38 Taylor 1989: 505.
39 Walzer 1983: 10.
40 *Ibid.*, chapter 1.
41 *Ibid.*, p. xiv.
42 Gray 1996: 45.
43 Labour Party 1995.

44 Collections of Macmurray's lectures include *Reason and Emotion* (1962) and *Freedom in the Modern World* (1968).

45 Including *Challenge to the Churches* (1941) and *Conditions of Freedom* (1949).

46 Including *The Self as Agent* (1957).

47 Macmurray 1968: inside front cover.

48 Rentoul 1996: 479.

49 *Ibid.*, p. 42.

50 Driver and Martell 1998: 27.

51 Driver and Martell 1997: 28.

52 Sopel 1995: 34.

53 *Ibid.*, p. 144.

54 Frazer 1999: 25.

55 Ahmed and Staunton 2000.

56 This is reported by Rentoul (1996: 51) who has Thomson going in alone; Sopel (1995: 34) says that 'a group' of Thomson's friends 'travelled to Scotland . . . and met John Macmurray'.

57 Quoted by Rentoul (1996: 42) who sources it to *Scotland on Sunday*, 24 July 1994.

58 Rentoul 1996: 44.

59 *Ibid.*

60 Blair 2000a: this paragraph alone covers community as location, as synonymous with society, as a means to individual fulfilment, as renewable, and as the solution to the problems of modernity.

61 Macmurray 1962: 97.

62 *Ibid.*, pp. 96–7.

63 *Ibid.*, p. 97.

64 *Ibid.*, p. 94.

65 *Ibid.*, p. 98.

66 Macmurray 1941: 23–4.

67 Macmurray 1968: 160–2.

68 Blair 2000b.

69 Brown 2000.

70 Blair 2000a. The terms are used interchangeably throughout this speech, and are also confused in Gordon Brown's speech (2000) to the NCVO.

71 The same distinction is made by Macmurray 1935: 97.

72 Driver and Martell 1998: 28–9.

73 Rentoul 1996: 42–3 (original emphasis).

74 Driver and Martell 1998: 27.

75 Macmurray 1957: 30.

76 Macmurray 1968: 59.

77 *Ibid.*

78 Giddens 1998: 66. Giddens does say in passing that the principle 'must apply not only to welfare recipients, but to everyone' – a point easily lost in New Labour politics.

79 Blair 2000b.

80 Blair 2000a. Both these examples in fact demonstrate a shift in which responsibilities are no longer exchanged for rights, but for mere 'opportunities'.

81 Blair 1997b.

82 Rentoul 1996: 42.

83 For example, in his speech to the Global Ethics Foundation, Blair (2000b) says that a

'covenant of opportunities and responsibilities' is a necessary condition of 'spending taxpayers' money on public services or social exclusion'.

84 Macmurray 1968: 215–16.
85 Macmurray 1941: 9.
86 Macmurray 1968: 48.
87 Active Community Unit 1999: 9.
88 See e.g. Labour Party 1997: 1, 4 and 6.
89 Active Community Unit 1999: 13.
90 Etzioni 1995: 113–15.
91 Macmurray 1968: chapter 9.
92 *Ibid.*, pp. 195–6.
93 *Ibid.*, p. 196.
94 *Ibid.*, p. 198.
95 *Ibid.* This ties in with Simon Prideaux's criticism of Etzioni's communitarianism in chapter 7 of this volume.
96 Macmurray 1968: 200–1 (emphasis added).
97 Tony Blair's maiden speech to the House of Commons, quoted in Blair 1996: 11.
98 Swift 2001: 40.
99 Hoggart 2002.

References

Active Community Unit (1999) *Giving Time, Getting Involved: A Strategy Report by the Working Group on the Active Community*, London, Cabinet Office.
Ahmed, K. and Staunton, D. (2000) 'Whose side is God on?', *Observer*, 25 June.
Anderson, P. and Mann, N. (1997) *Safety First: The Making of New Labour*, London, Granta Books.
Avnon, D. and de-Shalit, A. (1999) *Liberalism and its Practice*, London, Routledge.
Blair, T. (1995) Speech to the Labour Party Annual Conference.
Blair, T. (1996) *New Britain: My Vision of a Young Country*, London, Fourth Estate.
Blair, T. (1996a) 'The stakeholder society', in Blair, *New Britain*.
Blair, T. (1996b) 'Why I am a Christian', *Sunday Telegraph*, 7 April, reprinted in Blair, *New Britain*.
Blair, T (1997a) Speech on the launch of the Social Exclusion Unit, Stockwell Park School, 8 December.
Blair, T. (1997b) Speech to the Labour Party Annual Conference.
Blair, T. (1998) *The Third Way: New Politics for the New Century*, London, Fabian Society.
Blair, T. (2000a) Speech to the Women's Institute's Triennial General Meeting.
Blair, T. (2000b) 'Values and the power of community', speech to the Global Ethics Foundation, University of Tübingen, 30 June.
Bowring, F. (1997) 'Communitarianism and morality: in search of the subject', *New Left Review*, 222.
Brittan, S. (1997) 'Blair's real guru', *New Statesman*, 7 February.
Brown, G. (2000) Speech by the chancellor of the exchequer at the National Council for Voluntary Organisations' Annual Conference, 9 February.
Collins, P. (1996) 'Community, morality and fairness', *Renewal*, 4(3).

Driver, S. and Martell, L. (1997) 'New Labour's communitarianisms', *Critical Social Policy*, 17(3).

Driver, S. and Martell, L. (1998) *New Labour: Politics After Thatcherism*, Cambridge, Polity Press.

Etzioni, A. (1995) *The Spirit of Community: Rights, Responsibilities and the Communitarian Agenda*, London, Fontana.

Etzioni, A. (1997) *The New Golden Rule: Community and Morality in a Democratic Society*, London, Profile Books.

Etzioni, A. (ed.) (1998) *The Essential Communitarian Reader*, Lanham, MD, Rowman & Littlefield.

Etzioni, A. (2000) *The Third Way to a Good Society*, London, Demos.

Frazer, E. (1999) *Problems of Communitarian Politics: Unity and Conflict*, Oxford, Clarendon Press.

Giddens, A. (1997) 'Anomie of the people', *Guardian*, 31 July.

Giddens, A. (1998) *The Third Way: The Renewal of Social Democracy*, Cambridge, Polity Press.

Goodin, R.E. and Pettit, P. (eds) (1993) *Blackwell Companion to Contemporary Political Philosophy*, Oxford, Blackwell.

Gray, J. (1996) *After Social Democracy: Politics, Capitalism and the Common Life*, London, Demos.

Hansard, online: www.parliament.the-stationery-office.co.uk/pa/cm/cmhansard.htm.

Hattersley, R. (2002) 'So what is it that Tony believes in?', *Guardian*, 4 March.

Hoggart, S. (2002) 'Blair bamboozled when asked about his beliefs', *Guardian*, 28 February.

Kymlicka, W. (1993) 'Community', in Goodin and Pettitt (eds) *Blackwell Companion to Contemporary Political Philosophy*.

Labour Party (1995) *Safer Communities, Safer Britain: Labour's Proposals for Tough Action on Crime*, London, Labour Party.

Labour Party (1997) *Building the Future Together: Labour's Policies for Partnership Between Government and the Voluntary Sector*, London, Labour Party.

MacIntyre, A. (1985 [1981]) *After Virtue: A Study in Moral Theory*, London, Duckworth.

MacIntyre, A. (1995) 'The spectre of communitarianism', *Radical Philosophy*, 70.

MacIntyre, A. (1997) 'A philosophical self-portrait', in T. Mautner (ed.) *Penguin Dictionary of Philosophy*, London, Penguin.

Macmurray, J. (1935) *Creative Society*, London, Faber.

Macmurray, J. (1941) *Challenge to the Churches: Religion and Democracy*, London, Kegan Paul.

Macmurray, J. (1949) *Conditions of Freedom*, Toronto, Ryerson Press.

Macmurray, J. (1957) *The Self as Agent*, London, Faber.

Macmurray, J. (1962 [1935]) *Reason and Emotion*, London, Faber.

Macmurray, J. (1968 [1932]) *Freedom in the Modern World*, London, Faber.

McSmith, A. (1997 [1996]) *Faces of Labour: The Inside Story*, London, Verso.

Mautner, T. (ed.) (1997) *Penguin Dictionary of Philosophy*, London, Penguin.

Miller, D. (1999) 'Communitarianism: Left, Right and Centre', in Avnon and de-Shalit, *Liberalism and its Practice*.

Mulgan, G. (1995) 'Beyond the lure of off-the-shelf ethics', *Independent*, 30 January.

Mulhall, S. and Swift, A. (1992) *Liberals and Communitarians*, Oxford, Blackwell.

Phillips, M. (1995) 'The race to wake sleeping duty', *Observer*, 2 April.

Rawls, J. (1972) *A Theory of Justice*, Oxford, Oxford University Press.

Rentoul, J. (1996 [1995]) *Tony Blair*, London, Warner Books.

Sopel, J. (1995) *Tony Blair: The Moderniser*, London, Bantam.

Swift, A. (2001) 'Politics v. philosophy', *Prospect*, August–September.

Taylor, C. (1989) *Sources of the Self: The Making of Modern Identity*, Cambridge, Cambridge University Press.

Taylor, C. (1995) *Philosophical Arguments*, Cambridge, MA, Harvard University Press.

Walzer, M. (1983) *Spheres of Justice*, Oxford, Blackwell.

Walzer, M. (1990) 'The communitarian critique of liberalism', *Political Theory*, 18(1).

The Third Way and the politics of community

Introduction

This chapter argues that New Labour did not endorse a communitarian blueprint, but that it used communitarian ideas to revise traditional Labour values. In particular, it argues that the ideas of *duty* and *responsibility* defended by communitarianism were used by New Labour to water down the party's commitment to *equality*. In order to demonstrate this argument, New Labour's narratives on community, which were used to justify policies aimed at promoting work, are analysed.

The chapter begins with a brief explanation of communitarian ideas, focusing on the works of 'prescriptive communitarians', given that it was these thinkers who had an influence on New Labour's thinking. From there it explains the use that New Labour made of these ideas in the context of policies aimed at promoting work.

New Labour developed several narratives or subplots to the 'politics of community', which were fashioned by different actors at different times. The most salient subplot was the one developed by Tony Blair, who stressed the relevance of duty. The second subplot deals with the link between ideas on community and socialism. The third subplot concerns the narrative on social exclusion–social inclusion, which sheds light on New Labour's approach to poverty and social inequalities.

The final section assesses the impact of these ideas on New Labour's ideology and argues that New Labour did not endorse communitarianism, but simply used those ideas to revise the party's approach to equality. This is demonstrated by highlighting how New Labour endorsed *and* deviated from the communitarian agenda. The chapter ends with a discussion of the implications of those deviations for the party's ideology.

The narrative of community

Soon after Tony Blair became leader of the Labour Party, journalists and political commentators started to raise questions about the party's 'Big Idea'. The answer to this quest was quickly found in the national press. Melanie Phillips, in the *Observer*, wrote that Blair's speeches had the 'imprints' of the American communitarian thinker Amitai Etzioni;[1] and, in the *Guardian*, Seumas Milne claimed that Tony Blair's New Labour 'project' was 'communitarian to its fingertips'.[2] Peter Mandelson and Roger Liddle also helped to strengthen that perception. In *The Blair Revolution: Can New Labour Deliver?* they argued that New Labour's distinctive emphasis was 'on its concept of community', which was not a 'soft and romantic concept', but a 'robust and powerful idea' which meant teamwork, mutuality and justice.[3]

As the reference to Etzioni suggests, a particular type of communitarianism, which is defined here as prescriptive communitarianism, influenced New Labour's communitarian narrative[4]. But, in order to understand 'prescriptive communitarianism' we have to understand the starting-point of the communitarian debate. Sketchily explained, communitarianism draws from an academic debate fostered by thinkers who challenged Rawlsian liberal philosophy. Authors such as Charles Taylor, Michael Walzer, Alasdair MacIntyre and Michael Sandel, among many others, criticised the alleged individualistic and atomistic premises of procedural liberalism developed by Rawls and some of his followers, and argued instead that individuals were socially embedded.[5]

From this analytical framework, a group of thinkers, including Amitai Etzioni, Philip Selznick, Henry Tam and William Galston, developed a blueprint for political action which contained prescriptions on how to create the 'good society'.[6] It was this group of communitarian authors, here called 'prescriptive communitarians', which in part inspired New Labour's political agenda and language. The Scottish philosopher John Macmurray is also cited as one the main influences on Blair's communitarian thinking. His influence (or lack of it) is considered in chapter 5 of this book.

Prescriptive communitarians blamed excessive individualism and excessive neo-liberalism for the alleged moral drift of contemporary societies and also for the growth of a 'culture of dependence'. Excessive individualism was also perceived as a potential threat to individual autonomy.[7] In order to tackle such social ills, prescriptive communitarians developed a blueprint, the aim of which was the promotion of individual responsibility.[8] For instance, Amitai Etzioni proposed 'a moratorium on the minting of most, if not all, new rights; re-establishing the link between rights and responsibilities; recognizing that some responsibilities do not entail rights; and, most carefully, adjusting some rights to the changed circumstances',[9] and recommended a 'return to a language of social virtues, interests, and above all, social responsibilities'.[10] According to prescriptive communitarians, the implementation of such an agenda would lay the ground for inclusive communities, in which individual autonomy is fostered while all members contribute to the common good.[11]

The construction of inclusive communities presupposes the promotion of self-reliance through the work ethic and the support of family life. For prescriptive communitarians, work and family life have character-forming and 'community-building' qualities. Through work and through family life, they argue, people learn how to be self-reliant, responsible and civil, and how to contribute to the wealth of the community and of the country. Prescriptive communitarians argue that individuals have the 'moral responsibility' to be self-reliant – that is, to work for their own provision.[12] Work is important because it provides citizens with greater degrees of autonomy, self-esteem and sense of purpose in life, and gives people a sense of responsibility and fulfilment.[13] Philip Selznick argues also that policies for full employment should be part of a communitarian agenda given that, 'for most people of working age, the most important road to belonging and self-respect is a decent and steady job'.[14]

However, the duty to work is not of paramount importance. Individuals have the duty to work insofar as they are paid and the work is fulfilling, enabling individuals to live dignified and empowered lives. Prescriptive communitarians, such as Etzioni, opposed the imposition of penalties on those who refuse to work. Indeed, in those circumstances the state has the duty to provide them with basic goods. According to Etzioni, 'the state's duty in a good society is to ensure that no one goes hungry, homeless, unclothed or sick and unattended', given that 'providing essentials to people will not kill the motivation to work, as long as work is available and they are able'.[15]

Concerning the support of family life, the communitarian agenda is slightly more prescriptive. From the assumption that the consequences of family failure affect society at large, and, therefore, that questions of family structure are not purely private matters,[16] prescriptive communitarians defend the two-parent family on the grounds that 'the best antipoverty program for children is a stable intact family'.[17] But what prescriptive communitarians such as Etzioni or Tam defend is not the hierarchical family of the 1950s, but a democratic style of family in which men and women share equal rights and responsibilities.[18] Because they assume that two breadwinners form the typical family in contemporary societies, prescriptive communitarians argue that there must be a better balance between work and family life, in order to support families. To that end they advocate policies, which may or not be enforced by legislation, governing working hours, paternity leave, childcare facilities, and the distribution of welfare.[19]

Prescriptive communitarians also claim that the spirit of community must be promoted through 'moral suasion' and peer-pressure, and not by governmental decrees. Thus, they rely 'on moral dialogues, education, and suasion to win people to their ideals, rather than imposing their values by force of law'.[20] Likewise, the 'social order' can be established only voluntarily and chosen individually. In other words, in order to be accepted as legitimate by individuals, the new social order cannot be enshrined in legislation, but is to be promoted through the informal links of family, civic associations, churches, etc. This social pressure would then promote family life, faith,[21] a work-ethic and the mushrooming of social webs deemed essential for the creation of the good society. Communitarian thinkers like to stress that inclusive communities will not thwart individual autonomy, since their 'operative power relations' will enable all members to participate in collective decision-making.[22] Despite such assurances, several commentators have perceived the model of community defended by Etzioni as authoritarian and illiberal.[23]

The empowerment of the individual and of the community is considered necessary by prescriptive communitarians because they claimed that the state is partly responsible for the moral drift of society.[24] Hence they also aim at reducing the role of the state and at protecting individuals from state interference. However, communitarians stress that reducing the role of the state does not amount to replacing the state with other institutions. Indeed, communitarians like Etzioni and Tam reserve an important role for the state, namely the responsibility of ensuring that 'everyone has access to the basic necessities of life'[25] and the responsibility of limiting inequality.[26] Moreover, communitarians have shown some concerns about the promotion of a meritocratic society and the acceptance of socio-economic inequalities. Indeed, Henry Tam claims that 'progressive communitarians hold that power inequalities tend to undermine inclusive community life and, therefore, should be minimised as far as it is compatible with the maintenance of a reasonable degree of economic well-being'.[27] In a similar vein, Philip Selznick claims that 'meritocracy can undermine community'.[28] Furthermore, communitarians argue that to pay taxes is 'a civic virtue which good citizens are proud to display'[29] and that progressive taxation 'is a demand for responsible participation by those who gain most from the contributions of all', since 'people who gain most from the social and economic order, and from the benefits of community, have correspondingly greater obligations than those who get less, and especially those who get the least'.[30]

Though sketchily explained, these are the main points of the prescriptive communitarian agenda which have influenced New Labour's thinking. However, as I show, significant sections of this agenda were left out by New Labour, omissions which signal important aspects of its ideology.

The politics of community

The narrative on community was instrumental for New Labour to stress its ideological differences from the Conservatives, but it was equally important to emphasise its loyalty to the party's traditions. Community was thus presented as New Labour's 'Big Idea', the idea that would renew the party's electoral appeal. However, as a new idea, 'community' was used to mean different things at different times, as if the party was still trying to find the best formula for the presentation of New Labour's project.

Tony Blair was the strongest advocate of the 'politics of community'. Community and the communitarian themes of 'duty' and 'responsibility' were omnipresent in Blair's speeches, although his ideas on community underwent several metamorphoses. Gordon Brown developed a narrative on community, but his discourse was more consistent in the sense that he always linked communitarian ideas to the party's traditions, in particular the tradition of ethical socialism. And all Labour frontbenchers, especially those with social policy portfolios, spoke about community and about the ethos of 'rights and responsibilities', but those ideas were presented in simpler terms, in that there was no attempt to build bridges with the party's ideological past or to develop a grand narrative. For instance, Frank Field did not speak specifically of communities, but he argued that New Labour's welfare reform agenda aimed in part at 'reinventing and nurturing civil society'.[31] He also said that behind New Labour's values and principles 'lies the idea of the Good Society'.[32] On the theme of social morality, Field often stated that the welfare state does not operate in a moral vacuum, but that in fact it *teaches* values.[33] Similarly, David Blunkett often repeated the theme of 'rights and responsibility', and occasionally spoke about the need to create 'healthy, cohesive societies'.[34] Alastair Darling was the most pragmatic of the ministers involved in welfare policy since, in his speeches, he focused more on the practical aspects of policy than on the principles and values those policies were supposed to represent. Nonetheless, he occasionally referred to the ethic of 'rights and responsibilities', and about the need to change the culture of welfare claimants.[35]

The common thread to all the subplots of the politics of community is the relevance of duty. Indeed, duty and responsibilities are the core values of the communitarian blueprint, but they are also the distinctive trademark of the New Labour project. According to Blair and Brown, duty and responsibility are the forgotten values of the Labour tradition. But, more importantly, in New Labour's hierarchy of values, the concept of duty should be given priority over the concept of rights. Thus, 'duty', 'responsibility',or 'obligation', can be found in most of the speeches concerning the social policy developed by New Labour.

However, and despite the salience of these words in Blair's and other ministers' speeches, the nature of those duties and responsibilities was only vaguely specified, with the exception of the duty or responsibility to be self-reliant. New Labour's leaders perceived work as the means whereby individuals could feel connected to each other; thus, they claimed, the main duty in society was the duty to work. But more than promoting civic virtues and connectedness, the duty to work allowed New Labour to defend a new role for the State. In this new role, the State would be enabling, but it also would have fewer responsibilities.

Blair's spirit of community

Tony Blair started to use the idea of 'community' to convey the message that New Labour was not betraying the party's values, but renewing them. This linkage to the past was made by associating ideas of community with ideas of solidarity and collective endeavour. He was also trying to reassure the party by claiming that 'duty' was in fact a traditional Labour value. By defining his project in such terms, Blair was able to stress the differences between New Labour and the more individualistic and market-driven Conservatives.

However, Blair's discourse on community underwent several changes, with 'community' meaning different things at different times. In the first instance, Blair used communitarian ideas to establish a link with the party's past. For example, in a speech in 1993, he established the links between his ideas on community and early socialist political thinking by saying that 'the most basic belief of the Left is that people are not individuals in isolation from one another but members of a community and society who owe obligations to one another as much as to themselves and who depend on each other, in part at least, to succeed'.[36] In his speech to the 1994 Labour Party Conference, Blair defined *his* socialism as an 'understanding that the individual does best in a strong and decent community of people with principles and standards and common aims and values'.[37]

By establishing this link with the past, Blair was able to claim that communitarian themes, which sounded potentially authoritarian to some Labour supporters,[38] stemmed from traditional left-wing thought. The exercise of rooting his project in Labour's traditions was undertaken in parallel with a criticism of the recent past of the party. Blair argued that 'Old' Labour committed two major mistakes. On the one hand, it promoted a rights-based ethos that did not tackle individualism. On the other, it relied too much on the powers of the State and too little on the responsibilities of the individual[39]. The Labour leader also criticised the 'egalitarianism' of Old Labour, skilfully relating his argument to Etzionian and ethical socialist arguments. Moreover, he argued that a communitarian philosophy 'applied with common sense' would allow New Labour 'to move beyond the choice between narrow individualism and old-style socialism'.[40] This criticism prepared the ground for the reform of Clause 4. Indeed, the new Clause 4 replaced the commitment to the collectivisation of the means of production with a commitment to the market economy and a communitarian ethos.

But the criticism of the party's recent past also prepared the ground for the defence of a conservative version of community, which was illustrated by the adoption of a rather austere language. For example, at the 1994 Labour Party Annual Conference, Blair defined his socialism as the understanding 'that the individual does best in a strong and decent community of people with principles and standards and common aims and values'.[41] Blair also said that New Labour wanted 'to encourage people to make good and valuable choices, whether in terms of their own behaviour or their actions towards others'.[42] Moreover, and like Etzioni, Blair claimed that 'the only way to rebuild a social order and stability is through strong values, socially shared, and inculcated through individuals and families'.[43]

From here, Blair then moved on to the 'stakeholder society'. The ideas on the stakeholder society were first articulated by Will Hutton and John Kay. But, in the end, Blair's speech-writers were inspired by Francis Fukuyama's *Trust*, and Robert Putnam's ideas on 'social capital'.[44] Blair showed those influences when he said that his idea of stakeholder economy reflected 'new thinking about the economics of trust and social capital, as well as older ideas about rights and responsibilities of all those involved in wealth creation'.[45] For Blair, the stakeholder society is based on the communitarian principle of reciprocity, since it is a society 'based on a notion of mutual rights and responsibilities, on what is actually a modern notion of social justice – "something for something" – a society where every individual has a stake in the life of the community'.[46]

Though popular, the ideas on the stakeholder society were shortlived. According to an insider's account, Gordon Brown did not like stakeholding as an economic idea, because it would 'expose Labour to the risk of attack on grounds of social costs'.[47] In other words, stakeholding as an idea would jeopardise New Labour's relations with the business community and it therefore had to be discarded. Hence, stakeholding ideas were ditched, and the narrative of community once more assumed a highly normative gloss. The stress was again on the duties, and on the responsibilities, that individuals owed to their communities. In his first speech as prime minister, Blair said that his would be a 'government rooted in strong values, the values of justice and progress and community'.[48] At the 1997 Labour Party Conference in Brighton, Blair warned that a 'strong society cannot be built on soft choices', but 'is based on duty'.[49] The same idea of community was present in Blair's *Third Way* pamphlet, in which he defended a 'politics of "us" rather than "me"', one that would be based on 'an ethic of responsibility as well as [of] rights'.[50]

In more recent years, Blair has added a liberal finish to his ideas on community. At the Institute for Public Policy Research Conference, in January 1999, he proposed his 'modern idea of community'. In this new formulation, a far more liberal one than those articulated in previous years, the stress was more on what community could give to individuals. On that occasion, he described New Labour's idea of community as one 'which applauds and nurtures individual choice and personal autonomy and which recognizes the irreducible pluralism of modern society'.[51] Blair also expounded at great length his ideas about pluralism, tolerance and individual choice in connection with his ideas on community. What is not entirely clear is whether this later view is a complement to the previous ideas on community, or whether New Labour is experimenting with a less authoritarian conception of community.

From 1999 onwards the references to 'community' became rarer, and, when used, community was referred to as a means to liberate the potential of individuals, or to recognise the individuality of all. Until the end of New Labour's first term in government, Blair claimed that community was a central value of his project,[52] but communitarian ideas lost salience in his speeches. By contrast, meritocratic ideas gained a new prominence.

In short, from 1994, Tony Blair articulated different ideas on community, depending on his immediate political needs. However, in all the incarnations of the idea of community articulated by Tony Blair, we can find common threads. In all his communitarian visions, Blair mentions Etzionian themes: namely, the need to support the family, the need to promote work, and the need to promote 'decent values' for a 'decent society'.[53] Blair's decent and well-ordered society is based on the family, which, he argues, is the 'foundation for cohesive and for strong communities'.[54] Thus, Blair argues that the State should help the family, but he also uses this assumption to justify being more normative about the family.[55] For Blair, not to be morally neutral about the family is to state, as he did, a preference for the two-parent family.[56] However, Blair ignored important communitarian tenets: he addressed neither the question of rising inequalities nor the threats meritocracy can pose to inclusive communities.

Community and socialism

The second main subplot of New Labour's politics of community explored the links between New Labour and the traditions of the Labour Party. Gordon Brown was the main advocate of this subplot. Indeed, in most of his references to 'community' he tried to revive the link between New Labour and the intellectual traditions of the party.

For Brown, community 'properly understood' is the defining idea of socialism, since 'at its centre is the belief that society is a collective moral enterprise' in which all individuals are engaged. In addition, 'it stands in polar contrast to market individualism', and 'it offers a collective individualism' through which 'diversity and individuality are protected'.[57] Brown also claimed that the goal of individual emancipation, held by New Labour and by 'early socialists', would be achieved through, among other things, a 'strong community'.[58] He claimed that at the heart of New Labour's analysis was

> the enduring socialist message that it is only by using the power of community to spread opportunities to all that we can ensure that all our citizens are not only free from the threat of poverty, unemployment, disease and discrimination, but have the education, the skills and the opportunities to fulfil their potential to the full.[59]

Brown associated the idea of community with the 'historic socialist vision of working together for a greater good'.[60] The link with early socialism was also stressed when Brown articulated the idea that community can be a useful instrument to tackle the popular left-wing concern with the 'entrenched interests and accumulations of power that hold people back'.[61]

But community was used by Brown to say *other* things: namely, to defend a new role for the State. In this new role, 'community' would replace the State. 'Our new economic approach is founded on the socialist principle, that the community must accept its responsibilities for the goals of sustained growth and full employment', he argued.[62] The new policies represented something of a shift from Labour's traditional approach to the role of the State, but the way Brown phrased them diluted that impression, because he linked the proposed new role of the State to the socialist ideal of individual emancipation: 'For a hundred years the socialist message has inevitably had to be that the State should assume power on behalf of the people. Now it is time that the people take power from the State.'[63]

This diluted impression was reinforced by the ambiguous uses of 'responsibility' in Brown's discourse. He did not state in detail what the responsibilities of the community were, but simply that the community – meaning individuals – has responsibilities, including the responsibility to achieve sustained economic growth and full employment. But the most important change is Brown's perception of the State as inefficient and authoritarian.

Like Blair, Brown argued that individuals have the responsibility to take on the work opportunities given to them.[64] However, he refused to make moral judgements about unemployed individuals, 'because there are many people incapable of working'.[65] Again, like Blair, Brown talked about moral values. But unlike Blair he did not mention the need to 'inculcate moral values' in individuals, and he never addressed the issue of 'moral breakdown'. When he referred to the theme of 'moral purpose' he linked it to socialist aspirations.[66] In other words, Brown avoided addressing conservative themes, such as the 'culture of dependence', and always emphasised that New Labour was renewing Labour's traditions. But, like Blair, Brown ignored the issue of rising inequalities and defended a welfare-to-work programme which would punish those who refused to work.

The politics of inclusion

The communitarian tune of rights and responsibilities was also part of New Labour's discourse on social inclusion–social exclusion. This discourse was used mainly by Harriet Harman, Peter Mandelson, Alastair Darling and other ministers responsible for welfare policy, although tackling social exclusion was presented as a central governmental initiative. Unsurprisingly, the central plank of New Labour's strategy to tackle social exclusion and to promote social inclusion was work. The strategy 'to tackle the causes of poverty and social exclusion' was based on 'helping people find work',[67] because paid work was perceived as 'the best way to avoid poverty and social exclusion'.[68]

By 'social exclusion', New Labour meant a new social phenomenon which was different from 'poverty'. While 'poverty affects different aspects of people's lives, existing when people are denied opportunities to work, to learn, to live healthy and fulfilling lives, and to live out their retirement years in security', social exclusion 'occurs where different factors combine to trap individuals and areas in a spiral of disadvantage'.[69]

New Labour's approach to social exclusion suggests that, more than being concerned with the predicament of each individual, the Government was concerned with the impact of social exclusion on the wider society. Hence, fighting social exclusion was another way of saying that poverty is a problem that affects all members of the community, and that everybody has a duty to do something about it.[70] Moreover, social inclusion was presented as a replacement for egalitarian concerns. As John Gray put it, by talking of 'social exclusion' New Labour was able to 'escape more or less elegantly the egalitarian solutions that poverty problems traditionally required'; and on the other hand it was able to 'focus on the most serious problem of the break-up of communities'.[71]

There is another noteworthy aspect to this narrative of social exclusion: the absence, in New Labour's discourse on social exclusion, of any mention of the widening gap between rich and poor.[72] New Labour does not seem to be concerned with rising inequalities. Indeed, Brown accepted that 'not all inequalities are unjustified', but only those which are 'a standing affront to any notion of equal individual worth'.[73] In conformity with the acceptance of inequalities, New Labour adopted a new stance concerning redistribution – the traditional Labour way of promoting equality. Blair dismissed the idea of raising taxes on the grounds that to 'tax and spend is not the right way to run an efficient, dynamic, modern economy'.[74] However, New Labour did implement some redistributive policies; its rhetorical resistance to redistributing wealth in order to reduce inequalities is related to its concern with the idea of rewarding talent, effort and work, but also to its goal of promoting a meritocratic society. Even when New Labour became more vocal about redistribution, it was to argue for more investments in public services or to tackle poverty, but never to fight inequalities. Indeed, in a memorable interview before the 2001 general election, Blair argued that 'the key thing is not . . . the gap between the person who earns the most in the country and the person that earns the least', because what was important was 'to level up, not level down'. Moreover, Blair argued that if the Government chose to go after 'those people who are the most wealthy in society, what you actually end up doing is in fact not even helping those at the bottom end'.[75] On the same occasion, he said that it was not his 'burning ambition' to increase the taxes of the 'David Beckhams of this world'.[76] In terms of the communitarian blueprint outlined in the first section, this approach to equality has nothing distinctively communitarian – or, for that matter, social democratic – about it.

Conclusion

It is clear that prescriptive communitarianism inspired New Labour's policy-makers. New Labour figures such as Tony Blair, Gordon Brown, David Blunkett, Frank Field and others often spoke at length about their 'vision' and 'values', and 'community' or 'social cohesion' always featured in those visions. The words 'responsibility', 'obligation' and 'duty' – the cardinal values of the communitarian blueprint – and the critique of the 'rights-based culture', together with the themes of self-reliance, work, family and social order, are omnipresent in speeches by New Labour figures.

The way in which New Labour sought to transpose its politics of community was, however, highly selective, and it is this feature which is interesting. The selective use of the communitarian blueprint suggests that New Labour did not have as an aim the promotion of a communitarian project. Instead, its aim was to use the communitarian blueprint as a way to forward a rather different agenda, in particular to *revise* some traditional goals of the party.

Before discussing New Labour's agenda, I examine the points at which New Labour's narrative on community deviates from the prescriptive communitarian blueprint. The aim of this exercise is not to claim that New Labour is or is not communitarian. Political parties rarely, if ever, apply theoretical blueprints. However, the use they make of those blueprints can be quite revealing about their intentions.

The first striking deviation from the communitarian agenda is the absence of dialogue and consultation in the promotion of its welfare reform agenda. The farthest New Labour went in the process of consultation was the Green Paper on welfare reform, which anyway would, as all Green Papers do, involve a period of consultation. But New Labour did not use the Green Paper as an opportunity to engage in dialogue, but simply to promote its policies.

The second departure from the communitarian blueprint concerns aspects of policy on the family. New Labour adopted communitarian stances in some areas of family policy. However, in others it did not follow those prescriptions. Before showing how New Labour departed from communitarian prescriptions, there are some commonalities with communitarianism to be considered. Communitarians are strong defenders of the family. According to them, it is in the family that individuals learn about rules and values; therefore family life is perceived as having a civilising role. For those reasons, communitarian writers such as William Galston are strong supporters of marriage and argue that the state should make divorce for parents more difficult to obtain.[77] However, prescriptive communitarians do not support the patriarchal family, but rather families in which men and women are equal partners. Following the communitarian line of argument, Tony Blair, Gordon Brown and others make no apology for their defence of the family. As Driver and Martell put it, lack of economic opportunities and social exclusion are linked to problems of parenting and family.[78] Moreover, like most communitarian thinkers, New Labour's leaders have not been supporters of the 'traditional family'. Indeed, they want 'mothers' to participate fully in the labour market. However, New Labour deviates from the communitarian blueprint in one important aspect. Though Blair defended the two-parent family, the family policies implemented by his Government provide support for all family structures and not only to married couples. In fact, New Labour replaced the married couple's allowance with the child tax allowance, which is available to all forms of family. Moreover, New Labour did not try to re-engineer a particular type of family (in this case, with married parents) via its social policies, as the Clinton administration did in 1996 (the Personal Responsibility and Work Opportunity Reconciliation Act of 1996 established as a goal the reduction of out-of-wedlock pregnancies and encouraged the maintenance of two-parent families[79]).

The third departure from the prescriptive communitarian blueprint is apparent in the application of the ethic of 'rights and responsibilities'. New Labour seemed to agree with the communitarian argument that contemporary societies have been badly hurt by excessive individualism and by the so-called 'rights culture'. Like communitarian thinkers, New Labour argues that it is necessary to promote an ethos of mutual rights and responsibilities. But whereas communitarians claim that 'it is a grave moral error to argue that there are "no rights without responsibilities" or vice versa',[80] New Labour makes rights conditional on the performance of duties. Moreover, the strategy of distinguishing between the 'deserving' and the 'undeserving poor' may have a destabilising, instead of a strengthening, effect on communities.

The fourth main departure from the communitarian blueprint concerns the role of the State. Like communitarians, New Labour claims that the State has an important role in society, but the role it ascribes to the State departs in important respects from the communitarian blueprint. Communitarian writers want the State to have a smaller role in shaping the 'moral culture', since that is the role of individuals and communities and can be achieved only through a 'national conversation', and not through laws and governmental recommendations. By contrast, New Labour argues that the State does have an important role in shaping the moral culture, and attempts have been made to change and encourage different behaviour through legislation, governmental recommendations and guidelines, as illustrated by the New Deal and other policies. Furthermore, New Labour has not promoted a 'national conversation' on making work a condition to receive benefits, but has rather *assumed* that a consensus exists in society about what was necessary.

Communitarians are against State interference on matters of 'moral culture', but think that the state has an important social role in regulating equality of opportunity. Communitarians are concerned with the widening gap between rich and poor, arguing that 'society cannot sustain itself as a community of communities if disparities in well-being and wealth between elites and the rest of society are too great'.[81] Communitarians believe, therefore, that the state must ensure equality of opportunity for all and maintain progressive taxation.

New Labour has sidelined all these positions. First of all, the silence with which New Labour responded to the problem of rising inequalities suggests that it is not concerned with the issue. There is concern over 'social exclusion', poverty and deprivation, but not with inequality as such. New Labour claims to be committed to equality of opportunity, but its conception of 'equality of opportunity' differs from that espoused by communitarians. For communitarian thinkers, equality of opportunity means ensuring that everyone has a similar starting point.[82] Yet the equality of opportunity which underpins the welfare-to-work programme, the working families' tax credit and the 'baby bonds' proposal, for example, amounts more to 'minimum opportunities' than to equal opportunities,[83] given that as soon as some very basic needs are met the State is no longer worried over 'levelling up'.

Moreover, the discourse of duties and responsibilities does not apply equally to all members of society. Whereas the duties of the poor are clearly assigned,

the duties of the most successful members of society – who, according to prescriptive communitarians, have greater responsibility towards the community –
are not spelled out at all. In fact, what is hinted at is that these members of
society are necessary to create wealth for the country (no matter how unevenly
that wealth is distributed) and therefore should not be burdened with more
responsibilities.[84]

This approach once again suggests that New Labour is not inclined to vocally
defend redistribution to tackle inequality or to subsidise jobs for the unemployed. To date, New Labour has argued only for redistribution in order to invest
in public services, not to reduce inequalities. This reluctance to accept the idea
that government should be an employer of last resort and that the most successful members of a society have special duties also suggest an acceptance of all the
implications of the market economy. Again, this position reveals a selective
application of communitarian ideas. Communitarian writers hold that 'market
exchange makes no inherent contribution to autonomy' and therefore that
'market competition should be limited in contexts … where its impact on individual autonomy may be disabling rather than developing'.[85]

The selective endorsement of their agenda led some communitarian thinkers
to react to the appropriation of their ideas by New Labour and other governments. For example, Henry Tam acknowledged New Labour's creation of a
Social Exclusion Unit, but commented that the overall policy thrust of the
Government seemed 'to be more concerned with easing the plight of the poor so
that the drive for greater economic growth can roll forward without risking
social unrest'. In addition, he remarked that 'wealth redistribution as a tool for
tacking power inequalities does not feature at all' in New Labour's plans.[86] He
further concludes that, from a progressive communitarian point of view, 'there
is definitively a distinct way to practise politics, but it differs significantly from
what currently goes by the name of Third Way'.[87] Philip Selznick has expressed
similar concerns about the selective endorsement of the communitarian agenda.
Selznick admitted to being 'troubled' 'by a selective concern for personal responsibility, personal virtues, personal morality'. 'While these themes are music to the
ears of Conservative writers and politicians – whose main concerns are crime,
illegitimacy rates and similar offences, and who see immorality as a lower-class
evil appropriately addressed by punitive measures – they pay little attention to
the responsibilities of the affluent, or of business leaders, and, more importantly,
the moral responsibilities of the community as a whole are only dimly perceived
and given short shrift.'[88]

Amitai Etzioni also has been critical of New Labour, though his own position
changed over time. In an article published in *The Times* in 1997, Etzioni admitted that New Labour's Clause 4 'recognises that a communitarian society entails
much more than nurturing local residential communities, or building on small
platoons', and that New Labour understands 'that it is necessary to replace the
welfare state notion of entitlement'.[89] But he warned that 'the communitarian
paradigm does not call for closing down the welfare state and replacing it with

armies of volunteers', and that in an economy that still has considerable unemployment 'pushing welfare clients to work is likely to push others into unemployment and ultimately on to welfare'.[90] Etzioni also criticised the decision to cut benefits to lone parents as a 'not very communitarian' one, because 'the notion of getting people off benefit before there is real, solid evidence that we have provided them with work, or opportunities to find work, is too punitive'.[91] In 2001, Etzioni was more sympathetic towards New Labour. He praised Blair for making the concepts of community and responsibility 'a core element' of his first election campaign, but he argued that those were 'merely baby steps' towards the development of a genuinely communitarian approach.[92]

The discourse of 'duty', 'community' and 'self-reliance', and the absence of concern over rising social inequalities, suggest that New Labour aims at something different from the communitarian blueprint. With this discourse, New Labour seems to have found the arguments with which to justify a more modest role for the State. Indeed, if individuals work, the State does not need to provide for them. In fact, the State does not need to provide employment, and in the process work becomes a duty and ceases to be a right. This argument was strengthened by Blair's criticism of liberal individualism. Tony Blair made 'individualism' a synonym for 'redistributive policies'; therefore, 'community', a socialist value, meant independence from the State. From there it followed that, in order to achieve the 'communitarian' goals of the party, it was necessary to revise the role of the State as a distributor of wealth. New Labour policy-makers argue that the State must be an enabler and a provider of guidance about life choices.

By accepting social inequalities, by ascribing a more modest new role to the State and by defending a less regulated market economy, New Labour has redefined some of the ends of the Labour Party. Indeed, a more modest role of the State that coexists with an unequal society and an unregulated market is unlikely to deliver the stronger and fairer community, formed by freer and more autonomous individuals, which the Labour Party has traditionally promoted.

Notes

1 Phillips 1994.
2 Milne 1994.
3 Mandelson and Liddle 1996: 19.
4 Prescriptive or political communitarianism is diverse, but there are central themes which are shared by all varieties of prescriptive communitarianism, namely civic spirit, responsibility for self and for the community, mutuality and reciprocity (Frazer 1999: 35).
5 Raymond Plant (1991: 327) provides a useful description of the communitarian criticism of liberalism: 'Communitarians criticize the ontology and in particular the theory of the self put forward by liberal theorists and the conception of the human condition which follows from this. This involves making the case for arguing that the

self at least is part constituted by the values of the community within which the person finds him or her self and therefore that choosing values in some kind of abstract way as envisaged by liberal theory just embodies a false moral ontology.'

6 Mulhall and Swift (1996: xiv) also make a distinction between the 'communitarianism' of political philosophers and what they perceive as the 'popular appropriation' of the term by political parties, the media and political movements, such as the communitarian movement launched by Amitai Etzioni. See also Minogue 1997: 161.

7 Etzioni 1993: 40 and 1997a: 27; Tam 1998: 1–3.

8 Etzioni 1993: 4. More recently, Etzioni (2000: 29) has argued that rights are not conditional. 'Basic individual rights are inalienable, just as one's social obligations cannot be denied. However, it is a grave moral error to argue that there are "no rights without responsibilities" or vice versa . . . The number of basic rights we should have may be debated, but those that are legitimate are not conditional.'

9 Etzioni 1993: 4.

10 *Ibid.*, p. 7.

11 Gray 1996: 20–1.

12 Etzioni 1993: 144.

13 Tam 1998: 85–8.

14 Selznick 1996.

15 Etzioni 2000: 31–2.

16 Galston 1995: 285.

17 *Ibid.*, p. 284. Galston also argues for the active promotion of marriage and for making divorce more difficult for couples with children.

18 Etzioni 1997a: 74.

19 Frazer 1999: 217.

20 Etzioni 1997a: 74; see also Etzioni 1993: 39.

21 Most communitarian writers mention the role of churches in promoting communities and a sense of moral values. William Galston is perhaps one of the most vocal defenders of the 'civilising' role of religion in the United States: see Galston 1995: 276.

22 Tam 1998: 8.

23 Campbell 1995; Kenny 1996: 18; Walker 1998: 71; Price 1998: 65.

24 Etzioni 1993: 44.

25 Etzioni 2000: 32–3.

26 *Ibid.*, pp. 53–4.

27 Tam 1999: 4.

28 Selznick 1996.

29 Tam 1999: 5.

30 Selznick 1996.

31 Field 1998a.

32 Field 1998b: col. 686.

33 Field 1997a; 1997b: 38.

34 Blunkett 2000: 1; 1999.

35 Darling 1998: col. 340.

36 Blair 1993; reprinted: 1996: 221.

37 Blair 1994a; 1994b: 4.

38 Coote 1995; Gove 1996; Malik 1995; Mayo 1999.

39 About the 'mistakes' of the Left Blair (1995a: 236) said: 'a strong society should not be confused with a strong state, or with powerful collectivist institutions. That was

the confusion of the early Left thinking. It was compounded by a belief that the role of the state was to grant rights, with the language of responsibility spoken far less fluently'.

40 Blair 1995b.
41 Blair 1994a.
42 Blair 1999a.
43 Blair 1995b; see also 1995c: 13.
44 Gould 1998: 254; see also Driver and Martell 1998: 51–6.
45 Blair 1996a: 13.
46 Blair 1996b: 298.
47 Gould 1998: 255.
48 Blair 1997a.
49 Blair 1997b; this idea was repeated several times during the speech: 'I tell you: a decent society is not based on rights. It is based on duty. Our duty to each other. To all should be given opportunity, from all responsibility demanded.'
50 Blair 1998a: 14.
51 Blair 1999a; Blair developed this idea further: 'We are also about wanting to encourage people to make good and valuable choices whether in terms of their own behaviour or their actions towards others. This is not "new authoritarianism". There will be no nanny state. It is common sense: people want tolerance, but they also want rules.'
52 Blair 2000.
53 Blair 1998b.
54 Blair 1995c: 12.
55 Blair 1995d.
56 Blair 1995e, reprinted: 1996: 249.
57 Brown and Wright 1995: 24–5.
58 Brown 1994a: 118.
59 Brown 1994b: 25.
60 Brown 1995.
61 Brown and Wright 1995: 13–14.
62 Brown 1994c.
63 Brown and Wright 1995: 26.
64 Brown 1998a.
65 Brown 1998b.
66 Brown 1995.
67 Department of Social Security (DSS) 1999: 84.
68 DSS 1999.
69 *Ibid.*, p. 23.
70 Levitas 1998: 45.
71 Gray 1997a: 8–9; see also Levitas 1998: 35.
72 The few references to rising inequalities were exceptions. In the first report on social exclusion, the Government acknowledged that 'the benefits of growth have not been shared by all' (DSS 1999: 27).
73 Brown and Wright 1995: 20.
74 Blair 1997c.
75 Blair 2001.
76 *Ibid.*

77 *Ibid.*
78 Galston 1995: 284.
79 Driver and Martell 2000: 188.
80 Personal Responsibility and Work Opportunity Reconciliation Act of 1996.
81 Etzioni 2000: 29.
82 *Ibid.*, p. 53.
83 *Ibid.*, p. 54.
84 This point was made by Martell 2001: 211.
85 Blair (1999b: 2) said: 'If the markets don't like our policies they will punish you.'
86 Gray 1997b: 329–30.
87 Tam 1999: 5.
88 *Ibid.*, p. 11.
89 Selznick 1996.
90 Etzioni 1997b.
91 *Ibid.*
92 Etzioni, quoted in 'Labour attacked by guru', *Independent*, 27 December 1997, p. 2.
93 Etzioni 2001: 25.

References

Blair, T. (1993) 'New community, new individualism', speech given to the Charities' Aid Foundation 10th Arnold Goodman Charity Lecture, London, 8 July; reprinted in T. Blair (1996) *New Britain: My Vision of a Young Country*, London, Fourth Estate.

Blair, T. (1994a) Speech to the Labour Party Annual Conference.

Blair, T. (1994b) *Socialism*, Fabian Pamphlet 564, London, Fabian Society.

Blair, T. (1995a) 'The rights we enjoy reflect the duties we owe' (*Spectator* Lecture, 22 March); reprinted in T. Blair (1996), *New Britain: My Vision of a Young Country*, London, Fourth Estate.

Blair, T. (1995b) 'Is Labour the true heir of Thatcher?', *The Times*, 17 July, p. 17.

Blair, T. (1995c) 'Power for a purpose', *Renewal*, 13(4).

Blair, T. (1995d) Speech to the Labour Party Annual Conference.

Blair, T. (1995e) 'Valuing families', *Sun*, 31 May; reprinted in T. Blair (1996), *New Britain: My Vision of A Young Country*, London, Fourth Estate.

Blair, T. (1996) *New Britain: My Vision of a Young Country*, London, Fourth Estate.

Blair, T. (1996a) 'Switch on the bright ideas', *Guardian*, 27 May.

Blair, T. (1996b) 'Faith in the city – ten years on', in Blair, *New Britain: My Vision Of A Young Country*.

Blair, T. (1997a) The 'Downing Street speech', 2 May, available online (accessed 8 May 1998): www.number-10.gov.uk/publi..._display.asp?random=8215&index=56/.

Blair, T. (1997b) Speech to the 1997 Labour Party Annual Conference, 30 September.

Blair, T. (1997c) Speech on welfare, House of Commons, 17 December, available online (accessed 11 May 1999): www.number-10.gov.uk/public/info/...Speech_display.asp?random=2617&index=12.

Blair, T. (1998a) *The Third Way: New Politics For The New Century*, London, Fabian Society.

Blair, T. (1998b) 'Modernising the Welfare State', speech at Vauxhall Recreation Centre,

28 January, available online (accessed 8 May 1999): www.number-10.gov.uk/public.
info/...Speech_display.asp?random-2&index=17.

Blair, T. (1999a) Speech to the IPPR, 14 January, available online (accessed 15 January
1999): www.number-10.gov.uk/texts...p?random=0&index=1&sessionid=1386.

Blair, T. (1999b) 'Doctrine of the international community', speech in Chicago, 22 April,
available online (accessed 31 August 1999): www.number-10.gov.uk/publi..._display.
asp?random=2963&index=38.

Blair, T. (2000) 'Community for all', speech to the Women's Institute, 7 June, available
online (accessed 15 January 2001): www.labour.org.uk/lp/new/labour/U..._NEWS_
DISPLAY?p_rowid=AAAHIcAAFAAAQdAAAC.

Blair, T. (2001) Interviewed on *Newsnight*, BBC2, 5 June, available online (accessed 28 June
2001): www.news.bbc.co.uk/hi/english/events/newsnight/newsid_1372000/1372220.
stm.

Blunkett, D. (1999) *Social Exclusion and the Politics of Opportunity: A Mid-Term
Progress Check*, London, DfEE.

Blunkett, D. (2000) 'Enabling government: the welfare State in the twenty-first century',
speech to the Policy Studies Institute, 11 October.

Brivati, B. and Bale, T. (1998) *New Labour in Power: Precedents and Prospects*, London,
Routledge.

Brown, G. (1994a) 'The politics of potential', in R. Miliband (ed.) *Reinventing the Left*,
Cambridge, Polity Press.

Brown, G. (1994b) *Fair Is Efficient – A Socialist Agenda for Fairness*, Fabian Pamphlet 563,
London, Fabian Society.

Brown, G. (1994c) Speech to the Labour Party Annual Conference.

Brown, G. (1995) Speech to the Labour Party Annual Conference.

Brown, G. (1998a) Speech to the News International Conference, 17 July, available online
(accessed 30 April 2001): www.hm-treasury.gov.uk/press/1998/p117_98.html.

Brown, G. (1998b) 'The *FT* interview: a chancellor's progress', *Financial Times*, 18
February.

Brown, G. and Wright, T. (1995) *Values, Visions and Voices: An Anthology of Socialism*,
Edinburgh, Mainstream Books.

Campbell, B. (1995) 'Old fogeys and young angry men', *Soundings*, 1: Autumn.

Coote, A. (1995), 'A bit too much of a prig and a prude', *Independent*, 3 July.

Darling, A. (1998) *Hansard*, House of Commons, 28 October, col. 340.

Department of Social Security (1999) *Opportunity For All – Tackling Poverty and Social
Exclusion: First Annual Report*, London, DSS.

Driver, S. and Martell, L. (1998) *New Labour: Politics After Thatcherism*, Cambridge,
Polity Press.

Driver, S. and Martell, L. (2000) 'New Labour, work and the family: communitarianisms
in conflict?', in H. Wilkinson (ed.) *Family Business*, London, Demos.

Etzioni, A. (1993) *The Spirit of Community Rights, Responsibilities and the
Communitarian Agenda*, New York, Crown Publishers.

Etzioni, A. (1997a), *The New Golden Rule: Community And Morality in a Democratic
Society*, London, Profile Books.

Etzioni, A. (1997b) 'Tony Blair: a communitarian in the making?', *The Times*, 21 June.

Etzioni, A. (2000) *The Third Way to a Good Society*, London, Demos.

Etzioni, A. (2001) 'The third way is a triumph', *New Statesman*, 25 June.

Field, F. (1997a) 'Managing change in the welfare state', speech given to the Department of Social Security, 3 December, available online (accessed 2 March 1998): www.dss.gov. uk/hp/press/speeches/ff31297.htm.

Field, F. (1997b) Speech to the 'Beyond Dependency Conference: A Watershed For Welfare', New Zealand, reproduced in Field, *Reforming Welfare*, London, Social Market Foundation.

Field, F. (1998a) 'Social policy – a thirty year journey', Keith Joseph Memorial Lecture, 15 January, available online (accessed 28 February 1998): www.cps.org.uk/Field.htm.

Field, F. (1998b) Green Paper speech to the House of Commons, *Hansard*, 26 March, col. 686.

Frazer, E. (1999) *The Problems of Communitarian Politics: Unity and Conflict*, Oxford, Oxford University Press.

Galston, W. (1995) *Liberal Purposes: Goods, Virtues, and Diversity in the Liberal State*, Cambridge, Cambridge University Press.

Gove, M. (1996) 'New community is merely old coercion', *The Times*, 18 June.

Gould, P. (1998) *The Unfinished Revolution: How the Modernizers Saved The Labour Party*, London, Little, Brown & Company.

Gray, J. (1996) 'What community is not', *Renewal*, 4(3).

Gray, J. (1997a) 'Goodbye to Rawls', *Prospect*, November.

Gray, J. (1997b) 'After social democracy', in G. Mulgan (ed.) *Life After Politics*, London, Fontana.

Harman, H. (1997) 'Harriet Harman sets out principle for reforming welfare in DSS comprehensive spending review', DSS press release, available online (accessed 25 May): www.dss.gov.uk/mediacentre/pressreleases/1997/jul/97132.htm.

HM Government (1996) Personal Responsibility and Work Opportunity Reconciliation Act, available online (accessed 20 April 1998): http://thomas.loc.gov/cgi-bin/query/ D?c104:2:./temp/~c104RxzOt:e29376.

Kenny, M. (1996) 'After the deluge: politics and civil society in the wake of the New Right', *Soundings*,4: autumn.

Levitas, R. (1998) *The Inclusive Society? Social Exclusion and New Labour*, London, Macmillan.

Malik, K. (1995) 'Same old hate in the new byword for bigotry', *Guardian*, 12 August.

Mandelson, P. and Liddle, R. (1996) *The Blair Revolution: Can New Labour Deliver?* London, Faber & Faber.

Martell, L. (2001) 'Capitalism, globalisation and democracy: does social democracy have a role?', in L. Martell, C. van den Anker, M. Browne, S. Hoopes, P. Larkin, C. Lees, F. McGowan and N. Stammers (eds) *Social Democracy: Global and National Perspectives*, Basingstoke, Palgrave.

Mayo, M. (1999) 'New language, New Labour: exploring the politics of emotions', *Soundings*, 11: spring.

Miliband, D. (1994) *Reinventing the Left*, Cambridge, Polity Press.

Milne, S. (1994) 'Everybody's talking about', *Guardian*, 7 October.

Minogue, D. (1997) 'Etzioni's communitarianism: old (communion) wine in new bottles', *Politics*, 17(3).

Mulgan, G. (ed.) (1997) *Life After Politics*, London, Fontana.

Mulhall, S. and Swift, A. (1996) *Liberals & Communitarians*, Oxford, Blackwell.

Phillips, M. (1994) 'Father of Tony Blair's big idea', *Observer*, 24 July.

Plant, R. (1991) *Modern Political Thought*, Oxford, Blackwell.

Price, C. (1998), 'Commentary', in Brivati and Bale, *New Labour in Power*.

Riddell, P. (2001) 'Ministers tease voters with dance of five Euro tests', *The Times*, 6 November.

Selznick, P. (1996) 'Social justice: a communitarian perspective', *The Responsive Community*, 6(4).

Tam, H. (1998) *Communitarianism: A New Agenda for Politics And Citizenship*, Basingstoke, Macmillan.

Tam, H. (1999) '"Third way politics" and communitarian ideas: time to take a stand', *The International Scope Review*, 1(1).

Toynbee, P. (2001) 'Blair's community spirit needs to find its focus', *Guardian*, 28 March.

Walker, D. (1998) 'The moral agenda', in Brivati and Bale, *New Labour in Power*.

Wilkinson, H. (ed.) (2000) *Family Business*, London, Demos.

From organisational theory to the Third Way: continuities and contradictions underpinning Amitai Etzioni's communitarian influence on New Labour

Introduction

Across a wide range of social commentators there has been little doubt that New Labour is deeply influenced by the thoughts and sentiments of Amitai Etzioni and the new communitarian movement. Prideaux[1] and Heron[2] independently point to the original but persisting concept of 'stakeholding' and its emphasis on individuals taking an active 'stake' in a society or community. Powell, Exworthy and Berney[3] explore the connection through New Labour's *zeitgeist* of a 'partnership' between people, communities and government. Deacon[4] looks at the moral 'judgementalism' of Etzioni and New Labour,[5] whereas Levitas[6] points to the characteristic centrality that both give to 'family' and 'community' as theatres for learning and social control. All reinforce Driver and Martell's observation that if communitarianism 'is New Labour's answer to Thatcherism; so too is it Blair's rebuff to Old Labour. Community will restore the moral balance to society by setting out duties and obligations as well as rights.'[7]

Quite simply, it is this communitarian emphasis on family, community, social discipline, obligation and responsibility – as opposed to an indiscriminate conferral of rights – that lies behind New Labour's search for a 'Third Way' that would go 'beyond Left and Right'.[8] However, what is not common knowledge in the UK, and so has not been fully explored, is from where Amitai Etzioni actually drew his inspiration. Through a comparison of Etzioni's later works with those of earlier times, this chapter contends that Etzioni has not said anything new or innovative. Nor has he provided a social prescription that manages to traverse the old political and socio-economic boundaries. More to the point, this chapter shows how Etzioni continues to reiterate the thoughts and impressions he had gained during his functionalist days as an organisational theorist in the 1950s and 1960s: the only difference being that the earlier micro-theories of organisations have now been transposed to fit a macro-theory about the perceived ills and remedies pertinent to contemporary 'mainstream' society.

Although the point has already been made that organisational theorists characteristically restrict their search for efficiency within the confines of North

American relations of capital,[9] it is not a charge that has been rigorously applied to Amitai Etzioni, least of all to his US best-seller *The Spirit of Community* and his rather immodest *New Golden Rule*.[10] With a deeper analysis of the specific methodology employed, this chapter reveals the reliance Etzioni puts on his sociological origins and thus exposes the underlying limitations of his societal projections. Moreover, it will become apparent that this form of methodological analysis is used myopically to substantiate an argument for the promotion of a normative society remarkably reminiscent of America in the 1950s.

Finally, I discuss the ramifications of Etzioni's approach. Such theoretical and methodological limitations are bound to affect the efficacy and applicability of the communitarian ideal, especially when the revival of a sense of community is still reliant on the relatively unfettered continuation of a competitive market. More importantly, though, such limitations can also affect the policies of New Labour by virtue of the fact that it, too, has adopted a communitarian stance.

A wistful template of reference: American society in the 1950s

When introducing *The Essential Communitarian Reader*, Etzioni succinctly defines the communitarian movement. He is at pains to distinguish the new communitarians from the communitarianism of the nineteenth century by distancing his position from the old blinkered 'stress upon the significance of social forces, of community, of social bonds'[11] and of the elements that individualistic theory neglected. Instead, he argues, new communitarians concern themselves with 'the balance between social forces and the person, between community and autonomy, between the common good and liberty, between individual rights and social responsibilities'.[12] Elsewhere, Etzioni sees himself – and, for that matter, this new form of communitarianism – as a responsive harbinger of social equilibrium locked in a quest to revitalise society through a unique blending of some elements of 'tradition (order based on virtues) with elements of modernity (well protected autonomy)'.[13]

Pivotal to Etzioni's social deliberations is the wistful image he holds of America in the 1950s and his contrasting disdain for contemporary life as he sees it. These two polarised images deeply affect his ideas on how a communitarian alternative can be achieved. And both provide him with a rather circular argument that fails to address any of the problems that may be inherent to the socio-economic basis of Western society. Consequently, Amitai Etzioni's vision of a communitarian society is heavily predicated on what he sees as having gone wrong with present-day social relations.

As a starting-point for his argument, 1950s America becomes the baseline template of reference. Almost yearningly, he talks of that decade as in many respects a social ideal. Core values, he argues, 'were relatively widely shared and strongly endorsed', and so helped to promote a context in which societal members 'had a strong sense of duty to their families, communities and society'.[14] Pertinently,

morality and order during this period are seen by Etzioni to generate stable relations. Christianity was the dominant and guiding religion. Incidences of violent
crime, drug abuse, alcoholism and illegitimacy were low, or at least discreetly con-
cealed. The law made divorce difficult, abortion illegal throughout the USA, and
'the roles of men and women were relatively clearly delineated'.[15]

Despite a passing acknowledgement that women and ethnic minorities were
treated as second-class citizens, Etzioni still enthuses over this past society. In his
eyes, low autonomy for certain groupings is not always a bad thing. To that end
Etzioni ambiguously comments upon, but is not overly critical of, the fact that
college students then were expected to take a fair number of 'prescribed' courses
which 'reflected unabashedly (and often with little self-awareness) the dominant
set of values'.[16] While Etzioni concedes that American society of this yesteryear
was characterised by a high level of coercion, he nonetheless commends the fact
that it was offset with a similarly high presence of moral suasion. Coercion, for
Etzioni, is necessary at times, though it can be repressive and destructive if too
readily and too generously applied. On the other hand, a pervasive moral suasion
is one of his basic foundations for determining social order. An effective balance
between the two is, therefore, an integral aspect of Etzioni's communitarian
thinking, and it is precisely this detection of moral suasion, alongside elements
of coercion, which allows him to use 1950s' America as a measure of comparative social stability.

An irresponsible existence: from the promiscuous 1960s to the instrumentalist 1980s

In contrast, Etzioni's depiction of events in America from the 1960s to the end
of the 1980s amounts to a very tainted picture that allows him to hark back to
what he sees as the positive values of earlier times. Quite simply, '[i]f the hall-
mark of the 1950s was a strong sense of obligation, from 1960 to 1990 there was
a rising sense of entitlement and a growing tendency to shirk social responsibilities'.[17] Increasingly Etzioni claims to have witnessed the rise in a counter-culture
of individualism and instrumentalist reasoning that 'provided a normative seal
of approval to a focus on the self rather than on responsibilities to the community'.[18] For him, it was a self-interest that was soon to become an unacceptable,
if not distasteful, base for social disorder and misplaced virtues: a base from
which society would be riven by competition over individual entitlements arising
out of an increased political preoccupation with 'rights' at the expense of
'responsibilities'.

When tracing this later period of destructive change in social values, Etzioni
declares that with the rise in promiscuity from the 1960s onwards, the role and
influence of religion declined, divorce and abortion were eventually legalised,
and notions of what constituted a family were redefined to accommodate 'a
wider variety of households'.[19] The period saw a concomitant weakening of

respect for authority. No longer, he maintains, was there a confidence in, or a passive acceptance of, the actions of those empowered to lead. In fact, the exact opposite was to become the norm. Voter turnout decreased, feelings of aliena- tion were on the increase and, over the years, Americans would 'become a tribe that savages and consumes its leaders'.[20]

On the socio-economic front, Etzioni restricts his attention to the tensions and conflicts that were occasioned by the rising demands for autonomy, the unin- tended consequence of dependence and the increased individuation of society. Central to Etzioni's argument is the belief that, during this period, 'changes in socioeconomic conditions contributed both to enhancing autonomy – and dependency, and hence the loss of autonomy'.[21] This is a somewhat circular argument which rests on the belief that socio-economic policy had not only improved the living conditions of the disadvantaged but had created an unhealthy dependence on governmental support.

With regard to those in work, Etzioni points to the fact that household income was on the increase. But this had less to do with an increase in real income for individuals, and more with a greater financial need or reliance on more than one member of a household having to participate in the labour market. For Etzioni, this 'development had strong autonomy-reducing effects as more and more members of the family felt they were forced to work outside the household and had severely limited time for other purposes, including family, community, and volunteer action'.[22] Accordingly the family – the first institution of Etzioni's social chain – is seen to be the primary unit to suffer from such divisive trends. The proportion of nuclear families had declined from 42 per cent in 1960 to 26 per cent in 1990, while divorce rates doubled and illegitimacy rose sharply 'from 21.6 per 1000 births in 1960 to 41.8 in 1989'.[23] All of this, the argument goes, reflects a gradual erosion/disintegration of the moral order within society.

At the same time, Etzioni remarks, there was a diversification and fragmenta- tion of American society as a whole. The percentage of non-white and Hispanic Americans more than doubled and the 'percentage of the population that is foreign born increased from 5.4 percent in 1960 to 7.9 percent in 1990'.[24] Racial tensions started to come to the fore. African Americans felt under threat from the continued influx of new immigrants. They resented the special status accorded to new immigrants, and this fueled 'conflict with Hispanics and Asian Americans'.[25] Likewise, men and women were forming distinct groups, growing apart rather than continuing the 1950s' idyll of two 'human halves linked together in that basic human wholeness, the natural marital state'.[26]

In toto, Etzioni sees the 1960s and the 1970s as two decades characterised by a reduction in both coercive means of social control and a reliance on moral suasion to bring people into order. Coercion was seen to be reduced with the repeal of anti-sodomy laws, the gradual removal of abortion from the list of acts punishable by the State, the introduction of 'no fault' laws which made divorce even easier, and the diminution of public support for corporal punishment in schools. As for the reduction in moral suasion, Etzioni points to the effects of an upsurge in welfare liberal and *laissez-faire* conservative ideas as they took their respective turns to replace coercive measures. Traditional values lost much of their power. No strong new values arose, while the notion that one should not be judgemental gained currency to the extent that the 'rise of the counterculture in the 1960s further weakened the country's values of hard work and thrift, as well as compliance with moral codes of conduct'.[27]

Notwithstanding a partial return to coercive law enforcement and a revival in moral condemnation, the 1980s appeared to Etzioni to be worse than the previous two decades. This was not least because the intensification of *laissez-faire* individualist politics encouraged a culture of job insecurity and social greed which only helped to re-energise the social unrest that had been brewing in the 1960s and 1970s. For Etzioni, the end of the 1980s was the culmination of a growing state of 'normless anarchy'.[28] At its extreme, it was an anarchy epitomised by a lack of moral guidance that led to an increase in violent crime and to 'movies that romanticize incest, such as *Spanking the Monkey*; the campaign by NAMBLA (the North American Man/Boy Love Association) to repeal the age of consent for sex; [and] the spread of hard-core pornography and highly offensive sexually violent material'.[29] In short, the period was characterised by an unbounded autonomy that remains intolerable to Etzioni and his fellow communitarians.

The 1990s and a 'curl back' to social order

Despite all of this, Etzioni maintains, the 1990s, at last, began to curtail the libertarian excesses of the 1980s with a 'curl back'[30] toward societal stability. Not surprisingly, he sees himself and the communitarian movement as instrumental in furthering a moral regeneration designed to restore social order. Although Etzioni pays homage to the enhanced autonomy of many American women and minorities that the 1990s fostered, he still believes that autonomy should be curbed, even if not completely along the lines of America in the 1950s. To that end, he argues: 'American society requires a functional alternative to traditional virtue: a blend of voluntary order with well-protected yet bounded autonomy.'[31] Exactly how this should be done, however, is unclear to those not imbued by the communitarian ethos of today.

Even so, Etzioni and the communitarian movement have set themselves a comprehensive set of aims. They believe that America, and of course other Western societies of similar 'advancement', 'can attain a recommitment to moral values – without puritanical excesses'.[32] Law and order can be restored without the creation of a police state. The family can be saved without forcing women to stay at home, while schools can provide an essential moral education without resorting to methods of indoctrination. Concomitantly, a broader inclusion of the private sector alongside an emphasis on the market can enable the individual to become independent of the State yet reciprocally contribute to a thriving community.[33] After all, Etzioni asks, is it not 'better for all who seek work and are able to work to be employed than for some to have high salaries and benefits well protected, only to be taxed in order to pay unemplotment benefits?'[34] As a consequence, those who follow Etzioni's example firmly believe that people can overcome mutual hostilities and begin to live together in communities, since communitarian calls for increased social responsibility do not demean individual rights. Rather, the opposite is believed to be true: *strong rights presume strong responsibilities*.[35]

All-in-all, Etzioni's is an argument that is convinced by the feeling that a commitment to the community can counter the pursuit of self-interest and unbridled greed. Commitment would not represent a life of self-sacrifice, altruism or austerity. Instead, it would reflect a dedication to the pursuit of 'legitimate opportunities and socially constructive expressions of self-interest'.[36] In the same vein, these new communitarians hold that powerful interest groups can be constrained without limiting the constitutional right of the individual to lobby and petition those empowered to govern. Superficially it is an argument that appears to rearrange 'the intellectual–political map'[37] by offering 'a Third Way between anarchic individualism and repressive conformity'.[38]

But is this really the case? Could it be that this Third Way is more akin to repressive conformity than it would care to admit?

Reaching the communitarian ideal

To establish the means through which this new communitarian society will evolve, Etzioni re-emphasises the need to amend the existing imbalance within society. Through the use of a rather simplistic and not entirely representative metaphor, Etzioni constructs a working model as the basis for his continuing argument. His perspective is summed up with the claim that North American – and to a lesser extent British – society is like a stool with three uneven legs, the market and government representing the two longer legs, and community/civil society the third leg. The solution, he argues, is straightforward: simply lengthen the third leg through the propagation of a suitably modernised moral education.[39] With the necessary revival of the highly functional institutions of family, school, neighbourhood and community as its aim, this moral education would start with the reassertion of family values, and continue through the support – and reiteration – given during formal education and future life in a vibrant communal atmosphere.

Only in this way, continues Etzioni, can a moral basis for politics be rediscovered. This will provide, restore or nurture a sense of mutual responsibility to individuals. Ultimately, this would result in the creation of a virtuous cycle where the suasion of communities would be seen to 'gently chastise those who violate shared moral norms and express approbation for those who abide by them'.[40] Moreover, this vision of virtue would not confine itself to the sphere of local communities. It would continue to grow and spread nationally or possibly beyond. To underline the point, Etzioni cites the examples of Scotland and Wales. For him, they are countries that have already managed to embrace the communitarian ethic. They demonstrate to all and sundry that it is possible to 'combine regional identities with society-wide loyalties'.[41] They are Etzioni's proof that new communtarianism is not simply a utopian dream.

Etzioni's myopic constraints and solutions

Despite this, the more one reads Etzioni's writings the clearer it becomes that his brand of communitarianism is a highly conservative blueprint for future social relations. Realistically, it is a blueprint 'built around caricatures and straw men',[42] chosen by Etzioni to construct a highly relativistic argument against errant social configurations. In effect, Etzioni selects polarised extremes in an attempt to substantiate a middle course already determined by his own moral sensibilities. For example, Etzioni's positive recognition that America in the 1980s gave individuals more autonomy hardly compensates for his exaggerated insinuations that this very same society was liberally tainted by a growing mis-trustfulness, increased racial tension, rising street crime, rampant incest (*Spanking the Monkey*) and homosexual paedophilia (NAMBLA). The fatalis-tic inference is clear: unbridled autonomy for humankind leads to an extremely distasteful selfish excess.

In opposition, Etzioni's description of the US in the 1950s offers a picture more congenial to the palate. Notions of a strong sense of duty, shared core values, clearly delineated marital roles, respect for authority and a shared alle-giance to the nation state easily overcome the feeling that America in the 1950s may have been overly coercive. For the average reader this latter, more positive, image is the more preferable state of affairs, one which, according to Newman and de Zoysa,[43] suggests the stability of a *Gemeinschaft* where feelings of safety, comfort and a sense of belonging emanate out of face-to-face relationships, dependable values, freely shared norms, respect for standards and a paucity of deviance. It is the antithesis of the violent 1980s' *Gesellschaft* image of anxiety, isolation, insecurity and instrumentalistic reasoning. Deliberately, the effect of this comparison is to gently coax the reader into a more receptive disposition toward the society of 1950s' America.

Having created that impression, it is then easy for Etzioni to appear to build upon – not, he is at pains to point out, a harking back to – the ways of a bygone era, without being accused of nostalgia. He is suggesting, rather, that the cohe-sive values of American society in the 1950s have to be rekindled in order to curb the excesses of the 1980s, and so complement the advances made in the direction of liberty and independence. In reality, however, the favourable bias towards the past social configuration tends to sway suggested solutions to perceived ills towarda a reassertion of the mores and morals predominant in the 1950s. Hence the re-emphasis on the traditional roles undertaken by the family, education, community and society; hence also the attempt to reassert a moral consciousness capable of persuading individuals to conform to norms appropriate to the capitalism of America's past.

As was suggested earlier, another example of Etzioni's social conservatism is evident in the analytical and theoretical devices he deploys to make his case. They are techniques and understandings that are linked to 1950s' America. Such devices are characteristic of the social functionalism emerging in the USA during that period. In this respect, it is no coincidence that Amitai Etzioni specialised in the functionalist discipline of organisational theory from the 1950s to the 1970s. Importantly, it was a discipline that embedded itself in the capitalist system through its dedication to the improvement of organisational efficiency from within. And, crucially, this discipline rested on the belief that capitalism is the ultimate mode of human cohabitation. Questioning its sovereignty, therefore, was not an issue for the practitioners of such theory.[44]

Apart from the obvious references in his work to social equilibrium, balance, cohesion, functionality, dysfunctionality and centripetal or centrifugal forces, Etzioni also manages to apply other, less obviously but equally well-worn, organisational models to his examination of society today. In *The New Golden Rule*, Etzioni informs the reader that 'all forms of social order draw to some extent on coercive means (such as police and jails), "utilitarian" means (economic incentives generated by public expenditures or subsidies), and normative means (appeals to values, moral education)'.[45] This is not a particularly innovative observation. Nor are its assumptions objective. To emphasise the point, one has only to look back to 1973. In trying to trace a path towards 'a theory of societal guidance', Etzioni actually used the same analogy to stipulate that social structures are more than just patterns of interactions, expectations and symbols. They are also 'patterns of allocation of social assets, of the possessions of a social unit [which] can be classified analytically as coercive, utilitarian, and normative, concerning, respectively, the distribution of the capacity to employ means of violence, material objects and services, and symbols (especially values)'.[46]

In 1961 Etzioni had published *A Comparative Analysis of Complex Organizations*, a work that also centred around the same analytical triad. There, he attempted to place various organisations into a coercive–utilitarian–normative 'scheme … to clarify certain problems which emerge from this classificatory endeavor'.[47] Organisations, such as concentration camps, prisons and correctional 'institutions' were placed within the coercive category since the use of force 'is the major means of control over lower participants and high alienation characterizes the orientation of most lower participants to the organization'.[48] Business unions, farmers' organisations, and blue- and white-collar industries were said to typify utilitarian organisations in that 'remuneration is the major means of control over lower participants'[49] and calculative involvement distinguishes the orientation of the majority of participants. In contrast, organisations which use normative power as the major source of control over its highly committed 'lower' order are typical of religious and ideological movements, hospitals, social unions, voluntary associations, colleges and universities.

This 1961 application of the triad reveals the true character of such analysis. Consistent with organisational theory, it is a triad that is specifically designed to measure and define the degree of social control being exerted in the quest for efficiency and cohesion. In reality, it is about the exertion of power from above and the effectiveness of the response it elicits from the supposedly 'lower' participants. By implication, 'higher' participants must be the ones wielding the power. Exactly who they are, and how or why they are able to do this, are not the immediate questions; they simply are. Power over others, in some form or other, is deemed a prerequisite. Only the type, character and nature of that power is called into question. Nevertheless, it is this process of questioning that indirectly reveals who is thought best suited to actually wield the power concerned.

Critically, Etzioni's allegiance to the exertion of power, and to the stratified societal structures of hierarchy that allow for the exertion and distribution of it, is not limited to the study of organisations alone. The very notion of moving 'toward a theory of societal guidance' confirms this. Who, for instance, would be responsible for this guidance? What form would it take? Regardless of *The New Golden Rule*'s later call for open dialogue and the reassertion of a moral voice, the problem of who and how decides what is appropriate, right or wrong still remain. Likewise, problems over the preservation of individual freedom are still not tackled convincingly by Etzioni. Where can a consensus which is not tantamount to majority rule come from? Alternatively, if it is to be a minority voice that is heard, the danger could be that those most articulate would be best placed to determine the values and morals of future society. This, arguably, would fit Etzioni's tripartite model perfectly. In his eyes, it would be an informed exercise of normative power from above: an exercise that would emanate out of the highly articulate world of academia, which is where, as it happens, Amitai Etzioni practises his communitarian thinking.

What is more, Etzioni's use of this analytical triangle is in itself a serious – if not a dangerous – limit to the scope and breadth of any proposed solutions to the perceived moral decay. As we have seen, it is a model that encourages the use of linear polarisations to explain the intricacies of society. The 'problems of social order are thus reduced to finding an almost mythical balance between diametrically opposed dualities'.[50] As a result, investigation centres around the need to discover the point at which excessively coercive means can be effectively countered by utilitarian and/or normative means, and the point at which extreme utilitarian means may be countered by normative means alone. Therefore the search for an 'acceptable' equilibrium remains confined within the scope of the three power variants. This is not a true representation of social reality. Consequently Etzioni's call for the regeneration of a moral voice to help restore and strengthen the favoured variant of normative power does not offer a

> satisfactory answer to the disintegration of social bonds in . . . advanced societies,
> for . . . [Etzioni's] failure to defend the autonomy of individuals produces moral-

ity without value, a one-dimensional world in which communities are blessed with a cohesion that is neither chosen, intended, nor lived by the people who produce them.[51]

Social order cannot be reduced to simplistic expressions of teleology. One cannot simply detect a normative void and then assume that the missing components can be reinstated or reinvigorated through a recognition of their impotence. Even if they could, Norbert Elias would have been quick to point out that norms should 'be understood as a superimposed layer of social reality, varying in strength and scope but always partial and derivative'.[52] Moreover, Elias firmly believed that these norms should be analysed in terms of *shifting* power balances and power chances, since a neglect to do so would deny an examination of the fundamental question of 'how and under what circumstances relationships that are not regulated by norms can be brought under normative control'?[53]

In essence, such an analysis is not merely Etzioni's classificatory exercise of deciding which form of power is predominant and which is not. Nor is it a matter of Etzioni's tacit assumption that norms or rules are universally present from the outset. Rather, it is the recognition that norms and rules emerge out of the social process itself. By implication, this requires an awareness of the effects and consequences of changing political and socio-economic conditions in which multifarious human interactions are allowed to take place. In other words, norms and rules come and go from *within* society and cannot simply be applied or removed from without. Only a more 'processual' study of human interaction and social developments over a prolonged period would reveal this as distinct from the more 'snap-shot' style of comparative analysis indulged in by Etzioni. In truth, the flaws of Etzioni's analysis undermine the efficacy of the remedy. Etzioni fails to address the possibility that inherent contradictions within the capitalist system have played an integral role in the demise of normative social cohesion.

New Labour's communitarian myopia

In the light of both Etzioni's characteristic method and his subsequent failure to address any of the possible contradictions within the socio-economic foundations of society, it has become obvious that this communitarian Third Way is firmly premised on earlier functionalist interpretations of organisations. As a result, Etzioni restricts his arguments over the creation of a new communitarian society primarily to what he sees as the strengths and weaknesses of the country he has lived in since the 1950s. In this respect, Etzioni's '"New Communitarian Thinking" is myopically North American . . . revealing . . . [a] most informative self-interpretation of the United States. No more, no less.'[54] Moreover, by restricting his analysis to American relations of capital, Etzioni provides a micro focus on *community* that is also short-sighted in that it 'neglects and denies the importance of differences within communities and among communities, especially among communities in different countries'.[55] In sum, Etzioni mistakenly suggests that there is a single identity or a homogeneity of communities and, as a result, is guilty of attempting to impose his own Americanised version of community on the rest of the Western world.

The question remains, however, whether New Labour suffers from a similar form of myopia. Besides its repeated use of the *term* 'community',[56] New Labour's policy drive to reaffirm a *sense* of community is also permeated by Etzioni's influence. Without doubt, New Labour wants to reinvigorate the institution of the family[57] while also maintaining market relations by giving primacy to paid work.[58] Certainly, its moral evaluation of the 'irresponsible' welfare claimant has produced a rationale designed to provoke a change of 'culture'.[59] In short, New Labour envisages that its most fundamental task is to instil a sense of responsibility through the principle of welfare 'conditionality'.[60]

Given this, it is entirely consistent for New Labour to actively promote the welfare-to-work 'New Deals' and to expand the activities of the uncompromising Child Support Agency (CSA). Similarly, the introduction of the working families' tax credit (WFTC), alongside a 'National Childcare Strategy', also adheres to this communitarian logic. Equally, these measures have a judgemental approach. All include notions of obligation and behavioural change; and all signify the importance New Labour attaches to the traditional role of the family.

With the WFTC, the communitarian associations are particularly obvious. Work is inextricably entwined with conceptions of the family. Although the WFTC attempts to give better in-work benefits to both lone-parent and two-parent families in which there is an adult in full-time (sixteen hours or more) low-paid employment,[61] there is, nonetheless, the real possibility of a rather perverse consequence. By enabling men with limited earning power to support a non-working wife, the WFTC could help 're-establish the male breadwinner model among certain low-income households'.[62] Etzioni would not be too disturbed by such a trend. Nor, one suspects, would New Labour, even though its declared aim in this area is to promote the idea that all should be able to combine paid work and family life.

New Labour's plans for the CSA strengthen this suspicion. In keeping faith with the founding Conservative principle that 'no father should be able to escape from his responsibility',[63] the CSA under New Labour still maintains its draconian presence. Moreover, despite the failures of this agency New Labour are determined to link its activities with an effort to get lone parents who are on benefit back to work through the relevant New Deal scheme on offer. This, in itself, does not appear to question the family structure. Neither does it suggest that women should stay at home. However, the original – and little heard of – consultation proposal for a male mentoring scheme in the 'Sure Start' element of the New Deal for Communities[64] betrays New Labour's thinking. The whole idea of a male mentor for a male child undermines the responsibility of a single mother. It suggests a deep mistrust of a single mother's ability to cope alone. Instead, emphasis is placed on paid work and the inevitable involvement of others undertaking the necessary child-caring duties.

Similarly, in a follow-up document, New Labour's intention to 'improve couples' decision making about getting married, and to enhance services which prevent marriage breakdown',[65] further substantiates these misgivings. In spite of Driver and Martell's belief that *Supporting Families: Summary of Responses to the Consultation Document*[66] has a largely pragmatic view on family forms, the proposals given send a rather different message. True to maintaining the ideal of traditional family forms, the proposals recommend: 'an increased role for registrars in marriage guidance; a statement of the rights and responsibilities of marriage and the ceremony; the restructuring of marriage counselling to place greater stress on saving marriages; and funding for marriage advice centres'.[67] The wistful tone, content and intent of the document could easily have come from Etzioni's review of relationships in 1950s' America.

On a more general level, all of the 'New Deals' put forward by New Labour are designed to promote accepted 'mainstream' values and to inculcate a change in perceived behaviour. The four options – work with an employer who will receive a job subsidy of up to £60 per week; full-time education or training; work with a voluntary sector organisation; or work on the Environmental Taskforce[68] – are put forward to provide individuals with 'opportunities' to gain more independence – and responsibility – in their *'escape'* from poverty, dependence and the age-old *Gesellschaft* interpretations of life in the supposed 'underclass'.[69] Crucially, work is presented as the principal channel for social cohesion, since paid work is 'the main means of integration'.[70] As such, work is seen specifically as 'a route to an adequate income, social networks and personal fulfilment'. Therefore '[a]ttachment to the labour market ... is the key to breaking the vicious cycle of long-term unemployment and social exclusion'.[71]

Effectively, the whole scenario represents a graphic example of Etzioni's social engineering and sociological position. Quite simply, New Labour sees work, the family, community and 'schooling' as the bedrock for social development. As part of a virtuous cycle, families are seen primarily as institutions of social control and social welfare. They are 'where the difference between right and wrong is learned, and where a sense of mutual obligation is founded and practised';[72] and it is 'largely from family discipline that social discipline and a sense of responsibility is learned'.[73]

In support, education at school, at work and in the wider society provides more discipline and a further reinforcement of the basic values taught in the family. Finally (in a chronological sense), paid work and participation in the market generate responsibility, a moral sensibility, a feeling of belonging and, ultimately, stimulate the growth of a comforting and supportive community which, for New Labour, 'is not some piece of nostalgia [since community] means what we share, it means working together'.[74] In this way, the cycle of virtue is perpetuated as the community complements familial relations. Yet this reflects a negligently myopic position. As with Etzioni, the competitive and destructive machinations of capitalism are overlooked in their entirety. In contrast, an appreciation of these negative features of capitalism can reveal the first clues to the possible impotence, and failure, of this policy direction. After all, the same contradictions that beset and bedevil Etzioni's social diagnoses of the past – and, indeed of the present – remain as formidable obstacles in the social workings of the UK today.

One major concern, is that the combination of supply-side labour reforms[75] and the underpinning education, training and retraining principles that encapsulate the New Deal scenarios can have disastrous consequences. New Labour's call for education to go beyond the realms of academia and re-equip the British workforce to be more flexible (geographically as well as socially) and globally competitive[76] completely overlooks the problems surrounding job availability. While such innovations could well lead to the successful provision of a larger, more skilled workforce, if employment opportunities are limited competition for employment will intensify and the effects of an *immiserisation* process will still persist. Only this time, the unemployed may well possess more skills and greater levels of education. All the hours spent training in the aspirational pursuit of 'opportunity' could easily become a constant source of disenchantment and frustration. Moreover, the increasing availability of a reserve army of skilled labour would allow for some employers to reduce skilled wage levels much in the same manner as they have done to the unskilled workforce.

In the face of this cynical view of society-wide competition, exploitation, alienation and the possibility that *high-skilled immiserization*[77] could actually broaden the demographic composition of the 'underclass', it becomes less and less clear how New Labour hopes to stimulate a deep sense of community. Etzioni's call to redress individual rights with a collective responsibility could not be fulfilled under these conditions. In fact, the continuation of, let alone the possibility of an increase in, social exclusion can reflect only an imbalance in the opposite direction: an imbalance that could actually undermine the rights of the jobless poor and those with underpaid work in the name of competitive responsibility. This would be a direct contradiction of Tony Blair's declared mission to develop a better society around a community spirit built on a reduction in the 'moral and economic evil'[78] surrounding the 'underclass'. In sum, these formidable contradictions may well consign the New Deals' gift of 'opportunity' to the realms of fantasy rather than reality.

Betwixt two stools: a conclusion

By way of a conclusion, it is worth noting that New Labour's methodological approach to the problems facing British society displays similar failings to that of Etzioni. With a description of the communitarian dimensions of New Labour, Driver and Martell[79] provide a useful insight. In an approach which reflects New Labour's, Driver and Martell place the policies of New Labour within the confines of six polarities. Pluralist approaches are set against conformist; more conditional against less conditional; progressive against conservative; prescriptive against vol-

untary; moral against socio-economic, and individual against corporate. As with
Etzioni, the resulting prescription is clearly limited by the chosen polarities.

Again we see an inherent bias arising out of the portrayed images. Individual
responsibility is seen as the answer to the threat posed by a growing 'underclass';
a work-centred communal morality is preferred to hedonistic individuality and
materialism; while the 'job of Government is neither to suppress markets nor to
surrender to them but to equip people, companies and countries to succeed
within them'.[80] As this chapter has shown, the socio-economic consequences of
capitalism are not addressed. Moreover, it has become increasingly clear that the
creation of a nationwide sense of community would simply founder in the face
of rising job insecurity, flexible working practices, fewer welfare rights and an
increasing need to be socially and geographically mobile.

Put simply, *The Spirit of Community* under these conditions would have to be
so flexible that it would be unable to provide any lasting social cohesion. It would
be impossible to generate a united communal voice from a conception of community that had to mean different things to different people in different places, at
different times. As a result, the Third Way politics of New Labour can only
emulate Etzioni's failings by *imposing* its own personal vision of community.

Notes

 1 Prideaux 2001.
 2 Heron 2001.
 3 Powell *et al*. 2001.
 4 Deacon 2002.
 5 See also Deacon and Mann 1997, 1999; and Driver and Martell 2002.
 6 Levitas 1998.
 7 Driver and Martell 1998: 29.
 8 Giddens 1994.
 9 See Allen 1975.
10 Deacon 2002.
11 Etzioni 1998: x.
12 *Ibid*.
13 Etzioni 1997: xviii.
14 *Ibid*., p. 61.
15 *Ibid*.
16 *Ibid*., p. 63.
17 *Ibid*., p. 65.
18 *Ibid*.
19 *Ibid*.
20 *Ibid*., p. 66.
21 *Ibid*., p. 67.
22 *Ibid*.
23 *Ibid*., p. 68.
24 *Ibid*.

25 *Ibid.*

26 D. Miller and M. Novak (1977) *The Fififties: The Way We Really Were*, quoted Etzioni
    1997: 62.

27 Etzioni 1997: 64.

28 *Ibid.*, p. 72.

29 *Ibid.*

30 *Ibid.*, p. 73.

31 *Ibid.*

32 Etzioni 1995a: 1.

33 Heron 2001.

34 Etzioni 2000: 46.

35 Etzioni 1995a: 1.

36 *Ibid.*, p. 2.

37 Etzioni 1997: 7.

38 Levitas 1998: 90.

39 Campbell 1995.

40 Etzioni 1995: ix.

41 Etzioni 1995b.

42 Skoble 1998: 44.

43 Newman and de Zoysa 1997.

44 See Allen 1975.

45 Etzioni 1997: 13.

46 Etzioni 1973: 151.

47 Etzioni 1973: 26.

48 *Ibid.*, p. 27.

49 *Ibid.*, p. 31.

50 Prideaux 2002: 78.

51 Bowring 1997: 51.

52 Arnason 1987: 435.

53 Elias 1970: 435.

54 Bauer 1997: 73.

55 *Ibid.*

56 In a controversial and much heckled speech to the Women's Institute on 8 June 2000,
    Tony Blair made eighteen allusions.

57 Barlow and Duncan 1999; Driver and Martell 2002; Fox Harding 2000.

58 Levitas 1998.

59 Deacon 2002; Deacon and Mann 1997 and 1999; Department of Social Security 1998.

60 Dwyer 1998, 2000a and 2000b; Heron and Dwyer 1999.

61 Dean and Shah 2002.

62 Dean 2002: 6.

63 Margaret Thatcher quoted in Timmins 1996: 452.

64 Home Office 1998.

65 Driver and Martell 2002: 51.

66 Home Office 1999.

67 Driver and Martell 2002: 51.

68 DSS 1998.

69 See Bauman 1998; Bagguley and Mann 1992; Campbell 1995; Etzioni 1995a, 1997 and
    2000; Mann 1992; Murray 1984.

70 Levitas 1996: 13.
71 *Ibid.*, p. 14.
72 Mandelson and Liddle 1996: 125.
73 Blair 1994: 47–8.
74 Blair 1996: 64.
75 Driver and Martell 1998.
76 DfEE 1998.
77 Prideaux 2001.
78 Blair 1996: 59.
79 Driver and Martell 1997.
80 Labour's Economic Policy Commission 1995: 14.

References

Allen, V. L. (1975) *Social Analysis: A Marxist Critique and Alternative*, London, Longman.

Arnason, J. (1987) 'Figurational sociology as a counter-paradigm', *Theory, Culture & Society*, 4.

Bagguley, P. and Mann, K. (1992) 'Idle thieving bastards? Scholarly representations of the underclass', *Work, Employment & Society*, 6(1).

Barlow, A. and Duncan, S. (1999) 'New Labour's communitarianism, supporting families and the "rationality mistake"', *Centre for Research on Family, Kinship and Childhood*, Working Paper No 10, University of Leeds.

Bauer, R. (1997) 'A community is a community – but in reality roses are different, and bunches much more so', *Voluntas*, 8(1).

Bauman, Zygmunt (1998), *Work, Consumerism and the New Poor*, Buckingham, Open University Press.

Blair, T. (1994) *Socialism*, Fabian Pamphlet 565, London, Fabian Society.

Blair, T. (1996) *New Britain: My Vision of a Young Country* (*New Statesman* special selection) London, *New Statesman*–Fourth Estate.

Bowring, F. (1997) 'Communitarianism and morality: in search of the subject', *New Left Review*, 222.

Campbell, B. (1995) 'So what's the big idea, Mr Etzioni?', *Independent*, 16 March.

Deacon, A. (2002) *Perspectives on Welfare*, Buckingham, Open University Press.

Deacon, A. and Mann, K. (1997) 'Moralism and modernity: the paradox of New Labour thinking on welfare', *Benefits*, September–October.

Deacon, A. and Mann, K. (1999) 'Agency, modernity and social policy', *Journal of Social Policy*, 28(3).

Dean, H. (2002) 'Business versus families: whose side is New Labour on?', *Social Policy & Society*, 1(1).

Dean, H. and Shah, A. (2002) 'Insecure families and low-paying labour markets: comments on the British experience', *Journal of Social Policy*, 31(1).

Department for Education and Employment (1998) *The Learning Age: A Renaissance for a New Britian*, Cm 3790, London, HMSO.

Department of Social Security (1998) *New Ambitions For Our Country: A New Contract for Welfare* Cm 3805, London, HMSO.

Driver, S. and Martell, L. (1997) 'New Labour's communitarianisms', *Critical Social Policy*, 17(3).

Driver, S. and Martell, L. (1998) *New Labour: Politics After Thatcherism*, Cambridge, Polity Press.

Driver, S. and Martell, L. (2002) 'New Labour, work and the family', *Social Policy & Administration*, 36(1).

Dwyer, P. (1998) 'Conditional citizens? Welfare rights and responsibilities in the late 1990s', *Critical Social Policy*, 18(4).

Dwyer, P. (2000) *Welfare Rights and Responsibilities: Contesting Social Citizenship*, Bristol, Policy Press.

Dwyer, P. (2000) 'British Muslims, welfare citizenship and conditionality: some empirical findings', *Islamic Values, Human Agency and Social Policies*, RAPP Working Paper No 2, University of Leeds Race and Public Policy Research Unit.

Elias, N. (1970) 'Processes of state formation and nation building', International Sociological Association Paper, available online (accessed 21 March 1999): www.usyd.edu.au.

Etzioni, A. (1961) *A Comparative Analysis of Complex Organizations: On Power, Involvement, and Their Correlates*, New York, Free Press.

Etzioni, A. (1973) 'Toward a theory of societal guidance', in E. Etzioni-Halevy and A. Etzioni (eds) *Social Change: Sources, Patterns, and Consequences*, New York, Basic Books.

Etzioni, A. (1995) 'Nation in need of community values', *The Times*, 20 February.

Etzioni, A. (1995) *The Spirit of Community: Rights, Responsibilities and the Communitarian Agenda*, London, Fontana.

Etzioni, A. (1997) *The New Golden Rule: Community and Morality in a Democratic Society*, London, Profile Books.

Etzioni, A. (ed.) (1998) *The Essential Communitarian Reader*, Lanham, MD, Rowman & Littlefield.

Etzioni, A. (1998) 'A matter of balance, rights and responsibilities', in Etzioni (ed.), *The Essential Communitarian Reader*, Lanham, MD, Rowman & Littlefield.

Etzioni, A. (2000) *The Third Way to a Good Society*, London, Demos.

Etzioni-Halevy, E. and Etzioni, A. (eds) (1973) *Social Change: Sources, Patterns, and Consequences*, New York, Basic Books.

Fox Harding, L. (2000) *Supporting Families/Controlling Families? – Towards a Characterisation of New Labour's 'Family Policy'*, Working Paper 21, Centre for Research on Family, Kinship and Childhood, University of Leeds.

Giddens, A. (1994) *Beyond Left and Right: The Future of Radical Politics*, Cambridge, Polity Press.

Heron, E. (2001) 'Etzioni's spirit of communitarianism: community values and welfare realities in Blair's Britian', in R. Sykes, C. Bochel and N. Ellison (eds) *Social Policy Review*, vol. 13, Bristol, Policy Press.

Heron, E. and Dwyer, P. (1999) '"Doing the right thing": Labour's attempt to forge a new welfare deal between the individual and the State', *Social Policy & Administration*, 3(1).

Home Office (1998) *Supporting Families: A Consultation Document*, London, HMSO.

Home Office 1999) *Supporting Families: Summary of Responses to the Consultation Document*, London, HMSO.

Labour's Economic Policy Commission (1995) *A New Economic Future For Britain: Economic Opportunities for All*, London, Labour Party.

Levitas, R. (1996) 'The concept of social exclusion and the new Durkheimian hegemony', *Critical Social Policy*, 16(1).

Levitas, R. (1998) *The Inclusive Society? Social Exclusion and New Labour*, Basingstoke, Macmillan.

Levitas, R. (2000) 'Community, utopia and New Labour', *Local Economy*, 15(3).

Mandelson, P. and Liddle, R. (1996) *The Blair Revolution: Can New Labour Deliver?*, London, Faber & Faber.

Mann, K. (1992) *The Making of an English 'Underclass': The Social Divisions of Welfare and Labour*, Buckingham, Open University Press.

Murray, C. (1984) *Losing Ground*, New York, Basic Books.

Newman, O. and de Zoysa, R. (1997) 'Communitarianism: the new panacea?', *Sociological Perspectives*, 40(4).

Powell, M., Exworthy, M. and Berney, L. (2001) 'Playing the game of partnership', in R. Sykes, C. Bochel and N. Ellison (eds) *Social Policy Review*, vol. 13, Bristol, Policy Press.

Prideaux, S. (2001) 'New Labour, old functionalism: the underlying contradictions of welfare reform in the US and the UK', *Social Policy & Administration*, 35(1).

Prideaux, S. (2002) 'From organisational theory to the new communitarianism of Amitai Etzioni', *Canadian Journal of Sociology*, 27(1).

Skoble, A. (1998) 'Review of *The New Golden Rule*', *Policy*, 14(1).

Sykes, R., Bochel, C. and Ellison, N. (eds) (2001) *Social Policy Review*, vol. 13, Bristol, Policy Press.

Timmins, N. (1996) *The Five Giants*, London, Fontana.

Part IV

The discourse and strategy of the Third Way

Introduction

The Third Way, particularly in its New Labour form, is often presented as a triumph of style over substance and the product *par excellence* of a soundbite political culture. Far from dismissing the discourse of the Third Way, however, the contributions that comprise Part IV start from the position that discourse plays a key role in developing substantial political objectives. A critical engagement with the discourse of the Third Way is thus integral to an understanding of the political character of New Labour, as well as in the forging of viable alternatives. Interestingly, the importance of the discursive elements of political strategy are not lost on third-wayers themselves. Leading New Labour modernisers frequently call for the Centre-Left to develop a more robust narrative, linking in the public mind disparate policy mixes as part of a 'big picture'.

David Morrison traces how the key objectives of Centre-Left modernisers have been discursively articulated, both prior to and through the Third Way. He suggests that while labels such as 'stakeholding' and 'the Third Way' may be transient, a core modernising version of citizenship has been remarkably consistent since the early 1990s. Consequently, the Third Way theory offered by Giddens, like that of stakeholding before it, has been appropriated by New Labour and other Centre-Left actors only selectively, where it is of use in developing this enduring agenda. This is based on neo-liberal assumptions about the nature of a 'changed world' that must be adapted to, the perceived failure of both the Old Left and the neo-liberals themselves in responding to that change, and the need for a consensual society apparently free from antagonism in developing new responses. This analysis reveals the Third Way as an attempt to actively construct an economic 'Subject' appropriate to external imperatives such as economic globalisation and labour market flexibility.

Paul Cammack undertakes a similarly close reading of the language of the Third Way, focusing on the work of Giddens in particular. Like Morrison, he sees Third Way discourse as reflecting a definite and coherent project. For Morrison, that project is the attempt to reconcile social justice and economic efficiency. Alternatively, as Cammack sees things, Giddens has deliberately subverted the language of social democracy in order to usher in a new and aggressive phase of neo-liberalism. On his account, the Third Way is not an attempt to address the perceived failures of both the Old Left and neo-liberalism, but rather the ideological expression of a new phase of capitalist expansion into all areas of social life. The Third Way is thus, for Cammack, a reflection and an agent of the triumph of neo-liberalism, rather than an attempt to move beyond it.

In both contributions, the deeper structural imperatives of capital accumulation loom large. However, their authors imply that third-wayers could have *chosen* different – more progressive – strategies. This suggests a continuing role for political agency and room for alternative Third Way discourses.

The conditions for developing such alternatives are discussed in the concluding chapter, by Will Leggett. Leggett surveys the general state of criticism of the Third Way, in particular as illustrated by the contributors to this book. He suggests that critics are at their most convincing when they take the Third Way seriously, engage with the analysis it makes of social change, but show how such change can be taken in a more progressive direction than at present. He illustrates the importance of these features by considering our contributors' suggested reconstructions of Third Way themes and, in particular, by revealing an enduring role for the traditional leftist concern with the distribution of wealth and power.

Giddens's way with words

'When *I* use a word,' Humpty Dumpty said in rather a scornful tone, 'it means just what I choose it to mean – neither more nor less'.

'The question is,' said Alice, 'whether you *can* make words mean so many different things.'

'The question is,' said Humpty Dumpty, 'which is to be master – that's all.' (Lewis Carroll, *Through the Looking Glass*)

Introduction

If little remained that was revolutionary in the spirit or content of post-war social democracy, it still appealed to values that stood in direct or partial opposition to the logic of capitalist accumulation and exploitation. Principal among these were the ideals of emancipation and social justice. If social democracy increasingly came in practice to represent an accommodation with capitalism rather than an actual or potential alternative, it still evoked the possibility of an alternative and could advance independent values against which the limitations of capitalism might be exposed. These values informed social democracy's political agenda, as it looked to an active state to block or moderate the dynamics of capitalist reproduction. Even at its most reformist, then, social democracy represented a distinctly uneasy accommodation with capitalism, and a refusal to capitulate to values derived exclusively from the logic of capitalist accumulation and exploitation. In contrast, neo-liberalism looks to an active state first to restore and then to maintain and extend the conditions within which the logic of capitalist reproduction can work to the full. In this context, an essential component of its project – reflected in the claim that 'there is no alternative' – is the effort to re-align and redefine key social values in such a way that they confirm rather than challenge the logic of capitalism.

Anthony Giddens's *The Third Way* (published in 1998, and followed two years later by *The Third Way and its Critics*) was advertised and widely understood as presenting a new politics of the 'Centre-Left', adapted to the circumstances of globalisation – a 'Renewal of social democracy', as its sub-title proclaimed. Close examination of the text reveals something different – a process in which the vocabulary and values of social democracy are systematically redefined in order to bring them into alignment with an unabashedly pro-capitalist agenda. Giddens strongly resists the label 'neo-liberal', claiming to be steering a path between classical social democracy on the one hand and Thatcherite neo-liberalism on the other. He is able to do this, however, only because he equates neo-liberalism with an exclusive reliance on unregulated market forces – in other words with *laissez-faire* liberalism. However, if social democracy, as suggested above, is seen as looking to an active state to block or moderate the dynamics of capitalist reproduction, while neo-liberalism looks to such a state to restore and maintain the conditions within which the logic of capitalist reproduction can work to the full, his position is unambiguously neo-liberal. On issue after issue, he seeks to make the behaviour of individuals, corporations, 'third-sector' organisations and the State consistent with and supportive of a social system thoroughly permeated and ruled by capital. In other words, he is an active neo-liberal rather than a *laissez-faire* liberal. *The Third Way* reads not as an innocent manifesto for a resurgent Centre-Left, but as a systematic appropriation of the vocabulary and values of social democracy to legitimise and consolidate a new politics of the Centre-Right. In the Third Way vision, the State seeks to regulate capitalism not in order to soften its impact, but in order to bring its logic to bear on all aspects of existence. Acknowledging the continuing appeal of the core values of social democracy and of socialism, and invoking them in support of a diametrically opposed agenda, Giddens caricatures, subverts and neutralises those values, and promotes the hegemony of the neo-liberal project.

Viewed in the same perspective, New Labour's 'Third Way' rhetoric masks a shift within a neo-liberal project from an initial shock phase that unsettles 'anti-market' forces to a longer term second phase that builds positively 'pro-market' or (in World Bank-speak) 'market-friendly' institutions. The 'capitalistic communitarianism' identified by David Morrison (chapter 9, this volume) as informing Blair's understanding of citizenship provides this programme with ideological support. If that is so, to describe such elements of the programme as the New Deal as fitting with 'a progressive social democratic agenda on welfare reform', as Driver does (chapter 2, this volume), is to fall into the trap set by Giddens and others.

With that in mind, a detailed reading of Giddens's *The Third Way* is offered here. First, I analyse the text's rhetorical structure, showing how it caricatures and dismisses both socialism and social democracy. I then show how Giddens re-defines key terms in the social democratic lexicon – *solidarity*, *emancipation*, *security*, *community*, *redistribution*, *equality* and *welfare* – to suit the neo-liberal agenda. Finally, Giddens's project, like New Labour's, is shown to coincide with that of the IMF–World Bank, which is similarly presented as stepping away from the neo-liberalism of Reagan and Thatcher and towards a more socially inclusive agenda, yet seeks, nevertheless, to entrench the logic of capitalism. It is concluded that *The Third Way* should be understood not as crude sociology (although it is that) but as a sophisticated political intervention in support of the argument that 'there is no alternative' to all-out capitalism.

The rhetorical structure of *The Third Way*

The overt argument of *The Third Way* is straightforward. Social, economic and technological change have rendered classical social democracy obsolete. Social democrats must therefore continue the thorough revision of its content that is already underway, steering a middle course between the classical doctrine on the one hand and neo-liberalism on the other – hence the 'Third Way'. The resulting doctrine will still retain the core values of classical social democracy: 'The term "centre-left" thus isn't an innocent label. A renewed social democracy has to be left of centre, because social justice and emancipatory politics remain at its core.'[1]

Five 'dilemmas' are identified by Giddens: the transformation brought about by globalisation; the challenge posed by the new individualism; the weakening of the distinction between Left and Right; the question of the scope for political agency the parties and the State; and the need to respond to ecological issues. Against this background, Giddens sets out a new agenda for the Centre-Left, based on the twin principles: 'No rights without responsibilities'; and 'No authority without democracy'.[2] Proposals for social democratic policies modified to meet the needs of the age are then grouped in three chapters, addressing in turn the relationship between the State and civil society, and the role of the State in the domestic and global arenas.

On first appearances, then, *The Third Way* represents an honest effort to fashion a new social democratic agenda for the twenty-first century. But appearances are deceptive. Surrounding this expository framework is a rhetorical structure which subverts it. This structure, established in the opening lines and carried consistently through the text as a whole, trashes socialism and social democracy in turn, preparing the way for the redefinition of key entries in the social democratic lexicon in a way which assimilates them to the neo-liberal agenda. Far from being a 'Third Way', the doctrine proposed is a complete capitulation, all the more pernicious because it sows confusion and gets in the way of a genuinely social democratic alternative.

Giddens is quite explicit about his purpose at the outset. One might expect the text to begin with an exposition of the shortcomings of the neo-liberal project, as a prelude to setting out a renewed social democratic alternative. But it does not. Instead, it recalls Blair's ambition, announced after a seminar in Washington, in February 1998, to 'create an international consensus of the centre-left for the twenty-first century':

> The new approach would develop a policy framework to respond to change in the global order. [Quoting Blair] 'The old left resisted that change. The new right did

not want to manage it. We have to manage that change to produce social solidarity and prosperity.' The task is a formidable one because, as these statements indicate, pre-existing political ideologies have lost their resonance.[3]

The problem, then, is to create an ideology to underpin the political agenda of
New Labour, in circumstances where those of the old left (classical social democracy) and the new right (Thatcherism) have faltered. But this is not all. Giddens
moves immediately to recall *The Communist Manifesto*, and the continuing
appeal of overtly *socialist* values:

> A hundred and fifty years ago Marx wrote that 'a spectre is haunting Europe' – the
> spectre of socialism or communism. This remains true, but for different reasons
> from those Marx had in mind. Socialism and communism have passed away, yet
> they remain to haunt us. We cannot just put aside the values and ideals that drove
> them, for some remain intrinsic to the good life that it is the point of social and
> economic development to create. The challenge is to make these values count where
> the economic programme of socialism has become discredited.[4]

These opening moves disclose a highly political agenda. It is not so much that
'a renewed social democracy has to be left of centre because social justice and
emancipatory politics remain at its core';[5] rather, a New Labour project which is
resolved to turn its back on the past must *present itself* as renewing social democracy and advancing its emancipatory project, and must *position itself* at the 'left
of centre'. In the idiom of the Gramscian analysis of hegemony, Giddens is proposing himself as the organic intellectual of Blair's regime. In the vernacular, he
is saying: 'Look, Tony, you have a problem. You've got to dump socialism and
social democracy, but the values with which they are associated still appeal to
people. Never mind. Let me have a go at attaching those values to policies that
will enable you to manage and extend the neo-liberal programme.' In other
words, the rhetorical structure of the essay is as follows: socialism has failed;
classical social democracy is obsolete; solidarity, emancipation, security, community, redistribution, equality, and welfare can still be watchwords, but only if
they can be redefined to meet the needs of the age; appropriately redefined, they
can be achieved by pursuing neo-liberal policies, not by abandoning them; neo-
liberalism, therefore, can be presented as renewed social democracy. The proposal, in other words, is not to offer a social democratic alternative to
neo-liberalism, but to legitimise neo-liberal policies by clothing them in the
vocabulary of social democracy.

Trashing socialism

Giddens initially identifies three components to socialism – a critique of *individualism*, a critique of *capitalism* and an *economic programme* designed to
humanise or overthrow capitalism. The third of these – the economic programme – is identified exclusively with the Soviet Union, and the failure of the
Soviet Union is presented as the failure of socialism for all time:

> Socialism seeks to confront the limitations of capitalism in order to humanize it or to overthrow it altogether. The economic theory of socialism depends upon the idea that, left to its own devices, capitalism is economically inefficient, socially divisive and unable to reproduce itself in the long term. The notion that capitalism can be humanized through socialist economic management gives socialism whatever hard edge it possesses, even if there have been many different accounts of how such a goal might be achieved. For Marx, socialism stood or fell by its capacity to deliver a society that would generate greater wealth than capitalism and spread that wealth in a more equitable fashion. If socialism is now dead, it is precisely because these claims have collapsed.[6]

The demise of the Soviet Union does a lot of work here. First of all, it is made to stand for *all* the 'many different accounts' of how socialist economic management might come about. Second, its failure curiously disposes of the idea that capitalism can be either humanised or overthrown. Third, reference to the Soviet Union temporarily allows Giddens to pass in silence over the notion that capitalism, 'left to its own devices', is economically inefficient, or socially divisive, or unable to reproduce itself in the long term (a view which he elsewhere endorses). In other words, the failure of socialism in the Soviet Union disposes of the shortcomings and the critique of capitalism. The trick is a simple one – to dispose of the *idea* of socialism by equating it entirely with the specific form of one historical example – much disputed, as Giddens is perfectly aware – and to insinuate that the Marxist critique of capitalism falls at the same time. The view of socialism as monolithic, unreflective, ineffective and obsolete then becomes a key theme of the text, with socialists caricatured as limited moral beings out of touch with the times, anxious to surrender their personal autonomy and unthinking about the consequences of the lifestyles they adopt. Through this device Giddens avoids the central issues: if capitalism continues to be economically inefficient, socially divisive and unable to reproduce itself in the long term, then the Marxist critique is a relevant as ever. If the project of 'humanizing capitalism by socialist economic management' (not Marx's project at all, of course) has failed, it is social democracy rather than socialism that is called into question. If Giddens believes that capitalism cannot be humanised, but must be given its head, there is nothing social democratic about his project.

Trashing social democracy

Giddens employs the same method to dispose of classical social democracy. Classical or 'old-style' – for which, read 'obsolete' – social democracy is first equated with the Keynesian welfare consensus, despite acknowledgement of liberal and even conservative inspiration and support for the latter; it is then condemned for its limited ability to accommodate ecological concerns, and its association with a bipolar world;[7] before being equated with a social system in which the husband was the bread-winner and the wife the housewife and mother, and identified with such perversions as 'the social engineering which has left a legacy of decaying, crime-ridden housing estates'.[8] Social democracy, in short, is reduced to some highly selective features – not intrinsic to social democracy in itself – of the society in which it appeared. As with socialists, social democrats are caricatured throughout the text as being shy of taking responsibility for their own lives, passively dependent on the State and embracing collectivism as a safe refuge from responsibility and mutual obligation. Not to mince words, Giddens's argument rests upon a foundation of distortion, tendentious argument and vulgar abuse.

This underpinning rhetorical structure turns out to be essential to the case Giddens wishes to present. Against it, he makes a crucial move: 'Social democracy was always linked to socialism. What should its orientation be in a world where there are no alternatives to capitalism?'[9] The question is rhetorical. The answer, 'capitalist, stupid', not spoken here, is stated later:

> With the demise of socialism as a theory of economic management, one of the major division lines between left and right has disappeared, at least for the forseeable future. The Marxist left wished to overthrow capitalism and replace it with a different system. Many social democrats also believed that capitalism could and should be progressively modified so that it would lose most of its defining characteristics. No one any longer has any alternatives to capitalism – the arguments that remain concern how far, and in what ways, capitalism should be governed and regulated.[10]

Here the difference between Marxist and social democratic projects is clearly marked in a way that it could not have been earlier. At the same time, however, the perception of capitalism as 'economically inefficient, socially divisive, and unable to secure its reproduction in the long term' has entirely vanished, as has the idea of 'humanising' it. Giddens has concluded that the 'new social democracy' must unreservedly embrace the logic of capitalism. This in turn throws up the problem which dictates the course of the rest of the essay. Because he wishes to identify this proposition as somehow 'left of centre', he must redefine the key values with which social democracy is identified. From this point on the text is a work of 'semantic engineering' – of making words mean what Giddens chooses them to mean.

New meanings for new values

With the mood set by the trashing of socialism and social democracy, socialists and social democrats, the crucial task of appropriating the vocabulary and values of social democracy in the cause of neo-liberalism takes up the greater part of the essay. Giddens's method is disarmingly simple: he continues to use the social democratic vocabulary of solidarity, emancipation, security, community, redistribution, equality and welfare, but he gives to each term a new meaning. These key points of reference for social democracy are taken up, one by one, and redefined in terms appropriate to the market-friendly individualism of neo-liberal doctrine.

The first step is to replace solidarity or collective responsibility with individualism, thereby shifting from a socialist to a liberal value framework. The second is to propose that in the contemporary world, emancipated individuals are those who assume responsibility for their own future. The third is to have 'security' incorporate 'insecurity', in the form of *risk*. With this new framework in place, further key reference-points of social democracy – community, redistribution, equality and welfare – can be redefined in ways compatible with the social, economic and political demands of contemporary capitalism.

Solidarity

Giddens contrasts solidarity, or collectivism, with the narrow 'me first' individualism sometimes associated with neo-liberalism. He then slips in two characteristic moves before offering a more sympathetic version of contemporary individualism. First he remarks, almost as an aside: 'The idea of the "autonomous individual", after all, was the very notion that socialism grew up in order to contest.'[11] Then he implies that socialists have lacked authentic moral autonomy by presenting the 'new generations', in apparent contrast, as autonomous moral beings:

> The 'me' generation is a misleading description of the new individualism, which does not signal a process of moral decay. Rather to the contrary, surveys show that younger generations today are sensitized to a greater range of moral concerns than previous generations were. They do not, however, relate these values to tradition, or accept traditional forms of authority as legislating on questions of lifestyle.[12]

Socialists, one is led to infer, always have done. Worse, again by implication, socialists and social democrats alike have failed to live in an 'open and reflective manner':

> Social cohesion cannot be guaranteed by the top–down action of the state or by appeal to tradition. We have to make our lives in a more active way than was true or previous generations, and we need more actively to accept responsibilities for the consequences of what we do and the lifestyle habits we adopt. The theme of responsibility, or mutual obligation, was there in old-style social democracy, but was largely dormant, since it was submerged within the concept of collective provision. We have to find a new balance between individual and collective responsibilities today ... All of us have to live in a more open and reflective manner than previous generations.[13]

Socialists, note, are not implicated directly in the retrospective commentary, which refers exclusively to 'old-style social democracy'. In any case, Giddens cannot deny that 'responsibility' was one of its themes. But the idea that hovers in the air is that socialists lacked authenticity, moral responsibility, commitment to a set of values and a lifestyle reflective of that commitment. They failed, in other words, to live in an 'open and reflective manner'. The implication, put plainly, is that past generations of socialists, across the world, have surrendered active moral judgement in their mindless subjugation to state-imposed collectivism. There is no place here for conviction or commitment to principle, nor any recognition that the 'concept of collective provision', where it was advocated, was justified directly by appeal to the values of mutual obligation and responsibility. Giddens manages to find a way of presenting the 'me' generation as morally more authentic than committed socialists and social democrats, turning things on their head by depicting socialists as hedonistic and unthinking consumers of collective doctrine, and today's consumption-oriented generation as superior moral beings.

The best index of the sheer perversity of the argument is that the section opens with the acknowledgement that Marx envisaged a society in which 'the free development of each will be the condition of the free development of all',[14] and ends with the claim that 'leftish critics' dismiss ideas of self-fulfilment and the fulfilment of potential as 'just forms of therapy-talk, or the self-indulgence of the affluent'.[15] To be accurate, contemporary anti-Marxists have detached the idea of self-fulfilment from a context of political economy, interpreted it in purely individual, subjective and psychological terms, robbed it of its critical power and *converted* it into 'therapy-talk'. Of course, the association of contemporary individualism with 'me first' hedonism misses a great deal, as Giddens rightly notes. But he cannot also note, without destroying the false contrast on which his rhetorical structure depends, that those who are most 'sensitized to moral concerns' and most hostile to selfish consumerism, are also closest to 'traditional' socialist and social democratic values, and least committed to the all-out support for capitalism that he advocates. No matter. Giddens conjures up a new meaning for an old word: individualism, he contends, is the new solidarity.

Emancipation

What, then, of the emancipatory project of social democracy? How is the new individual to be 'emancipated'? Commenting on Bobbio's association of 'the Left' with the idea of equality, Giddens begins by detaching the notion of 'emancipation' from 'social justice':

> Although it can be interpreted in quite different ways, the idea of equality or social justice is basic to the outlook of the left. It has been persistently attacked by those on the right. Bobbio's definition, however, needs some refining. Those on the left not only pursue social justice, but believe that government has to play a key role in furthering that aim. Rather than speaking of social justice as such, it is more accurate to say that to be on the left is to believe in a politics of emancipation.[16]

'Emancipation' is next associated with an entirely new set of issues. Immediately after declaring that there is no longer any alternative to capitalism (thereby ruling out a whole set of meanings 'emancipation' might have), Giddens claims:

> To the emancipatory politics of the classical left we have to add what I have elsewhere called life politics. The term may or may not be a good one. What I mean by

it is that, whereas emancipatory politics concerns life chances, life politics concerns life decisions.[17]

In sum, he replaces emancipation from capitalist exploitation with respect for different lifestyle choices and adherence to a new politics of 'choice, identity and mutuality'.[18] The direction in which the argument tends becomes clear later, when Giddens sets out the 'framework of emancipatory politics' that forms the core of the Third Way:

> Third way politics should preserve a core concern with social justice, while accepting that the range of questions which escape the left/right divide is greater than before. ... Freedom to social democrats should mean autonomy of action, which in turn demands the involvement of the wider social community. Having abandoned collectivism, Third Way politics looks for a new relationship between the individual and the community, a redefinition of rights and obligations.
> One might suggest as a prime motto for the new politics, *no rights without responsibilities*.[19]

In Giddens's land of wonders wild and new, then, emancipation comes not via deliverance from the social oppression inherent in the unequal structures of capitalism, but from the individual exercise of personal responsibility in a context where government is emphatically *not* responsible for furthering social justice. Responsibility, it turns out, is the new emancipation.

Security

The focus of Giddens's 'renewed social democracy', then, is on individuals taking responsibility for themselves. Underlying the shift to the 'new individualism', and acting as a unifying principle for the text as a whole, is the idea of 'risk' as a central and essential element of contemporary social life. The topic is introduced by way of a lengthy discussion of ecological risk and the BSE crisis, and the problem posed for the Government of managing the presentation of the risk posed for citizens. But at the end of the section entitled 'Ecological issues' Giddens leaps onto an entirely different terrain, moving beyond the narrow issue of 'ecological risk' to a broader framework within which the 'successful market economy' is taken as the ultimate point of reference. All of a sudden, and unannounced, the emphasis is on the structures and institutions needed to shape the 'risk environment' in which individuals are placed, in order to maximise the likelihood that they will play the roles required of them by the market economy:

> Providing citizens with security has long been a concern of social democrats. The welfare state has been seen as the vehicle of such security. One of the main lessons to be drawn from ecological questions is that just as much attention needs to be given to risk. The new prominence of risk connects individual autonomy on the one hand with the sweeping influence of scientific and technological change on the other. Risk draws attention to the dangers we face – the most important of which we have created for ourselves – but also to the opportunities that go along with

them. Risk is not just a negative phenomenon – something to be avoided or mini-mized. It is at the same time the energizing principle of a society that has broken away from tradition and nature.[20]

Passing over the preposterous implication that BSE should be embraced as an opportunity to take an energising risk, the same technique is to be observed here as was applied to 'solidarity' – where the link between mutual responsibility and collective provision was broken, allowing the two terms to be contrasted, and the values of social democracy were attached to the former in apparent *opposition* to the latter. Here, the proposition that the welfare state protects citizens from risk – the risk of illness, the risk of starvation, the risk of unemployment, the risk of homelessness – is turned around. The suggestion is allowed to slip in that the welfare state reflected a continuum with 'tradition and nature', rather than a principled attempt to protect citizens from risks 'which we have created our-selves'. The issue of responsibility in this topsy-turvy account arises *after*, not before, the introduction of social provision through the welfare state.

At this point Giddens sidles up to his ultimate objective – the presentation of the risk involved in direct exposure to market forces as an integral and appropri-ate part of the 'renewal of social democracy':

> Opportunity and innovation are the positive side of risk. No one can escape risk, of course, but there is a basic difference between the passive experience of risk and the active exploration of risk environments. A positive engagement with risk is a necessary component of social and economic mobilization. Some risks we wish to minimize as far as possible; others, such as those involved in investment decisions, are a positive and inevitable part of a successful market economy.[21]

As he elaborates later:

> A high rate of business formation and dissolution is characteristic of a dynamic economy. This flux is not compatible with a society where taken-for-granted habits dominate, including those generated by welfare systems. Social democrats have to shift the relationship between *risk* and *security* involved in the welfare state, to develop a society of 'responsible risk takers' in the spheres of government, business enterprise and labour markets.[22]

Giddens is of course quite at liberty to embrace the logic of New Right public choice theory, and propose the explicit redefinition of the role of the State and the rights of the individual in ways that make them entirely open to the logic of capital. He is entitled to adopt as his own the agenda of the World Bank – on which more below. But it is adding insult to injury to seek to legitimise the process in the language of social democracy. To recapitulate: in a section entitled 'Ecological issues', launched by a discussion of BSE, Giddens has found his way to the conclusion that a contemporary understanding of security must incorpor-ate structured insecurity through exposure to the risk of market forces, and has claimed that this thought can sit comfortably within the tradition of social democracy. The John Selwyn Gummer of the risk society, Giddens would compel us to bite into the beefburger of market forces. Risk, it seems, is the new security.

Community

With the conceptual framework of individualism, responsibility and risk in place, and the connection made to the broad theme of furthering capitalist reproduction, Giddens makes short work of reinterpreting key social democratic watchwords in explicitly pro-market, neo-liberal, terms. To start with community: '"Community" doesn't imply trying to recapture lost forms of local solidarity; it refers to practical means of furthering the social and material refurbishment of neighbourhoods, towns, and larger local areas.'[23] The 'practical means' in question are to be activated by unleashing the spirit of entrepreneurialism: 'The renewal of deprived local communities presumes the encouragement of economic enterprise as a means of generating a broader civic recovery.'[24]

So the heroes of renewed social democracy are 'young business leaders' and private corporations, and the preferred 'social democratic' policy options are the introduction of 'time–dollar' accounting systems to create financial assets from individual charitable activity and incentives for private corporations to make investments; 'tax breaks for corporations that participate in strategic planning and offer investment in designated areas'.[25] In other words, Giddens proposes the commodification of community activity, and its explicit placing under the sway of capital. Enterprise, it seems, is the new community.

Redistribution

With entrepreneurs established as the new heroes of social democracy, Giddens is now well on his way. Having explained earlier that where social democrats have wanted to expand the State and neo-liberals to shrink it, he suggests that, for the Third Way, 'what is necessary is to reconstruct it'.[26] This 'reconstruction' proceeds in ways that are entirely supportive of the market economy. Proposing that '[g]overnment has an essential role to play in investing in the human resources and infrastructure needed to develop an entrepreneurial culture', he declares that the 'new mixed economy' looks for 'a synergy between public and private sectors, utilizing the dynamism of markets but with the public interest in mind'.[27] This requires a radical reformulation of redistribution, in which the transfer of resources from the rich to the poor has little place:

> For reasons I shall give below, redistribution must not disappear from the agenda of social democracy. But recent discussion among social democrats has quite rightly shifted the emphasis towards the 'redistribution of possibilities'. The cultivation of human potential should as far as possible replace 'after the event' redistribution.[28]

Redistribution, then, is not actually redistribution as such, at all. On the contrary, opportunity is the new redistribution.

Equality

It is already clear that Giddens will have no truck with equality as generally understood in the social democratic tradition. Having first announced that '[e]quality and individual liberty can come into conflict, and it is no good pretending that equality, pluralism and economic dynamism are always compatible',[29] he offers the following thought, for once overtly signalling the process of the redefinition of key terms: 'What then should equality be taken to mean? The new politics defines equality as *inclusion* and inequality as *exclusion*, although these terms need some spelling out.'[30] 'Education and training' turn out to be the key: 'Governments need to emphasize *life-long education*, developing education programmes that start from an individual's early years and continue on even late in life.'[31]

There is, however, the neo-liberal proviso: 'Instead of relying on unconditional benefits, policies should be oriented to encourage saving, the use of educational resources and *other personal investment opportunities*.'[32] Inclusion, optimally at one's own expense, is the new equality.

Welfare

What then of the central principle of social democracy: welfare? Adherents to the ideals of social democracy have, according to Giddens, unaccountably got this completely wrong:

> When Beveridge wrote his *Report on Social Insurance and Allied Services*, in 1942, he famously declared war on Want, Disease, Ignorance, Squalor, and Idleness. In other words, his focus was almost entirely negative. We should speak today of *positive welfare*, to which individuals themselves and other agencies besides government contribute – and which is functional for wealth creation. Welfare is not in essence an economic concept, but a psychic one.[33]

It follows, naturally, for example, that 'counselling ... might sometimes be more helpful than direct economic support'. This leads in turn to a straightforward 'New Right' stance on unemployment benefits:

> Old-style social democracy ... was inclined to treat rights as unconditional claims. With expanding individualism should come an extension of individual obligations. Unemployment benefits, for example, should carry the obligation actively to look for work, and it is up to governments to ensure that welfare systems do not discourage active search.[34]

Later, the circle back to *risk* (the new word for security) is completed in true New Right style: 'Benefit systems should be reformed where they induce moral hazard, and a more active risk-taking attitude encouraged, wherever possible through incentives, but where necessary by legal obligations.'[35]

Such are the virtues of this 'progressive' stance – reflected in suggestions that pensions could be abolished and children obliged to care for elderly parents –

that, in its turn, it frees resources so that 'welfare' as traditionally understood can be directed to those who have most need of it. Once the poor learn to invest in their own education, to spare the State the expense and to keep themselves attractive to capitalists,

> [g]overnment policy can provide direct support for entrepreneurship, through helping create venture capital, but also through restructuring welfare systems to give security when entrepreneurial ventures go wrong – for example, by giving people the option to be taxed on a two- or three-year cycle rather than only annually.[36]
>
> [...]The public sector can . . . provide resources that can help enterprises to flourish and without which joint projects may fail.[37]

Giddens has squared the circle. The inner secret of social democracy is revealed: properly understood, it is functional for wealth creation. For capitalists, welfare is the redistribution of real resources. For the working class, on the other hand, self-help is the new welfare.

The politics of *The Third Way*

At the start of *The Third Way and its Critics,* Giddens endorses the 'new progressivism' of the US Democratic Party, praising the Clinton agenda of fiscal discipline, healthcare reform, investment in education and training, welfare-to-work schemes, urban renewal programmes, a hard line on crime and punishment and active interventionism on the international scene.[38] He then cites approvingly the Blair–Schröder argument that 'the essential function of markets must be complemented and improved by political action, not hampered by it'.[39]

As the last sentence suggests, what is proposed is not an agenda of passive submission to market forces. Nor does it recommend that the State should be the instrument of the large corporations, or of industrial or financial capital. It is a call for the State to exercise a degree of autonomy, over capitalists and workers alike, in order to ensure as best it can that all act in ways compatible with the logic of capitalist accumulation. The State is to be reconstructed as a regulator and a support for markets, as, left to themselves, they breed crisis and instability. The claim that '[t]hird way politics is not a continuation of neoliberalism, but an alternative political philosophy to it' depends on the assertion that 'the neoliberal idea that markets should almost everywhere stand in place of public goods is ridiculous'.[40] But this is only half right – the idea is ridiculous, but it is *not* neo-liberal. To think that it is confuses neo-liberalism with *laissez-faire* liberalism, and overlooks the neo-liberal call for a strong State selectively engaged in a new set of active policies aiming to create a framework within which markets can flourish – exactly the position Giddens adopts. He goes on to argue, energetically and consistently, that governments today must work with the market, not against it:

> The left has to get comfortable with markets, with the role of business in the creation of wealth, and the fact that private capital is essential for social investment.[41]

> [... But] markets [cannot] nurture the human capital they themselves require –
> government, families and communities have to do so. Market economies generate
> externalities, whose social implications have to be dealt with by other means.
> Environmental damage, for instance, can't be dealt with purely by market mecha-
> nisms.[42]
>
> [...] Government must play a basic role in sustaining the social and civic frame-
> works upon which markets actually depend.[43]

This perspective leads naturally to the already familiar contrast between the old
politics and the new:

> Old-style social democracy concentrated on industrial policy and Keynesian
> demand measures, while the neoliberals focused on deregulation and market liber-
> alization. Third way economic policy needs to concern itself with different prior-
> ities – with education, incentives, entrepreneurial culture, flexibility, devolution
> and the cultivation of social capital. Third way thinking emphasizes that a strong
> economy presumes a strong society, but doesn't see this connection as coming from
> old-style interventionism. The aim of macroeconomic policy is to keep inflation
> low, limit government borrowing, and use active supply-side measures to foster
> growth and high levels of employment.[44]

Following this, Giddens argues that 'the key force in human capital development obviously has to be education'; that 'product, capital and labour markets
must all be flexible for an economy today to be competitive'; that 'third-sector
groups can offer choice and responsiveness in the delivery of public services'; and
that 'social democrats should continue to move away from heavy reliance on
taxes that might inhibit effort or enterprise, including income and corporate
taxes'.[45] He then calls at the global level for: 'the development of appropriate reg-
ulations providing for surveillance of financial transactions'; the extension of
IMF functions in the short term pending the creation of a global central bank; a
'global war on poverty' subject to internal reform in poor countries and the
adoption of 'domestically sound social and economic policies'; the enforcement
of competition policies nationally and internationally and encouragement to
'corporations and unions to work together on economic restructuring in the face
of technological change'.[46]

This is precisely the agenda that has been promoted by the World Bank since
1990. The *World Development Report 1990: Poverty*, promoted 'investment in
people', an improved climate for enterprise, the opening of economies to trade
and investment and 'getting macroeconomic policy right'. It called for common
action to preserve the world's environment and a war on poverty, accompanied
by debt relief for middle- and low-income countries that would pursue recommended domestic reforms. The following year's *Report* set out with absolute
clarity exactly the position adopted by Giddens:

> A central issue in development, and the principal theme of this Report, is the inter-
> action between governments and markets. This is not a question of intervention
> versus laissez-faire – a popular dichotomy, but a false one. Competitive markets are
> the best way yet found for efficiently organizing the production and distribution of

goods and services. Domestic and external competition provides the incentives that unleash entrepreneurship and technological progress. But markets cannot operate in a vacuum – they require a legal and regulatory framework that only governments can provide. And, at many other tasks, markets sometimes prove inadequate or fail altogether. That is why governments must, for example, invest in infrastructure and provide essential services to the poor. It is not a question of state or market: each has a large and irreplaceable role.[47]

The antecedents of Giddens's *Third Way* are here rather than in the social democratic tradition. It reflects the 'second-phase' neo-liberal approach which moves on from initial short-term 'shock treatment', aimed at dismantling structures hostile to the operation of markets, to the construction for the longer term of enduring institutions which will sustain markets and capitalist disciplines into the future. It is not surprising, then, that the policies Giddens recommends can all be found in subsequent *World Development Reports* through to 2002, and in programmes developed by the World Bank jointly with the IMF since the late 1990s. These place the same emphases on the protection of the environment, the importance of education and the knowledge economy, the need to discipline capitalists and workers alike, and to develop civil society and the role of 'third-sector' actors in the provision of local services.[48] Giddens's original contribution to this agenda – taken up zealously by Tony Blair and Gordon Brown since New Labour came to power – has been to dress it up in the language of social democracy in an effort to broaden its appeal. As we have seen, *The Third Way* systematically redefines social democratic values in order to give them neo-liberal content. Casting himself in the role of Blair's Minister of Truth, Giddens offers New Labour a set of slogans tailored to the needs of the age: individualism is solidarity; responsibility is emancipation; risk is security; enterprise is community; opportunity is redistribution; inclusion is equality; self-help is welfare. It obviously won't do to pass this off as renewed social democracy.

Notes

1 Giddens 1998: 45.
2 *Ibid.*, pp. 65–6.
3 *Ibid.*, p. 1.
4 *Ibid.*, pp. 1–2.
5 *Ibid.*, p. 45.
6 *Ibid.*, pp. 3–4.
7 *Ibid.*, p. 11.
8 *Ibid.*, p. 16.
9 *Ibid.*, p. 24.
10 *Ibid.*, pp. 43–4.
11 *Ibid.*, p. 35.
12 *Ibid.*, pp. 35–6.
13 *Ibid.*, p. 37.

14 *Ibid.*, p. 34.
15 *Ibid.*, p. 37.
16 *Ibid.*, p. 41.
17 *Ibid.*, p. 44.
18 *Ibid.*
19 *Ibid.*, p. 65.
20 *Ibid.*, pp. 62–3.
21 *Ibid.*, pp. 63–4.
22 *Ibid.*, p. 100.
23 *Ibid.*, p. 79.
24 *Ibid.*, p. 82.
25 *Ibid.*, pp. 83, 88.
26 *Ibid.*, p. 70.
27 *Ibid.*, pp. 99, 100.
28 *Ibid.*, pp. 100–1.
29 *Ibid.*, p. 100.
30 *Ibid.*, p. 102.
31 *Ibid.*, p. 125.
32 *Ibid.* (emphasis added).
33 *Ibid.*, p. 117.
34 *Ibid.*, p. 65.
35 *Ibid.*, p. 122.
36 *Ibid.*, p. 124.
37 *Ibid.*, p. 125.
38 Giddens 2000: 3.
39 *Ibid.*, p. 6, quoting Blair and Schröder 1999.
40 Giddens 2000: 32.
41 *Ibid.*, p. 34.
42 *Ibid.*, p. 36.
43 *Ibid.*, p. 38.
44 *Ibid.*, p. 73.
45 *Ibid.*, pp. 73, 75, 81, and 100.
46 *Ibid.*, pp. 126, 127, 129, 131, 143, and 150.
47 World Bank 1991: 1.
48 See Cammack 2002.

References

Blair, T. and Schröder, G. (1999) *Europe: The Third Way/Die Neue mitte*, London, Labour Party and SPD.
Cammack, P. (2002) 'Attacking the poor', *New Left Review*, 2(13).
Giddens, A. (1998) *The Third Way: The Renewal of Social Democracy*, Oxford, Polity Press.
Giddens, A. (2000) *The Third Way and its Critics*, Oxford, Polity Press.
Work Bank (1990) *World Development Report 1990: Poverty*, Washington, DC, World Bank.
World Bank (1991) *World Development Report 1991: The Challenge of Development*, Washington, DC, World Bank.

9 David Morrison

New Labour, citizenship and the discourse of the Third Way

In this chapter I analyse the content and evaluate the significance of the discourse of 'the Third Way', disseminated by the New Labour Government. I argue that the Third Way is a brand name that may well be transient. However, while the label may be transient, the content of Third Way discourse does contain substance, much of which predated the use of the term 'Third Way' by several years. At the heart of New Labour's Third Way is the claim that economic efficiency and social justice can be symbiotic. I argue that the articulation of a particular concept of citizenship is a crucial element of the framework that New Labour believes is necessary in order to achieve this. This argument is supported by evidence drawn from a discursive analysis of various New Labour texts that utilises a method of critical discourse analysis adapted from the work of Fairclough and of Laclau and Mouffe.[1] Furthermore I argue that this particular concept of citizenship is inherently exclusionary in its operationalisation within policy. These exclusionary effects can be seen in New Labour's operationalisation of their particular discourse of citizenship in the New Deal programme for the unemployed.

The temporary embrace of stakeholding

The utilisation of the concept of the 'Third Way' by New Labour is arguably largely a political marketing strategy. Its primary purpose is to differentiate the ideology of New Labour from that of its opponents. These opponents are the Old Left within the Labour Party and the New Right, who comprise the first and second ways, respectively.[2] The 'Third Way' was not the first big idea to be utilised by New Labour in this manner. During the early months of 1996 the predominant label utilised by New Labour was that of 'stakeholding'.[3] Tony Blair embraced the idea of stakeholding in a speech in Singapore in January 1996.[4] It proceeded to feature in New Labour's public discourse throughout the early part of that year. However by the start of the following year, the stakeholding theme had largely been dropped.

The appeal of stakeholding to New Labour was that it could signal a new political project, but be ambivalent with regard to that project's policy content. Thus stakeholding could act as a discursive umbrella for New Labour's particular policy content. The problem with this approach was that Will Hutton had already established in his book *The State We're In*[5] a series of policies derived from the notion of stakeholding. Hutton also wrote articles for the *Guardian* newspaper which exposed his thinking to an audience made up largely of Labour voters. Hutton's policy programme contained a higher level of wealth redistribution and greater regulation of capitalism than New Labour was prepared to embrace. Attempts were made to mark out a different form of stakeholding based on the changing of cultural attitudes rather than by a regulatory approach.[6] However, these attempts had little to say with regard to policy and failed to have any significant impact within the arena of political discourse.

The emergence of the Third Way: Giddens and Blair

By the time of the 1997 general election, the public had not really identified New Labour with a big idea. New Labour fought the election using a discourse that stressed its newness and its claims to pragmatism and trustworthiness, which were discursively contrasted with the outdated dogma and sleaze of the Conservatives. While this was a discourse that could be effective for winning an election from a position of opposition against an unpopular government, it was unlikely to be a discourse that would maintain popular support for a government over several elections. It was from this background, of the transition from opposition to government, that the articulation of a 'Third Way' emerged in 1998.

There were two publications that marked the emergence of a 'Third Way' discourse: *The Third Way: The Renewal of Social Democracy*, by Anthony Giddens of the London School of Economics, and *The Third Way: New Politics for the New Century*, by Tony Blair.[7] Both publications were given considerable media coverage, with exposure being particularly given to the personal links between the two authors. For example, coverage was given to the flight to New York that the two shared to attend a seminar on the Third Way organised by Hillary Clinton. The cover of Giddens's book claims that Giddens is 'allegedly Tony Blair's favourite intellectual'.[8] There is mutual advantage in this claim. Giddens is posited as an intellectual who is close to and influential with the Government, while Blair has the advantage of being able to claim intellectual support from the academy for his own position.

Giddens's book has the advantage for New Labour of being rather abstract, with few policy prescriptions. There is not the space here to detail Giddens's account of the Third Way.[9] However, there are themes within Giddens's book which coincide with New Labour's thinking and which are worth highlighting. A key theme is the rejection of Old Left and New Right positions, hence a *Third Way*. Another is an account of a society undergoing change through the pressures of globalisation. A third is a call for the renewal of civic society. A fourth is the belief that welfare should deliver opportunities. Giddens also uses the alliterative slogan 'No rights without responsibilities',[10] which has been utilised in New Labour's public discourse. Giddens's approach is underpinned by what he describes as 'philosophic conservatism', which, he explains, is a commitment to modernisation in order to pursue a pragmatic programme that can cope in a world which is 'beyond tradition' and which requires new responsibilities to meet the demands of new risks.[11]

However, there are elements of Giddens's account that are lacking in Blair's. One is Giddens's stress on the importance of equality. He argues that '[a] democratic society that generates large-scale inequality is likely to produce widespread disaffection and conflict'.[12] Giddens argues that promoting equality means more than merely promoting equality of opportunity[13] and that equality should be seen as inclusiveness.[14] He explains: 'Inclusion in its broadest sense refers to citizenship, to the civil and political rights and obligations that all members of a society should have not just formally but as a reality of their lives.'[15] It is notable that Giddens does not mention the social rights that were once seen as integral to post-war social democracy. In contrast, Blair's account of the Third Way barely mentions equality. Instead it offers 'opportunity', with but a single reference to 'equal worth'.[16] Gordon Brown, who argued that in the context of the 1990s equality meant equality of opportunity and not equality of outcome, made clear the meaning of equality for New Labour.[17]

Giddens stresses the dangers of social exclusion, a concern shared by New Labour; hence the setting up of the Social Exclusion Unit. However, New Labour only emphasises the exclusion of those at the margins of society. Therefore its social and economic policies for tackling social exclusion are aimed at these marginalised groups. In contrast, Giddens argues that exclusion takes place both at the bottom and the top of society. The top of society is prone to voluntary exclusion, described by Giddens as 'the revolt of the elites'.[18] Giddens argues for both a revival of civic liberalism and sustained levels of welfare spending that benefit most of the population, in order to limit the exclusion of those at the top and at the bottom of society.[19]

So, to what extent has New Labour been influenced by Anthony Giddens? It is arguable that the answer to this question is 'very little'. Matthew Taylor of the Institute of Public Policy Research (IPPR) argues that an intellectual can really be said to influence a political organisation only when the whole framework of that intellectual's approach is adopted by the organisation.[20] It is clear from the above analysis that this is not the case with regard to the influence of Giddens on New Labour. Giddens's work has been utilised by Blair as support from a prominent member of the academy for positions that Blair had already established, rather than being an influence shaping new approaches. Consequently, only those elements of Giddens's approach that already coincided with Blair's thinking have been included in Blair's version of the Third Way.

New Labour's discourse of citizenship

If, as I am claiming here, the use of the label 'the Third Way' is little more than a potentially transient political marketing strategy, how can we best characterise the actual substance that is mobilised by New Labour under the brand name 'the Third Way'? A valuable approach to answering this question is to apply a method of discourse analysis to New Labour texts. This has the advantage of identifying both New Labour's discursive strategies and those strategies' development and consistency. The application here of a method of discourse analysis adapted from that constructed by Norman Fairclough identifies a specific discourse that is both explicitly and tacitly articulated within a wide range of New Labour texts.[21] My argument is that this discourse is based on a particular concept of *citizenship* that was first clearly articulated by Tony Blair in 1993, and which has remained a remarkably consistent, albeit developed, discourse within New Labour texts ever since.[22] This discourse was a central element of the substance of New Labour's temporary embracing of stakeholding and is a central element of the substance of its current embracing of the Third Way. Thus, during the 1990s it was the labels of New Labour's philosophy that changed rather than the fundamentals of that philosophy.

In 1993 Blair, while shadow home secretary, wrote an article for *Renewal*, a journal that has always been close to the New Labour modernisers. The article, entitled 'Why modernisation matters',[23] was in effect a rallying call for the modernising faction of the Labour Party, at a time when the modernisers in the party had temporarily lost momentum.[24] In this article, Blair claims that both the Old Left and the New Right have failed, and that the pace of change in the modern world demands a new approach to tackle social fragmentation. Thus the idea of a 'first' and 'second' way that have failed, necessitating a Third Way, is implicit in this article – five years before the public embracing of the Third Way in 1998.

All the main themes found in Blair's and Giddens's accounts of 'the Third Way' can be found also, at least in rudimentary form, in this 1993 article. Those themes are: the failure of Left and Right, globalisation, social exclusion, and an idea of citizenship in which responsibilities and community are emphasised. At the centre of the new approach suggested in this article is the articulation of a new conception of citizenship. Blair argues: 'Rebuilding Britain as a strong community, with a modern notion of citizenship at its heart, is the political objective for the new age. Labour must transform itself into a credible vehicle for achieving it.'[25] The terms 'at its heart' and 'political objective for the new age' emphasise the importance and relevance of 'a modern notion of citizenship'. The sentence 'Labour must transform itself into a credible vehicle for achieving it' indicates a very strong commitment by Blair to creating this effective notion of citizenship and the percieved need to transform the Labour Party in order to achieve that end; hence the need for modernisation. The phrase 'for the new age' is of crucial importance as it creates a sense of a changing world that makes new demands that have to be met with new requirements. This sense

is enhanced elsewhere in the article by the statement: 'What is required today is
to define a new relationship between citizen and community for the modern
world.'[26] This discursive sense of a changing world is initiated in the phrase that
informs the reader of 'what is required today'. The phrases utilised here are presuppositions[27] in that they presuppose a modern world or new age that has the
requirements of a strong community and a modern notion of citizenship. It is
also notable that the phrases 'modern world' and 'new age' are, within this discourse, nominalisations: they are in effect posited as actors that demand
requirements from specific societies.[28] The agency of the members of a society
to be able to formulate their own requirements is absented. The phrases 'new
relationship' and 'modern notion' indicate that this notion of citizenship constitutes a break with previous ones. This modern notion of citizenship is posited
as a requirement in order to meet the demands of the modern world.

New Labour utilises a number of phrases such as the 'modern world', the
'new age', the 'changing world', 'new times' and the 'global economy' to construct a context for the necessity of a new approach with a modern notion of citizenship at its heart.[29] This context is presented as a given fact, disguising the
neo-liberal presuppositions on which it is predicated; for example, the limitations of the nation state, the inevitability of capitalist deregulation, flexible
labour markets and privatisation.[30] The 'modern world', or 'global economy', is
presented as a reality and is posited as the central process that necessitates the
development of a new notion of citizenship.[31] This has two notable effects.
Firstly, the responsibility of managing global economic change is partially
shifted from being a governmental responsibility to being the obligation of a
responsible citizenry.[32] Secondly, citizenship is articulated as inextricably linked
to economic requirements. Inclusion into citizenship becomes, in practice, the
fulfilment of the obligation to participate in both labour and consumer markets,
in order to enable Britain to compete as a nation within the global economy.

This notion of citizenship is defined in these terms:

> A modern notion of citizenship gives rights but demands obligations, shows
> respect but wants it back, grants opportunity but insists on responsibilities. So the
> purpose of economic and social policy should be to extend opportunity, remove the
> underlying causes of social alienation, but it should also take tough measures to
> ensure that chances that are given are taken up.[33]

The first phrase of this passage begins the process of decontesting citizenship as
a concept. By positing '*a* modern notion' – in the singular – of citizenship, the
statement absents other, potentially competing, conceptions of citizenship. It
does not define the rights that are to be given and what obligations are being
demanded. However, the use of 'demands' signals that whatever these obligations are, they are to be taken seriously. It is an example of a discourse of tough
authority, which also surfaces in the statement in the forms 'insists', 'takes tough
measures', and 'to ensure that chances that are given are taken up'. The implication is that previous notions of citizenship have lacked this toughness.

The idea of 'opportunity' is included within this 'modern notion of citizenship' and is grouped along with rights and respect as the elements given by this new notion. In contrast, obligations, respect and responsibilities are grouped together as the elements demanded by the new notion. The linking of 'rights' and 'opportunities' allows slippage between these two terms. This is not in itself new. T. H. Marshall's concept of citizenship implicitly linked rights and opportunities, in that the establishing of social rights was seen as the means of guaranteeing opportunity by alleviating poverty and disadvantage.[34] Within Blair's notion of citizenship, opportunity is not something that is necessarily created via the establishing of social rights. It is open to the idea that opportunities can function in place of social rights. This slippage, of opportunities replacing social rights, can be seen in the New Deal policy under which universal unemployment benefit is replaced by benefit that is conditional on the uptake of one of the opportunities offered. Thus the principle of ensuring that chances that are given are taken up is embedded within the New Deal policy.

During 1995 there was an important development in Blair's articulation of a concept of citizenship. This development concerns the relationship between the notions of *rights* and *responsibilities*. In the 1993 articulation of citizenship the implied relationship between these two elements was one of balance. Duties/obligations were stressed as an element that had previously been neglected, leading to an imbalance in favour of rights. In Blair's *Spectator* lecture, in March 1995, this relationship of balance was replaced with one of hierarchy. This is most clearly seen in the statement: 'The rights we receive should reflect the duties we owe.'[35] The key word in this statement is the seemingly innocuous 'reflect', as it is this word that indicates the shift from a relationship of balance to a relationship of hierarchy. A reflection is a copy of an original. The existence of the original manifestation is prior to and conditions the existence of the reflection. Therefore in this case, it is the existence of duties that is both prior to and conditions the existence of rights. Duties come above rights in a relationship of hierarchy. Rights no longer have a status in which they are justified by their own inherent value. Instead their justification is determined by the need and capability to perform duties. Rights are given so that duties can be performed. This is not an overestimation of the significance of the word 'reflect'. Consider this statement from the same speech: 'Duty is the cornerstone of society. It recognises more than self. It defines the context in which rights are given.'[36] It is made explicit that the context in which rights are given is defined by duty, which is implicitly posited as the first priority of citizenship.

This new – hierarchical – notion of citizenship was institutionalised in the new Clause 4 of the Labour Party's Constitution in April 1995. Close attention is often rightly paid to Labour's embrace of the 'dynamic market economy' within this clause. Less attention is paid to the phrase found in the first article of the clause: 'where the rights we enjoy reflect the duties we owe'.[37] The key word is again 'reflect', although the phrase is more appealingly packaged, with the word 'receive' in the earlier articulation being replaced by 'enjoy'. Thus the prioritisation of duties over rights was embedded in the founding statement of New Labour's values, which the new Clause 4 undoubtedly represents.

It could be argued that the above analysis demonstrates merely that Blair and New Labour passed through a phase in which citizenship was articulated as a key concept. However an analysis of later New Labour texts indicates that, while the influence of a modern notion of citizenship is rarely explicitly referred to, the discourse of citizenship established in this earlier phase is notable in these texts. Consider these examples drawn from a speech delivered by Blair at Southwark Cathedral in 1996, during the 'stakeholding' period:

> Above all, however, we must create a society based on a notion of mutual rights and responsibilities …We accept our duty as a society to give each person a stake in its future. And in return each person accepts responsibility to respond, to work to improve themselves.[38]

Although citizenship is not articulated in these statements, a discourse of citizenship is clearly present, as it is in these examples taken from the 1997 Labour Party general election manifesto: 'New parental responsibility orders will make parents face up to their responsibility for their children's misbehaviour';[39] and 'The unemployed have a responsibility to take up the opportunity of training places or work.'[40] These statements also indicate the intention of New Labour that this discourse of citizenship be operationalised within specific policies.

The Third Way and New Labour's discourse of citizenship

This discourse of citizenship is also present in Blair's account of the Third Way. Again the phrase 'the rights we enjoy reflect the duties we owe' is utilised within the text, invoking the subordination of rights to responsibilities.[41] Responsibility is a key theme that enjoys its own subsection and is repeatedly utilised throughout the text. Consider these examples:

> For too long the demand for rights from the state was separated from the duties of citizenship and the imperative for mutual responsibility [...] Strong communities depend on shared values and a recognition of the rights and duties of citizenship – not just the duty to pay taxes and obey the law, but the obligation to bring up children as competent, responsible citizens.[42]

Blair's account of the Third Way contains no fewer than thirty-five instances of the concepts of responsibility, duty and obligation. In contrast there are only ten instances of the concept of rights. There are eight instances in which rights and responsibilities are collocated as concepts (this technique also has alliterative value) of which five refer to rights and responsibilities going together and three stress increased responsibilities as a response to the perceived previous excessive emphasis on rights (for example, consider the first sentence in the above axtract). There are only two instances within the text of the concept of rights standing alone, whereas there are twenty-seven instances of the concepts of responsibility, duty or obligation standing alone. However, this apparent imbalance of repetitive use between rights and responsibilities has not yet taken account of the usage of a concept of opportunity. That concept appears twenty times in this text, of which fifteen instances utilise opportunity where the concept of rights *could* have been utilised instead, indicating a tendency to replace the concept of rights with that of opportunity.[43] Consider this statement which summarises the core values of Blair's Third Way: 'Our mission is to promote and reconcile the four values which are essential to a just society which maximise the freedom and potential of all our people – equal worth, opportunity for all, responsibility and community.'[44] There are no *rights* in this mission statement: instead, responsibility is balanced by opportunity.[45] Equality is reduced to the classical liberal concept of equal worth and the slippery concept of community is invoked.[46] There is also the presupposition that these are indeed the values that are essential for a just society.

It is not being claimed here that the substance of Blair's Third Way consists only of a particular articulation of citizenship. The big idea at its heart is the belief that economic efficiency and social justice go together and have wrongly been considered as antagonistic in the past.[47] This belief is articulated in Blair's *Third Way* and is widely articulated across New Labour's public discourse. My own study of 100 textual examples of New Labour's public discourse reveals that in 83 per cent of these texts the idea of social justice and economic efficiency going together is at least implicit.[48] In 34 per cent the same idea has a high salience in that it is a central theme of the text. The idea that past antagonisms can be transcended is a key feature of Blair's Third Way. Underlying this idea is a belief that there can be a fully consensual society,[49] and this becomes explicit in New Labour's articulation of the 'shared values' that are established in 'strong communities'. The possibilty of shared values is dependent on the reality of a fully consensual society without underlying antagonisms.[50] This is a very idealistic perspective, which implicitly denies other values formed within different perspectives. It is inevitable that the operationalisation of 'shared values' will identify certain values as normative and therefore prove exclusionary for some – non-conformist and marginal – individuals and groups.[51] The operationalisation of a normative concept of citizenship inevitably results in distinctions between *good* and *bad* citizens. The latter are invariably found among the poor and the marginalised: for example, single mothers, young unemployed men, travellers and the homeless. The wealthy who avoid taxes and pay low wages are rarely highlighted for their lack of responsibility.[52]

New Labour's belief in a consensual society is expressed in its confidence in the potential of 'partnership' – the term is utilised eighteen times in Blair's *Third Way* and twenty-three times in the 1997 Labour Party general election manifesto. Partnership is posited as the mechanism by which national renewal can be achieved. As such, it is explicitly presented and also nominalised as a panacea which can overcome previous antagonisms at all levels of society: for example, between public and private sectors, or parents and schools. Such a wide application of the concept of partnership presupposes that there can always be shared objectives derived from shared values.

The same presupposition informs New Labour's concept of *community*, which is usually presented in the singular and is invoked as the source of 'shared values'.[53] Community is rarely defined clearly in New Labour texts. Marquand has noted that the term is used interchangeably in New Labour texts with 'society', 'nation', 'country' and 'people'.[54] The articulations of these terms lack analytical rigour, but they do invoke a broad sense of inclusiveness. 'Community' is utilised by New Labour as a floating signifier that acts as an overarching concept for developing consensus within the electorate, in that all of the electorate are members of at least one community. The implication is that Britain can function as a fully consensual society that shares the same set of values, which then operate as the basis for social rules and norms.[55] This is a highly modernist perspective, one which asserts that the appropriate social rules and norms can be correctly identified and universally applied, as this statement by Blair demonstrates: 'We understand the scale of change and are willing to organise our society to meet it. We recognise the need for a new moral purpose in politics and have the individual family and social values capable of sustaining it.'[56] The claim that accepted social rules might be identified and achieved is an ideological articulation that attempts to deny the inevitability of social and political antagonism. Therefore those who are antagonistic to New Labour's shared values are posited as irresponsible citizens who need to become better citizens or should be denied elements of citizenship. For example, a key New Labour 'shared value' is the work ethic, as seen in this statement by Gordon Brown: 'The task is to revitalise the work ethic in our society.'[57] Consequently there is no fifth option of remaining on benefit under the New Deal policy, a policy that attempts to operationalise New Labour's concept of citizenship by matching opportunities with the responsibilities of the good citizen. Either the social rights of citizenship have to be earned by the responsible taking up of one of the opportunities offered, or they are denied via the practice of sanctioning benefits.

In short, for New Labour, citizenship is not an automatic right; it is earned by the fulfilling of responsibilities. Therefore, inclusion in citizenship becomes a personal responsibility. This has the discursive effect of absenting structural social and economic barriers to full participation in society. Opportunities are consistently substituted for rights, thus increasing the conditionality of this notion of citizenship. Responsibility and duty are posited as the prime concern of citizenship, with rights and opportunities given in order that citizens are able dutifully to fulfil their responsibilities, as seen in the New Deal programme for the unemployed. The social rules and norms of the responsible, or good, citizen are claimed to be derived from shared values found in strong communities, thus introducing a strong normative content to New Labour's concept of responsibility.

The functions of citizenship in New Labour's Third Way

New Labour's Third Way is predicated on three key presuppositions. These are the presupposition, firstly, of a neo-liberal narrative of a changing world that demands adaptation; secondly, of a consensual society that can agree shared values and work in partnership; and, finally, of the failure of both the Old Left and the New Right, characterised respectively as the first and second ways, hence the required *Third Way*.[58] New Labour's articulation of its concept of citizenship is a crucial part of the party's response to the demands, or requirements, of these three presuppositions.

First, this concept of citizenship plays a large part in differentiating the Third Way from both the first and second ways. It could be argued that New Labour's embracing of the 'dynamic' market economy, its support for privatisation and its acceptance of the majority of the Conservative's trades union legislation already constitute a sufficient break with Old Labour, or the first way, to make unnecessary a new notion of citizenship. However, these breaks, while representing a rupture with Old Labour, represent also continuity with a New Right agenda. The particular value of New Labour's discourse of citizenship is that it represents a simultaneous break with both Old Labour and the New Right, or second way. Thus New Labour is able to differentiate itself further from Old Labour while avoiding the charge that it is merely embracing a New Right agenda.

It is this discourse of citizenship, with its particular articulation of community, inclusion, equality of opportunity and personal responsibility, that differentiates New Labour from the individualistic and purely market-based ethos of the new right. It is this discourse that offers a vision of social inclusion that can potentially appeal to centre-left academics, old Labour Party personnel and traditional Labour Party voters, alleviating the discomfort that many would feel at New Labour's embrace of a neo-liberal political economy.[59] It also allows an attempt to construct chains of equivalence across a wider range of social groups than the socialist discourse of Old Labour. For example, the absence of any socialist intertextuality in this discourse, along with its stress on personal responsibility, enables it to appeal to voters who have formerly voted Conservative out of fear of socialism. Therefore it is a discourse that can both substantiate New Labour's newness and have wide electoral appeal.

Second, responsible citizenship is presented as socially inclusive of all and therefore as the basis of a fully consensual society based on partnership. The presupposition that there can be a fully consensual society without antagonism and polarity posits the prospect of a society without sides, where there are only varying degrees of winning and no losing. New Labour advocates the view that such a consensual society can be created by socially responsible citizens taking up the opportunities offered, in order to fulfil obligations derived from shared values. The development of the good citizen is an ongoing long-term project aimed at creating strong communities and, therefore, social cohesion.[60] It could be argued that citizenship, for New Labour, is a moral crusade to sustain society, over the long term, against the fragmentation resulting from the amorality of market forces, which are accepted by New Labour as dynamic and beneficial.[61]

Third, responsible citizenship is linked to economic competence and the ability to compete in the global marketplace. If citizens act responsibly in taking up the opportunities to learn new skills and enhance present skills, then, it is claimed, the overall economic efficiency of the nation will be better equipped to compete in the global marketplace. In their proposal of a European Third Way, Blair and Gerhard Schröder argue: 'The most important task of modernisation is to invest in human capital: to make the individual and business fit for the knowledge-based economy of the future.'[62] With regard to citizenship it is significant that individuals are to be made fit for the supposed economy of the future. Citizens are to be equipped with the appropriate competences in order to meet the economic context that New Labour have discursively constructed via their discourse of globalisation. The second and third of the functions described above (social inclusion and economic competence) are crucial to New Labour's central aim of facilitating a symbiosis between social justice and economic efficiency. It is implied that it is precisely the operationalisation of a responsible citizenship – one that both observes the shared values of community, equal worth and opportunity and is competetive in labour markets – that can facilitate this symbiosis. In this regard, New Labour's operationalisation of citizenship, along with that of partnership, underpinned by a commitment to a neo-liberal political economy, represents the mechanisms by which social justice and economic efficiency can be made to reinforce each other.

The foregoing discursive analysis of New Labour's articulation of a concept of citizenship, and of its functions as a crucial pillar of the Third Way, elucidates the ideological characteristics of New Labour. It is Blair's claim that the Third Way stands for a modernised social democracy.[63] This claim does not seem viable in the light of the above analysis. New Labour has embraced a neo-liberal political economy by accepting the neo-liberal presuppositions of its perspective of globalisation.[64] New Labour has adopted a classical liberal concept of equal worth, rather than the socialist or social democratic concepts of equality of outcome or redistributive equality. It has adopted a modern liberal concept of opportunity for all, but even this, within Blair's Third Way, is separated from the concept of equal worth, and therefore only represents a commitment to providing *some* opportunity rather than *equality* of opportunity.

New Labour expresses a commitment to the fulfilling of duties and obligations that is reminiscent of civic republican approaches, although for the majority of citizens there has been no evidence of a civic republican commitment to increased participation in the political process, but only a partial commitment to citizen consultation. However, such an emphasis on personal responsibility without increased political participation is a feature of a number of American versions of capitalistic communitarianism. New Labour has had strong links with Etzioni's brand of communitarianism.[65] Etzioni and New Labour share an emphasis on the responsibilities of the citizen, a condemnation of excessive rights and a belief in a consensual society based on shared values found in strong communities; and both embrace the market economy while largely failing to identify the responsibilities of capitalist enterprise.[66] Thus the collectivist element of New Labour's Third Way that surfaces in the form of community is not a renewal of social democracy. Rather, it is a commitment to a British version of capitalistic communitarianism. Stephen Driver is therefore correct when he argues, as he does in chapter 2 of this book, that New Labour cannot be dismissed as merely Thatcherism Mark II. However, the difference between New Labour and Thatcherism stems not from the former's modernisation of social democratic principles, but from its adoption of a version of capitalistic communitarianism.[67] In short, New Labour combines a neo-liberal political economy with a communitarian social perspective. There is very little here that is recognisable as even a modernised social democracy, and certainly no trace of socialism.

The consumption of New Labour's discourse of citizenship and its prospects for the future

The distinction that New Labour articulates between the good, or deserving, citizen and the bad, or undeserving, citizen clearly has some resonance with the general public. The findings of the 1999 annual *British Social Attitudes* survey suggest that New Labour's emphasis upon the importance of imposing a work ethic with regard to welfare claimants has widespread public support, although the same survey also found that most respondents still believed that adequate welfare should be paid to those who become unemployed.[68] This would suggest that a significant part of the general public accept a distinction between those welfare claimants who are deserving because of their willingness to take up opportunities of work and training, and those who are undeserving on account either of their reluctance to work or their engagement in the 'black economy'. It is the latter group which is identified by New Labour as those who are 'other' and who represent a threat to the consensual achievements of the rest of society.

While the public appears broadly to support the principles of New Labour's operationalisation of citizenship in the New Deal policy, such support may not be so strong among the clients of welfare who are its targets. Geoff Mulgan, formerly a member of the No. 10 Policy Unit, states that independent survey evidence indicates that the majority of clients who have experienced the New Deal programme believe it to be broadly fair in its implementation.[69] However, my own research, carried out with the New Deal clients of a training provider contracted to the Employment Service in Swindon, indicates a high degree of dissatisfaction with the New Deal for the unemployed.[70] Out of fifty-three clients interviewed, all but one claimed that they were only taking part in the New Deal because they had been threatened with sanctions on their benefit payments. Clearly, within this particular case study, the element of compulsion, via the threat of benefit sanctions is the main method of recruitment to the New Deal programme. The use of compulsion also had the effect of creating resentment towards the New Deal policy among those particular clients. With two exceptions, these clients were not aware of the existence of a new conceptualisation of citizenship.[71] They were, however, familiar with many of the elements of New Labour's discourse of citizenship. In particular, many had become familiar with New Labour's use of the terms 'opportunity' and 'responsibility' though their experience of the New Deal programme,. Many of these New Deal clients expressed concern that they had experienced a greater emphasis on responsibility than on opportunity. Some clients complained of churning – that is, the constant recycling of claimants through training programmes and employment schemes. Others complained of being denied the information of which opportunities were actually available to them. Many felt that the New Deal policy was a 'window-dressing scheme', which may have political advantages for the New Labour Government but only made their own lives more difficult.

My research also involved interviewing various people employed to deliver the New Deal programme.[72] In general, these people had a much more positive view of the New Deal programme than did the clients. Although these individuals displayed little awareness of the utilisation of a particular discourse of citizenship within the New Deal programme, they were both very aware and generally supportive of the usage of the concepts of opportunity and responsibility, and had actually widely utilised these concepts themselves. Several of these individuals had a rather paternalistic attitude towards the delivery of the programme. These respondents considered the use of compulsion necessary in bringing opportunities to people who could not see those opportunities for themselves. References to 'tough love' and 'having to be cruel to be kind' were made by some as justification of the use of compulsion in the form of benefit sanctions.[73] In general, these New Deal providers displayed a relatively high degree of internalisation of elements of New Labour's discourse of citizenship as operationalised in the programme. This is in considerable contrast to the relatively high degree of resistance to this discourse and operationalisation that was displayed by the clients who were interviewed.

One provider, however, took rather a different perspective from the other providers.[74] He did not support the use of compulsion, claiming that it was undermining the attempt to establish a positive ethos among New Deal clients. He also suggested that the New Deal programme was having exclusionary effects, in two respects. First, the reluctance on the part of some clients to integrate with the disciplinary regime of the New Deal programme was resulting in their withdrawal and consequent sanctioning of their benefits.[75] Second, clients were entering the programme with raised expectations concerning their future. Some clients were finding their expectations to be realistic, but for others the experience of 'churning' prior to their eventual return to unemployment only frustrated their expectations, leading to considerable disappointment and even resentment. The interviews with the clients revealed that most of them *had* experienced such frustration, disappointment and resentment.

The future success of New Labour's hegemonic articulation of citizenship is uncertain. In May 2001 the party won a second general election, with another large majority, albeit on a very low turnout. Therefore its overall popularity among electors is still strong. However, many promises were made concerning the successful delivery of the symbiosis of economic efficiency and social justice during their second term. The successful operationalisation of New Labour's concept of citizenship is a crucial element of its project to combine economic efficiency and social justice. As such it provides rather shaky foundations for this project. While its discourse of citizenship has so far had a clear appeal to the general electorate, it appears from my own research to have considerably less appeal for some New Deal clients, who are the targets of the attempt to socially construct better citizens from among the ranks of the unemployed. Their resentment, frustration and, in some cases, exclusion will remain as a visible sign of the failure of the attempt to socially shape the good citizen.[76]

Ultimately, New Labour's discourse of citizenship faces a fundamental problem. It is a discourse which attempts to suture the social by articulating the particular as the universal.[77] This can be clearly seen in the articulation of supposedly shared values that are both found within and form the basis of strong communities. This perspective denies the possibility of social antagonism concerning these shared values. It is always particular values that are articulated as values which are universally shared. Consequently other values are either absented or marginalised. The holders of these other values represent the social antagonism that negates New Labour's claim to represent universal values. This social antagonism is always already there and as such performs a constant undermining of the credibility of New Labour's discourse of citizenship. Whether, or when, this process of undermining results in both a public and an elite rejection of the credibility of this discourse of citizenship is a question that only the unfolding of events over time can answer. However, a discourse of citizenship which emphasises a normative conception of responsibility above the holding of universal rights is particularly prone to rejection on the basis of its prescriptive content, and to the inevitable associated social antagonism associated with such a rejection.

Conclusion

This chapter has argued that 'the Third Way' is, for New Labour, primarily a convenient and possibly temporary brand name for their agenda. I have argued that 'stakeholding' also was utilised as a brand name for its agenda until it was dropped because of its policy implications. A crucial element of this agenda is New Labour's commitment to operationalising a particular concept of citizenship, one which has been articulated with considerable consistency since 1993. This discourse of citizenship has remained reasonably consistent through the stages of its development, while it is the public labels of New Labour's philosophy that have changed. From this perspective it can be seen that the Third Ways of Blair and Giddens did not emerge as simultaneous projects. Giddens's approach has been utilised by Blair only where it is already compatible with the philosophy that the prime minister has consistently developed since 1993. For Blair, it was only the name of the Third Way that was new in 1998, not the substance. It has been argued that this notion of citizenship is crucial in that it aids differentiation of the Third Way from the first and second ways, and is a key mechanism in the task of meeting the claimed challenges both of responding to globalisation and of developing a consensual society derived from shared values, thus combining the twin aims of economic efficiency and social justice.

New Labour's concept of citizenship is characterised by its prioritising of responsibilities above rights, with the latter largely replaced by opportunities. This concept is predicated on presuppositions that are drawn, in the economic sphere, from neo-liberalism and, in the social sphere, from capitalistic communitarianism, very little being drawn from socialist or social democratic perspectives. Consequently, New Labour's articulation of a concept of citizenship can be interpreted as an attempt to develop greater social cohesion within contemporary Britain while positively embracing the private sector and the market economy. It is part of an attempt to create a basic level of social justice while avoiding any elements of socialism. However, beyond the rhetoric, this discourse of citizenship indicates both an institutionalising of a normative and moralistic conception of the good citizen which simultaneously defines the identity of the bad citizen, and a shift in the responsibility for ensuring social justice away from both the government and the social sector to individual citizens themselves, but without an equivalent shift in the rights of political participation or economic power for those same citizens.

Notes

1 This method of critical discourse analysis uses techniques of textual analysis drawn from the work of Norman Fairclough, but applied within a post-structuralist theoretical framework drawn from the work of Ernesto Laclau and Chantal Mouffe. See Fairclough 1995 and Laclau and Mouffe 1985.
2 Blair 1999.
3 New Labour's embrace of stakeholding led to a flurry of academic interest; see e.g. Kelly, Kelly and Gamble 1997.
4 Blair 1996: 291.
5 Hutton 1996.
6 See e.g. Darling 1997; Metcalf 1996.
7 Giddens 1998; Blair 1998.
8 Giddens 1998: dust cover.
9 See the previous chapter, by Paul Cammack, for a detailed discursive analysis of Giddens's version of the Third Way.
10 Giddens 1998: 65.
11 *Ibid.*, p. 68.

12 *Ibid.*, p. 42.
13 *Ibid.*, p. 101.
14 See chapter 8, this book, for Paul Cammack's critical account of Giddens's interpretation of 'equality'.
15 Giddens 1998: 102.
16 Blair 1993: 3.
17 Levitas 1998: 134.
18 Giddens 1998: 103.
19 *Ibid.*, pp. 107–8.
20 Interview with Matthew Taylor, at the IPPR, 12 January 2000.
21 Fairclough 1995.
22 This is a very different argument from that of Finlayson (1999: 274) , who claims that New Labour only flirted with a new notion of citizenship.
23 Blair 1993.
24 This was during Smith's leadership of the party, which was seen by the modernisers as a time of stagnation; (see Gould 1998: 175–82.
25 Blair 1993: 11.
26 *Ibid.*, p. 4, reprinted in Blair 1996: 215.
27 Presuppositions are the taken for granted assumptions of a text, or the 'unsaid' of a text; that is, what it taken as a given and is already said elsewhere. Therefore it is the form in which a text is shaped and penetrated by elements of prior textual practice. Presuppositions are evidence of the presence of specific intertextualities. See Fairclough 1995: 4–6.
28 'Nominalisations' are processes that have been turned into noun-like terms (nominals), which can then function as participants in other processes. When a process in nominalised some or all of its participants are obscured. See Fairclough 1995: 110.
29 Fairclough 2000: 23–9: Fairclough considers New Labour's globalisation thesis to be a major discursive strategy in creating an apparently objective context of necessity. However, whilst Fairclough notes the presence of a discourse of rights and responsibilities, he does not identify a specific cohesive articulation of a concept of citizenship by New Labour.
30 Hay (1999: 30) argues that this set of prescriptions is presented as the only alternative available.
31 For a critical account of this globalisation thesis derived from persuasive if inconclusive empirical evidence, see Hirst 1999.
32 Freeden (1999: 42) offers a similar argument.
33 Blair 1993: 7.
34 Marshall 1950.
35 Blair 1996: 238.
36 *Ibid.*, p. 237.
37 The new Clause 4 of the Labour Party Constitution.
38 Blair 1996: 298.
39 Labour Party 1997: 23.
40 *Ibid.*, p. 19.
41 Blair 1998: 4.
42 *Ibid.*, pp. 4 and 12.
43 Gordon Brown in particular utilises a discourse of opportunity rather then a discourse of rights. For example, in his speech to the East London Partnership, in

February 2000, Brown referred to opportunities twenty four times without once referring to rights.

44 Blair 1998: 3.

45 White (1998: 17–30) notes that the concepts of opportunity and responsibility are centre stage in what he terms a recent attempt to articulate a Centre-Left philosophy of government, but he does not connect this to an articulation of citizenship.

46 In chapter 6 of this book Eunice Goes demonstrates that the term 'community' has been used in divergent ways by various New Labour personnel.

47 Blair 1998: 1.

48 These 100 texts were articulated by a range of New Labour authors over the period from 1993 to 2000, and were disseminated in media including Labour movement journals, broadsheets, tabloids, television appearances and speeches (drawn from relevant websites).

49 Fairclough (2000: 44–5) draws a similar interpretation and argues that New Labour implicitly claim to be able to reconcile irreconcilables.

50 Hall (1998) argues that New Labour's Third Way suggests that there are no longer any conflicting interests that cannot be reconciled, and therefore envisages a politics without adversaries. It is arguable that it was this belief that left New Labour so unprepared to deal with the fuel protests of September 2000, and that their belief in the absence of adversaries resulted in them being unable to see the adversaries who were organising against them.

51 It is inevitable due to the impossibility of a fully sutured society. Any discursive construction of a reality of shared values can never have an unmediated relation with the real. Such a construction will always be particular rather than universal and will therefore always be antagonistic to other particular accounts of shared values. See Laclau and Mouffe 1985.

52 Matthew Taylor of the IPPR expressed in interview (12 January 2000) concern that New Labour's discourse of responsibility appeared to be targeted at those at the bottom of society rather than those at the top.

53 Blair 1998: 12.

54 Interview with David Marquand, Mansfield College, Oxford, 18 January 2000.

55 Blair 1995: 11.

56 *Ibid.*

57 Brown 1998.

58 The 'Old Left' refers to the Keynesian egalitarian social democrats of the post war period. The 'New Right' refers to Thatcherite conservatism underpinned by neo-liberalism; see Driver and Martell 2000.

59 Many of the commentators in the Nexus Online Third Way Debate who demonstrate guarded support for New Labour, dwell on these particular concepts in their discussion; notably, Julian LeGrand, David Halpern, Stuart White and John Browning; see Halpern and Mikosz 1998.

60 In this regard, New Labour's discourse of citizenship can be seen as an attempt to constitute new political subjects.

61 Blair 1998: 7.

62 Blair and Schröder 1999.

63 Blair 1998: 1. Giddens subtitles his own version of the Third Way 'The renewal of social democracy'. Giddens may have a stronger claim in that he does demonstrate a commitment to equality that is greater than just equality of opportunity.

64 For a detailed account of the neo-liberal character of New Labour's political economy, see Hay 1999.
65 Etzioni 1993. Both Blair and Gordon Brown were introduced to the ideas of Etzioni by Elaine Kamark, who was a special advisor to President Clinton; see Sopel 1993: 145.
66 For a detailed analysis of the similarities and differences between New Labour's agenda and various communitarian theorists see chapter 8 of this volume.
67 See chapter 3 of this collection, in which Steven Driver offers what is ultimately a defence of New Labour's claim to be modernising social democratic principles.
68 National Centre for Social Research 1999; Riddell 1999.
69 Interview with Geoff Mulgan, held at 10 Downing Steet, London, 22 March 2000.
70 These interviews were carried out in groups at a training centre run by Taurus, under contract to the Employment Service, between the Autumn of 2000 and the Summer of 2001. All interviewees were guaranteed anonymity.
71 The two exceptions were particularly articulate clients who were well read. Both were critical of New Labour's conception of citizenship and both expressed great reluctance regarding working within capitalist labour markets.
72 This involved interviewing nine individuals who were employed by the Employment Service and other organisations associated with the delivery of the New Deal programme. These interviews took place between late 1999 and the summer of 2001 in Bristol, Reading, Swindon and London. Again all interviewees were guaranteed anonymity.
73 These phrases were articulated by Employment Service Job Centre business managers in Reading and Bristol.
74 This individual, interviewed during the summer of 2000, was working for a New Deal provider in the Swindon area.
75 Between January 1998 and June 1999, 40,000 individuals dropped out of the New Deal programme. The destination of many of these individuals is unknown; see *Times* 1999.
76 See chapter 2 of this book, in which Stephen Driver offers a more positive account of the effects of the implementation of the New Deal policy.
77 The 'suturing of the social' is a Lacanian concept that describes the attempt of particular discourses to present themselves as being universally applicable; see Laclau and Mouffe 1985.

References

Blair, T. (1993) 'Why modernisation matters', *Renewal*, 1(4).
Blair, T. (1995) 'Power for a purpose', *Renewal*, 3(4).
Blair, T. (1996) *New Britain: My Vision of a Young Country*, London, Fourth Estate.
Blair, T. (1998) *The Third Way: New Politics for the New Century*, London, Fabian Society.
Blair, T. and Schröder, G. (1999) *Europe: The Third Way/Die Neue mitte*, available online: www.labour.org.uk/views/items/00000053.html.
Brown, G. (1998) Speech to News International Conference, Sun Valley, Idaho, 17 July.
Brown, G. (2000) Speech to the East London Partnership, Newham, 29 February.
Darling, A. (1997) 'A political perspective', in G. Kelly, D. Kelly and A. Gamble (eds) *Stakeholder Capitalism*, London, Macmillan.

Driver, S. and Martell, L. (2000) 'Left, Right and the third way', *Policy and Politics*, 28(2).

Etzioni, A. (1993) *The Spirit of Community: Rights, Responsibilities and the Communitarian Agenda*, London, Fontana.

Fairclough, N. (1995) *Critical Discourse Analysis: The Critical Study of Language*, Harlow, Longman.

Fairclough, N. (2000) *New Labour, New Language?*, London, Routledge.

Finlayson, A. (1999) 'Third way theory', *Political Quarterly*, 70(3).

Freeden, M. (1999) 'The ideology of New Labour', *Political Quarterly*, 70(1).

Giddens, A. (1998) *The Third Way: The Renewal of Social Democracy*, Oxford, Polity Press.

Gould, P. (1998) *The Unfinished Revolution: How the Modernisers Saved the Labour Party*, London, Abacus.

Hall, S. (1998) 'The great moving nowhere show', *Marxism Today*, November–December.

Halpern, D. and Mikosz, D. (eds) (1998) *The Third Way: Summary of the NEXUS Online Discussion*, London, NEXUS.

Hay, C. (1999) *The Political Economy of New Labour: Labouring Under False Pretences?*, Manchester, Manchester University Press.

Hirst, P. (1999) 'Has globalisation killed social democracy?', in A. Gamble and T. Wright, *The New Social Democracy*, Oxford, Blackwell.

Hutton, W. (1996) *The State We're In*, London, Vintage.

Kelly, G., Kelly, D. and Gamble, A. (eds) (1997) *Stakeholder Capitalism*, London, Macmillan.

Labour Party (1997) *New Labour: Leading Britain into the Future*, London, Labour Party.

Laclau, E. and Mouffe, C. (1985) *Hegemony and Socialist Strategy: Towards a Radical Democratic Politics*, London, Verso.

Levitas, R. (1998) *The Inclusive Society? Social Exclusion and New Labour*, London, Macmillan.

Marshall, T. H. (1950) *'Citizenship and Social Class' and Other Essays*, Cambridge, Cambridge University Press.

Metcalfe, P. (1996) 'Stakeholding versus corporatism', *Renewal*, 4(4).

National Centre for Social Research (1999) *British Social Attitudes*, London, National Centre for Social Research.

Riddell, P. (1999) 'Third way in search of a coherent idea', *The Times*, 30 November.

Sopel, J. (1995) *Tony Blair: The Moderniser*, London, Penguin.

The Times (1999) 'New Deal: is it working?', 22 June.

White, S. (1998) 'Interpreting the third way: not one road, but many', *Renewal*, 6(2).

10 Will Leggett

Criticism and the future of the Third Way

Introduction

It is ironic that the surest indication of the durability of the Third Way is the continuing attention paid to it by its critics. This collection has provided a flavour of the range of such criticism from different disciplinary, analytical and political perspectives. But what general conclusions can be drawn from contributions such as these as to the prospects for a successful critique of the Third Way and a reconstructed project for the (Centre) Left? This concluding chapter reviews existing critical strategies towards the Third Way, as illustrated by contributions to this volume. It divides the various criticisms from what are broadly the neo-Marxist and the social democratic Left into those which dismiss the Third Way as a 'smokescreen', with no substance in itself, and those which recognise that if it is to be critically engaged with the Third Way has to be taken seriously.

This overview reveals that, at present, the various critical approaches expose significant weaknesses, tensions and dangers in the Third Way project. However, critics representing both these perspectives are often too quick to dismiss outright some of the claims made by the Third Way as to the changing social and political terrain on which the 'actually existing' Centre-Left finds itself. It is suggested here that a productive critique of the Third Way should do three related things. First, it needs to take the Third Way seriously. To dismiss the Third Way as 'mere' spin, or simply a smokescreen for a more traditional agenda, is to misconceive it: the Third Way is a distinctive political project that draws on different political heritages in novel ways. Second, having acknowledged that the Third Way merits serious engagement, critics must recognise and attempt to understand the new landscape against which the Third Way claims to operate. The Third Way is a response to empirical shifts that have significant implications for constructing political strategies: the changes posited by the Third Way (such as globalisation) are not simply fabricated. However, the picture the Third Way paints of the world is not the only possible one. Too often third-wayers treat the dramatic social transformations they have identified as a fact of nature, rather than historical constructions that can be steered by purposeful political interventions. Thus, the third and most important criterion for a successful critique of the Third Way is to show how what Giddens calls the 'social revolutions of our time'[1] can be taken in a more progressive direction by a revitalised politics of the Left.

Contributors to this volume begin to meet this third criterion in their reworkings of the Third Way's understanding of the individual, community and wider social transformations. I suggest that Third Way theory itself, particularly the earlier work of Giddens, contains the basis of a more progressive vision than that which is being pursued by current practitioners. However, for this to take meaningful shape it needs to be supplemented by a re-introduction of more traditional Left concerns, the salience of which have been highlighted throughout the chapters of this collection.

Existing critical strategies

The Third Way as smokescreen

Much of the criticism in this volume reflects a general tendency to dismiss the Third Way as of no substance in its own right, or to reject the idea that it represents something meriting serious engagement on its own terms. Instead, the Third Way is seen as a distraction from, or smokescreen for, some alternative (and usually less desirable) agenda. In Britain, this has been the oppositional strategy adopted by the Conservative Party in trying to present the Third Way as masking New Labour's unreconstructed Old Left threat. This involves high taxation, over-regulation on business and centralised State power. While there is no doubt that New Labour is vulnerable to libertarian charges of representing a 'nanny state', the Conservatives have thus far failed to capitalise on this opportunity; and trying to paint Blair's New Labour with the brush of the red menace is, to say the least, unconvincing.

It is from the Left's criticism that the idea of the Third Way as smokescreen has gained greater purchase. Much of this can be seen in the broadly Marxist tradition of viewing changing political formations and projects as masking enduring social relations. These consist in ongoing capitalist domination and exploitation, as social forms are restructured in the relentless drive towards profit maximisation. As capital seeks to colonise ever more areas of social life, governors are forced to develop corresponding political strategies that seek to maintain the ensuing social tensions. The Thatcherite neo-liberal strategy proved remarkably successful in this role over an extended period, to the extent that a number of this book's commentators grant neo-liberalism a hegemonic status. On this view, the Third Way is simply an elaborate rhetorical device that seeks to legitimise the capitulation of the Centre-Left to the triumph of neo-liberal ideology and practice. Giddens and other advocates of the Third Way have simply reconciled themselves to neo-liberalism. The Third Way is a project that looks to 'adapt to the existing order, seeking marginal improvements inflated by self-deceiving rhetoric'.[2] Such a position is taken by David Morrison (chapter 9) when he suggests that New Labour has adopted a neo-liberal political economy which is given a 'human face' by communitarian rhetoric in social policy.

There are also social democratic critics who, while not speaking the Marxian language of exploitative capitalist relations, also dismiss the notion of a meaningful Third Way. Of course, social democracy can itself lay claim to being the original Third Way; between state socialism and *laissez-faire* capitalism. The numerous individuals and groups that remain true to the European social democratic heritage are thus understandably put out by claims for a 'new' Third Way. From what might be called the Old Right of the Labour Party, approaches of this sort would like to place New Labour in the long tradition of revisionist Labourism and forget talk of Third Ways. The task of a Labour government is to maintain economic growth, high levels of employment and well-funded public services, and to alleviate the inequalities of the market through modest redistribution. Those more sanguine about New Labour's social democratic credentials, such as Stephen Driver (chapter 2), believe that it *has* been largely true to these goals, but are often frustrated that Third Way rhetoric refuses to be explicit about this fact and to develop a bolder social democratic narrative. As one chronicler of Labour revisionism has argued: 'Third Way discourse has been conscientiously devised to disguise the real continuities between New Labour's policy agenda and the traditional social democratic agenda in Britain.'[3]

However, social democrats who are more critical of the Third Way see it as masking not a 'real' social democratic agenda but, like their neo-Marxist counterparts, as a collapse before neo-liberalism. This reflects the steady encroachment of the market into all areas of social life. Thus, having examined the case of the PFI, Eric Shaw (chapter 4) concludes that, far from being a technocratic exercise of the 'what matters is what works' variety, the Third Way in fact represents the incorporation of key neo-liberal nostrums within Labour ideology, or what he calls the 'operational code' which informs policy choices. Similarly, having charted in detail the use of the term 'community' in Third Way discourse, Eunice Goes (chapter 6) argues that it has come to act as a means by which to abandon more traditional social democratic themes such as a commitment to reducing inequality.

Following New Labour's second landslide election victory, that of 2001, some social democratic critics of this type have been given heart by the apparent reemergence of taxation and a commitment to public services as a defining difference between Labour and the Conservatives. New Labour has apparently realised that to promise investment in public services without making the case for taxation to fund those services is to make an unsustainable commitment. Driver points to Labour's increasingly 'social democratic' budgetary decisions. The 2002 spending review recognised that 'stealth' taxation was neither a long-term policy option nor sensible politics. A rise in national insurance contributions, coupled with massive investment in the NHS, was even being described by party modernisers and an excited *Observer* editorial as 'the most significant restatement of the British social democratic tradition for a generation'.[4] It has been the longstanding hope of many social democrats that, once these *real* political battle lines re-emerge, inflated claims about a Third Way will cease to be made.[5]

The Third Way as real, but wrong

In contrast to these 'smokescreen' approaches which largely dismiss the Third Way, neo-Marxist and social democratic accounts contain a strand which accepts that the Third Way represents something new and significant, reflecting wider social and economic change.

Neo-Marxist approaches of this sort concur with the smokescreen theorists that the Third Way is the product of global capitalist restructuring. However, rather than see the Third Way as a relatively passive conduit for such restructuring, it identifies a more *aggressive* role for Third Way politics. In this view, the Third Way not only legitimises the neo-liberal hegemony, but is a strategy for its active reinforcement, promotion and development. Furthermore, dressed up as it is in the language of the Centre-Left, the Third Way is able to extend the dominance of capital in ways that would have been off limits to traditional Conservatives and even neo-liberals. This is evidenced, for example, in the extension of private sector involvement in the public services or the charging of university tuition fees.

Paul Cammack's polemical intervention (chapter 8) provides a forceful example of this approach. Cammack takes what might be called a strong view of neo-liberalism, arguing that it is not concerned just with leaving be markets in *laissez-faire* fashion but looks to the State to actively promote conditions ripe for the logic of capitalist reproduction. On this account, by accepting neo-liberalism, the Third Way seeks not to humanise capitalism but to impose its logic on all areas of social life. Cammack explains in detail how the language of social democracy has been subverted as part of this aggressive neo-liberal project.

This sense of the Third Way, as actively representing what might be called the neo-liberal moment within social democracy, is evident also in Morrison's analysis of the function of the discourse of citizenship. Morrison argues (chapter 9) that the label 'Third Way' is merely a transient piece of branding. However, his analysis of citizenship discourse and the New Deal suggests that, far from being insubstantial or a smokescreen, the Third Way is a definite attempt to construct the *mindsets* of individuals necessary to support a new phase of capitalist development. By ostensibly empowering citizens to help themselves ('a hand up and not a hand-out'), the strategy is one of displacing, from the level of the State to that of the individual, some of the contemporary problems of government. Morrison suggests that a key objective of New Labour's 'rights and responsibilities' citizenship discourse is that citizens are to be equipped as competent members of the global information age. This is further reflected in Goes's assessment that the Third Way selectively deploys communitarian rhetoric to justify a retrenchment for the State's role in addressing inequality, again shifting the burden to the individual.

This view of the Third Way as an active governing strategy, the rhetoric of which is aimed at constructing specific types of political subject, is evident also in the deconstruction of Etzioni's communitarianism offered by Simon Prideaux (chapter 7). Prideaux sets out to show how Etzioni's version of community is influenced by his organisational theory work in the 1950s. Interestingly, whereas Morrison, and implicitly Cammack, suggest that the Third Way is a strategy aimed at constructing economic subjects appropriate to the (perceived) new global economic context, for Prideaux the communitarian strand of Third Way thought is in fact a regressive strategy. On this view, the Third Way is more appropriate to the social and economic conditions that ushered in Taylorism in the 1950s and 1960s. The criticism is that, far from representing the leading edge of social change, the present Third Way is based on *outdated* sociological assumptions.

There are also social democratic critics willing to recognise that the Third Way is more than a smokescreen and needs to be engaged with in its own right. Rather than wanting the Third Way dropped in favour of a traditional social democratic agenda of the type discussed above, these critics want to see Third Way modernisation as the *completion* of an unfinished social democratic project. They are willing to engage with the Third Way as long as it has the potential for delivering their enduring agenda of a modernising, often liberal, social democracy. Thus, Will Hutton retains his commitment to the idea of a stakeholder society, despite, as both Morrison and Goes point out, New Labour having discarded such a discourse. This envisages a more radical restructuring of British capitalism. It would involve a robust and active role for the State, particularly in terms of promoting sustainable growth beyond the short-term drive for maximal shareholder returns, and would protect the public interest through the regulation and enforcement of service agreements.[6]

The critics assessed

It was suggested at the outset that a successful and productive critique of the Third Way needs, first, to recognise that it has substance in its own right; second, to identify where it has responded to significant social change; and, third, show how such change may be appropriated for progressive ends. Existing critical approaches have been broadly grouped into those which tend to see the Third Way as insubstantial and as masking an alternative agenda, and those which recognise it as a project in its own right, albeit one with which they disagree. These positions cross-cut what have been identified as neo-Marxist and social democratic perspectives.

Critics who largely dismiss the Third Way as a smokescreen do touch upon important issues to which any successful reconstruction must be alert. The neo-Marxist account is the result of privileging economic relations over mere political analysis. Marxian approaches remain compelling in terms of locating the development of a set of theories and practices such as the Third Way in the context of definite dynamic relationships of economic and social power. At the same time, traditional social democrats tend to take a longer view of the Centre-Left which puts some of the more excited claims about the Third Way being 'beyond Left and Right' into a more sombre perspective. They ask *exactly* why is there such urgent need to abandon social democratic values and policy mechanisms? This poses the possibility that the Third Way mantra of 'traditional values in a modern setting' simply represents the jettisoning of certain values, as a matter of ideological preference on the part of current party elites.

However, on the smokescreen neo-Marxist accounts, attempts to delineate the complex normative and empirical assumptions that underpin the Third Way are rather a waste of time. The action remains at the level of global class relations and it is through understanding these that the Third Way is exposed as a sham which diverts from the real issues of power and domination. While it is important to reveal how political projects may be subservient to enduring material interests, how they are deployed to contain contradictory and potentially antagonistic social relations or even represent a *coup d'état* within existing parties, the cry of 'sell-out' is all too easily made. It is not sufficient to account for the Third Way as the result of academic theoreticians, or even Labour politicians, simply choosing to turn their backs on socialism. If a broadly materialist approach to the production of political ideas is to be true to itself, it should consider the possibility that the emergence of an entity such as the Third Way is a response to definite changes in the world within which it operates.

There are similar problems with the traditional social democratic criticism that the Third Way simply masks continuities with previous Labour governments, or that it has erred from that past and should return to its true path. This perspective, like the neo-Marxist accounts, neglects the fact that its preferred model (the post-war social democratic welfare state) was tied to a specific social formation which has been radically altered. Specifically, the institutions of the Keynesian welfare state presumed a greater degree of national economic sovereignty, a largely homogenous working class based on the male bread-winner model and a greater degree of social solidarity, primarily through collective class identities. The desire to recreate a traditional Labour Party based on this model neglects what the Third Way recognises: that processes such as economic and cultural globalisation, changes in employment and the decline of collective solidarities have radically altered the frame of reference for any political strategy. It also rests upon the spurious notion of a fixed 'Old Labour', a Labour that was in fact complex, diverse and contested. The Third Way has emerged as a response to a whole range of social, economic and cultural shifts, an understanding of which is of paramount importance.

The smokescreen approaches highlight important issues about the relationship between ideological projects and material interests. However, they broadly fail on all three criteria suggested for a successful critique: dismissing the Third Way itself as spin; claiming that the empirical changes posited have been exaggerated or distorted for ideological purposes; and being consequently unwilling to address how such changes may be engaged with as a new set of challenges for the Left.

Approaches that recognise the Third Way as a largely coherent body of ideas with important effects have a greater critical purchase than do those which dismiss it out of hand.

Neo-Marxists who see the Third Way as more than a smokescreen suggest that it provides the ideological repertoire for managing a whole new phase of capitalist expansion. This colonises the language and politics of social democracy, which at least used to be about containing capitalism and ameliorating its worst effects. However, those who follow this line grant a vast amount of agency to the political elites who are held to have ushered in this new justification for capitalism, almost to the point of a conspiracy theory. They tend to understate the extent to which projects such as the Third Way are a contested response to definite social changes, and once again are consequently unwilling to elaborate on how such social transformations might need addressing. Although perhaps not quite as mechanical as those theories which dismiss the Third Way outright, neo-Marxist approaches which grant substance to the Third Way are still ultimately reducible to an enduring struggle between capital and labour, with the predictable prescription that the latter must be strengthened.[7]

Social democrats who engage with the Third Way, but disagree with the form it is taking, show more promise. They share with the Third Way the perception that the 'social revolutions of our time' necessitated a shift in Centre-Left strategy, but are concerned that such a shift need not have entailed what they perceive as the abandoning of the social democratic project. However, there is still the sense here, as in more traditional social democratic accounts, that Labour needs only to return to its true path. For political economists such as Hutton and Hay, the goal appears to be a more interventionist state that can at last modernise the British economy by transforming its fundamental structural weaknesses: a lack of investment and chronic short-termism.[8] For those such as David Marquand, the golden path appears to be a journey towards a form of liberal social democracy, perhaps healing the rift that has famously split Labour and the Liberals and enabled the Conservatives to dominate the twentieth century.[9]

However laudable these models for a revitalised social democracy are, there remains a sense of wanting to steer the Third Way towards the longstanding projects of the authors. While there is nothing illegitimate in this, it fails to appreciate the extent to which the challenges posed by new social and economic conditions have called for a rethinking of many of the assumptions of social democracy itself. Despite granting the Third Way significance in its own right, these versions of the neo-Marxist and social democratic approaches still ultimately fail to perceive the significance of the economic and social transformations that informed the development of Third Way theory. They do not address how the empirical changes identified by the Third Way, such as economic and cultural globalisation and increased individualisation, may have necessitated a revision of their *own* strategy, as well as that of the ruling elites.

The problem remains, then, that in a productive critique of the Third Way, both these conditions and Third Way ideas themselves need to be more fully engaged with. In what follows, those elements of the contributions to this volume that suggest a more productive critique of the Third Way are identified and elaborated. This account is presented against the stated criteria of: taking the Third Way seriously; engaging with social change; and showing where progressive political interventions might lead.

Towards a productive critique

Taking the Third Way seriously

Taking the Third Way seriously is the first task in any successful reconstruction. Some critical approaches, as has been seen, achieve this to the extent that they view the Third Way as an extended, more aggressive, neo-liberalism or a misguided attempt at reforming social democracy. However, the Third Way is clearly more complex than both these things, and the contributors to this volume have attempted, in places, to pin down exactly what is distinctive about the Third Way enterprise.

Armando Barrientos and Martin Powell (chapter 1) caution against lazy references to a homogenous Third Way by assessing tensions between its discourse, values, mechanisms and policies; illustrated by significant national variations. The value of this reminder is that it highlights where, for example, the rhetoric of the Third Way may depart significantly from what is being implemented in terms of policy, or where values that purport to be in harmony may in fact be irreconcilable. Such an examination should encourage critics to specify those areas of the Third Way, as both ideology and policy vehicle, to which they are firmly opposed and those with which they might engage. The Third Way is too complex to be uniformly endorsed or rejected.

Driver (chapter 2) tries to capture the distinctiveness and complexity of the Third Way from a more sympathetic perspective than other contributors to this collection. He agrees with critics such as Goes and Shaw that the Third Way is not particularly social democratic in the traditional sense, but argues forcefully that it is certainly not neo-liberal as authors such as Cammack suggest. Like Powell, Driver teases out what is specific about Third Way policy mixes, and goes on to show how in his view it is possible to *combine* elements of what are broadly social democratic and neo-liberal approaches, if not *reconcile* them. This poses a question, for those who dismiss the Third Way as an attempt to create an artificial consensus: could such a recombining of elements of Left and Right actually form the basis of a progressive project?

Engaging with the 'social revolutions of our time'

If the first step to a successful critical engagement with the Third Way is to take it seriously as an ideology and governing strategy, the second is to then critically engage with the analysis of the world on which it is based. A number of contributors to this volume are clearly sceptical about Third Way claims as to dramatic social shifts such as economic and cultural globalisation, increasing individualisation and the rise of the knowledge society.

What was labelled above as the 'smokescreen' approach to the Third Way sees such claims as merely discursive, ideological justifications for the reconfiguration of enduring capitalist relations. Others such as Cammack, who see a more aggressive role for the Third Way, tend to regard phenomena such as globalisation as the outcome of the intended strategies and actions of elite actors. On this view, to amend or reverse such changes is simply a matter of political *will*, and hence the charge of betrayal levelled at the leaders and theoreticians of Centre-Left parties. Similarly, Morrison suggests that New Labour's discursive articulation of a new type of citizenship is first and foremost a *political* project. This is aimed at recasting the relationship between the State and the individual, and marginalising opponents on both Left and Right. In other contributions, doubts over the extent of social change are implicit. Thus, Goes's detailed account of New Labour's retrenchment on social democratic values, or Shaw's claim that it has opted for greater use of the private sector as a matter of *ideological preference*, again suggests that the wider structural changes which third-wayers invoke are not as important as their own ability to select various ideological guides and policy options.

There is no doubt that critics are right to challenge the fatalism that seems to underpin the Third Way's claims about sweeping processes such as globalisation. Norman Fairclough has shown elsewhere how, in New Labour rhetoric, such processes are treated as agents in their own right rather than uneven and contested processes deeply influenced by the decisions and strategies of social actors.[10] However, although it is important to demystify overblown claims that 'there is no alternative' to the trajectory laid out by uncontrollable social forces, the effect of those forces still needs to be kept in mind. Certainly, much of the current social and political climate was deeply fashioned by an extended neo-liberal project, but the effects of this cannot be simply wished away. This is recognised in those contributions which identify the Third Way as grappling with how to bring social democratic values and policies to *bear upon* this new environment.

Regardless of previous ideologically motivated political choices, the scale of many of the social changes identified by the Third Way are such that it is plausible to suppose they would have occurred whatever the ideological colour of administrations from, say, the 1970s onwards. Where political choices make a difference is in shaping the particular forms in which social transformations manifest themselves, and how they come to be understood in the public imagination. The contributors' perspectives, on how the types of social change that inform the Third Way can be appropriated for a more progressive project, are identified below.

Reconstructing Third Way themes

Once willing to take the Third Way seriously, and engage with its analysis of social change, the third, most significant and (as ever) most difficult task for critics is to demonstrate how the existing Third Way might be moulded in a more progressive direction. A number of possible themes for such a reconstruction have been hinted at in this collection. They relate to alternative interpretations of the theoretical assumptions of the Third Way as well to as its understanding of the social transformations to which it purports to be a response. In both cases, there are signs of more progressive possibilities within existing Third Way theory itself, most notably in the earlier work of Giddens. But what critics here have shown is that developing these possibilities involves re-introducing some of the core Old Left themes which third-wayers have jettisoned or underplayed. In particular, there is a need for greater attention to the persistence of material inequality and unequal power relations in undermining the progressive vision to which Third Way theory occasionally points.

Theoretical influences

The Third Way is sometimes criticised for being merely a technocratic response to perceived social changes, without a guiding political philosophy of its own. However, the contributors to this collection have identified the distinctive recurrent themes that could be said to constitute a Third Way – 'no rights without responsibilities' – philosophy, grounded in a recasting of the Left's understanding of the relationship between the community and the individual.

The Third Way's understanding of 'community' has been queried in this collection primarily on the grounds that it has misappropriated the term. Sarah Hale (chapter 5) shows how key concepts deployed by communitarian philosophers diverge significantly from what is offered by the Third Way. She reveals how material redistribution plays a role in communitarianism, and points to a version of community based more on fraternity and spontaneous care than the duty-bound instrumental model offered by the Third Way. Hale's alternative reading of community is complemented by that of Goes, who suggests that the Third Way departs significantly from the communitarian blueprint. She notes how New Labour has departed from communitarianism in its attitude to public dialogue (superficial), the family (*less* concerned with the traditional family than are communitarians), rights and responsibilities (creating an undeserving poor while neglecting the responsibilities of the wealthy and powerful) and use of the State (interventionist on moral culture, but not on alleviating inequality – the inverse of progressive communitarianism). Neither Goes nor Hale seeks to demonstrate crudely whether or not the Third Way is communitarian, and Hale challenges the possibility of trying to map abstract philosophy onto political projects. However, by contrasting the Third Way in practice with an ideal-type communitarian blueprint, both authors implicitly point to an alternative trajectory for the Third Way's understanding of community. This would pay greater attention to Old Left concerns of solidarity, redistribution and unconditional rights.

A recasting of the Third Way's understanding of the individual is attempted by Pete McCullen and Colin Harris (chapter 3), who also re-introduce a role for material redistribution. Just as Hale and Goes have compared the Third Way understanding of community with the original ideas of key thinkers, McCullen and Harris identify a distinction between the rhetoric and practice of Third Way politics and the work of Giddens himself with regard to the status of the individual. Given Giddens's central role in the development of Third Way ideas, this represents one of the more promising routes for an immanent critique and reconstruction. Driver and Martell have pointed out that, for Giddens, individual*isation* consists in the choice and uncertainty that characterise a 'detraditionalised' society, in which individuals are increasingly freed from binding structural constraints. Alternatively, Blair and other third-wayers understand individual*ism* as signifying a growth in egoistical behaviour, stemming from flaws in the approaches of both the Old Left and the New Right. Consequently, as a response to individualisation, the

> active, reflective citizen in a radical democracy is Giddens' model. Blair puts more emphasis . . . on the notion of duty, on moral cohesion and those institutions . . . which he believes can and should enforce good behaviour . . . In this respect, third way ideas can be divided between 'post-traditionalists' like Giddens and 'social moralists' like Blair.[11]

Drawing on management and organisation theory literature, McCullen and Harris point to how this notion of the post-traditional individual has elements that should be attractive to progressives. If a core goal for the Left has been creating the conditions that allow for individual autonomy as human fulfilment, then Giddens's reflective, creative individual would seem to be true to that tradition. There are similarities here with MacIntyre's richer version of human fulfilment *per se*, as pointed to in Hale's overview, in contrast to the instrumentalism of the Third Way individual. Using Maslow's hierarchy of needs, McCullen and Harris show how, in the management literature itself, for this high-order need to be met distortions created by want of material resources need to be addressed. These have been glossed over in Giddens's account, which has a tendency to assume that the structural conditions for such individual liberation are already in place, rather than constituting an enduring problem for a Left politics to resolve. Again, traditional Left themes have been discarded too hastily.

Alternative readings of social change

Our contributors have thus shown how there is significant room for alternative, more progressive, understandings of both community and the individual to be gleaned from Third Way thought. However, the problem remains that these alternative versions invest a great deal in the significance of political will. If only Third Way strategists *chose* those alternative definitions, more progressive political projects would ensue. This neglects the possibility, iterated throughout, that such is the scope and rapidity of social change that the existing Third Way really is the 'only game in town' as a viable response. Third-wayers themselves offer up this 'there is no alternative' line, with the implication that the Third Way is merely a technocratic, functional project of the sort identified here by Morrison,

Prideaux and Shaw. However, alongside the alternatives to the Third Way's theoretical understanding of the community and the individual, identified above, are
different readings of its analysis of the character of the social change within
which they are located, and the implications of this for politics. Interestingly, as
with the example of individualisation, it is by returning to the Third Way theory
of Giddens himself that some possible alternatives are to be found. In particular, Giddens's notions of globalisation, a dialogic democracy and what he calls
'life politics' and 'generative politics' serve to map out a bolder progressive vision
than the more technocratic versions of the Third Way. Again, though, this vision
needs fleshing out with more traditional Left concerns if it is to be viable.

The critical concept in the Third Way's understanding of social change is
undoubtedly *globalisation*.[12] Where New Labour sees the new global economy
as something to which we must simply adapt, Giddens suggests a more active
response via the establishing of global democratic institutions.[13] It is true that
Giddens has increasingly endorsed New Labour's acceptance of the reality and
desirability of economic globalisation, and the importance of developing human
capital against a background of 'sound money'. He suggests that 'Economic globalisation, by and large, has been a success. The problem is how to maximise its
positive consequences while limiting its less fortunate effects'.[14] However, while
Giddens is an advocate of the benefits of economic globalisation, he differs from
New Labour in acknowledging that it was a deliberate project, constructed by
concrete actors to meet particular interests. Accordingly, Giddens identifies – up
to a point – the powerful interests at work in the process of globalisation and
argues that they need to be counterbalanced, suggesting that

> Third way politics as a matter of principle must not be complacent or collusive in
> the face of power. There are interest groups, and groups of the powerful, that any
> self-respecting left-of-centre government must confront, face down, or regulate.[15]

The impetus for this checking of powerful interests resides in Giddens's account
of the 'social revolutions of our time', which leads from globalisation to the new
epoch he refers to as reflexive modernity.[16] Politically, this is characterised by a
communicative ideal of 'dialogic democracy'. This is a space in which rational
decisions can be made on an issue-to-issue basis, free from traditional, given
authority and totalising ideological claims. Giddens sees this as 'a way of creating a public arena in which controversial issues – in principle – can be resolved, or
at least handled, through dialogue rather than through pre-established forms of
power'.[17] It is in this space that the boundaries of what, for example, should be
preserved from colonisation by the imperatives of economic globalisation can be
negotiated. To that end, Giddens and others such as David Held are strong advocates of extending democratic processes so as to create global dialogic spaces.[18]

In terms of the political agency that might facilitate this dialogic democracy,
Giddens introduces ideas of what he calls 'life politics' and 'generative politics'.
Generative politics provides the institutional framework that both draws upon
and encourages individualisation and the development of an 'active trust', based

on reason rather than on embedded forms of power. Giddens sees generative politics as creating the conditions for desirable outcomes to be reached through negotiated reason, rather than being imposed top–down as in hierarchical notions of politics. He envisages active trust being built and sustained at all levels of society. Autonomy is to be encouraged through the provision of sufficient material resources and the decentralisation of political power.[19] Within this framework, Giddens depicts the flourishing of 'life politics', based around the continually fluctuating issues arising from the active construction of individual identities. He contrasts this with the hitherto predominant 'emancipatory politics', which was primarily concerned with freedom from arbitrary power and material deprivation.[20]

It is thus possible to discern in the earlier work of Giddens a number of more progressive themes for the Third Way than those envisaged by its present practitioners. The ideal type Giddens sketches, based on what he suggests are implicit trends, is of a dialogic democracy of active, reflective citizens able to bring their life-political concerns from outside the traditional top–down statist model of politics. Entrenched interests, including spurious claims to expertise, will no longer be able to carry the day without being able to justify their actions on the basis of dialogue.

There is plenty in Giddens's broad-brush vision that should appeal to the Left. However, there is a tendency in Giddens's work, illustrated by his later elaboration of the Third Way, to imply that the conditions for this new polity are already in place, or at least that they are being ushered in by benevolent social forces which Third Way governments need only manage competently. This volume has pointed to where, on the contrary, a revitalised Left politics is vital in overcoming the barriers that remain to the realisation of Giddens' vision. Material inequality, asymmetrical power relations and the continuing tendency of capital to undermine the kinds of dialogic spaces Giddens envisages present formidable obstacles. They cannot yet, unfortunately, be consigned to a past era of emancipatory politics.

Conclusion

From its inception, the Third Way has been dismissed and ridiculed, occasionally with good reason. But it is now clear that whatever happens to the expression itself, the Third Way identifies the ongoing challenges that the Left must adapt to and provides the closest thing to a governing philosophy for Centre-Left administrations. For this reason, it has been suggested here that a critical engagement must take the Third Way seriously, understand the problems it identifies yet show how they can be converted into progressive outcomes. The various contributions to this volume, often reflecting the wider state of criticism, have both neglected and fulfilled these criteria at different moments. To be sure, outright rejection is always the easiest critical strategy, and that is reflected where the Third Way is dismissed as mere spin or a sell-out in what was labelled the 'smokescreen' tendency in criticism. Others are more willing to give the Third Way credence, but fail to take on board the extent to which it reflects real and dramatic social transformations that do call into question aspects of traditional Left strategies.

Critics, here and elsewhere, are most compelling when they have recognised the Third Way as an attempt to address these challenges, but endeavoured to show that there are many possible responses and how these can appeal to progressives. This has included contrasting the Third Way's selective use of 'community' with the richer understanding of that term offered by progressive communitarians, and suggesting a model of the reflective, active individual in a genuinely post-traditional order. This is in contrast to the atomised individual implicit in the commodified image of society that informs the present Third Way. It has been stressed that realising these alternative visions means re-introducing traditional Left concerns of addressing the material inequality and unequal power relations that distort the possibility of a dialogic democracy.

What stands out from all the contributions is that this process, of reconstructing the Third Way along more progressive lines, involves first and foremost its *repoliticisation*. A discourse which claims to have obliterated Left and Right when, as this volume shows, the terms still have real purchase will always be exposed by the irreducible nature of political conflict. By repoliticising the Third Way, its advocates can become explicit about their objectives, friends and enemies. This collection illustrates that the multitude of Left critics will never all be satisfied – that's politics. But recognising that in the face of revolutionary social transformations, political interventions matter and can be more or less progressive, would be a start.

Notes

1 Giddens 1994: chapter 3.
2 Callinicos 1999: 102.
3 Larkin 2000: i.
4 Editorial, *Observer*, 21 April 2002.
5 Keegan 2000.
6 Hutton 1997.
7 E.g. Callinicos 1999.
8 Hutton 1997; Hay 1999.
9 Marquand 1999.
10 Fairclough 2000.
11 Driver and Martell 2000: 157.
12 See e.g. Dearlove 2000; Wickham-Jones 2000.
13 Driver and Martell 2000.
14 Giddens 2000: 124.
15 *Ibid.*, pp. 37–8.
16 For a detailed discussion of the relationship between Giddens's theory of reflexive modernity and the Third Way, see Mouzelis 2001 and the response by Leggett 2002.

17 Giddens 1994: 16.
18 See e.g. Held 1998.
19 Giddens 1994: 93.
20 *Ibid.*

References

Callinicos, A. (1999) 'Social theory put to the test of politics: Pierre Bourdieu and Anthony Giddens', *New Left Review* (I), 236, July–August.

Dearlove, J. (2000) 'Globalisation and the study of British politics', *Politics (PSA)*, 20(2).

Driver, S. and Martell, L. (1998) *New Labour: Politics After Thatcherism*, Oxford, Polity Press.

Driver, S. and Martell, L. (2000) 'Left, Right and the third way', *Policy and Politics*, 28(2).

Fairclough, N. (2000) *New Labour, New Language?*, London, Routledge.

Giddens, A. (1994) *Beyond Left and Right: The Future of Radical Politics*, Oxford, Polity Press.

Giddens, A. (1998) *The Third Way: The Renewal of Social Democracy*, Oxford, Polity Press.

Giddens, A. (2000) *The Third Way and its Critics*, Oxford, Polity Press.

Hay, C. (1999) *The Political Economy of New Labour: Labouring Under False Pretences?* Manchester, Manchester University Press.

Held, D. (1998) 'The timid tendency', *Marxism Today* (special issue), November–December.

Hutton, W. (1997) *The State to Come*, London: Vintage.

Keegan, W. (2000) 'An end to public squalor', *New Statesman*, 24 July.

Larkin, P. (2000) 'Blair's third way: its emergence and prospects', Paper presented at the workshop 'Competing Models of European Social Democracy', University of Sussex European Institute, Brighton, 26 May.

Leggett, W. (2002) 'Reflexive modernization and reconstructing the third way: a response to Mouzelis', *Sociological Review*, 50(3).

Marquand, D. (1999) *The Progressive Dilemma: From Lloyd George to Blair*, 2nd edn, London: Phoenix Giant.

Mouzelis, N. (2001) 'Reflexive modernization and the third way: the impasses of Giddens's social-democratic politics', *Sociological Review*, 49(3).

Wickham-Jones, M. (2000) 'New Labour in the global economy: partisan politics and the democratic model', *British Journal of Politics & International Relations*, 2(1).

Index